DEEP AND SHELTERED WATERS

DEEP AND SHELTERED WATERS

DAVID R. GRAY

THE HISTORY OF TOD INLET

Royal **BC** Museum

VICTORIA, CANADA

Published by the Royal BC Museum, 675 Belleville Street, Victoria, British Columbia,
v8w 9w2, Canada.

The Royal BC Museum is located on the traditional territories of the Lekwungen
(Songhees and Xwsepsum Nations). We extend our appreciation for the opportunity
to live and learn on this territory.

Cover and interior design by Lara Minja/Lime Design Inc.
Index by Catherine Plear

Cover photo, Chinese workers at the Tod Inlet wharf (see p. 85); and back cover photo,
SS *Charmer* (see p. 43). Photos on p. i, cement plant at Tod Inlet in the 1920s (see p. 127);
pp. ii–iii, Tod Inlet wharf (see p. 64); p. vi, excursion ship arriving in Tod Inlet (see p. 145);
p. 220, waterfall at Tod Creek (note the old waterline pipe; David R. Gray photograph);
and p. 250, mossy tree branch (David R. Gray photograph).

Library and Archives Canada Cataloguing in Publication

Title: Deep and sheltered waters : the history of Tod Inlet / David R. Gray.
Names: Gray, David Robert, author. | Royal British Columbia Museum, issuing body.
Description: Includes bibliographical references and index.
Identifiers: Canadiana (print) 20200276417 | Canadiana (ebook) 20200276581 |
     ISBN 9780772672568 (softcover) | ISBN 9780772679437 (EPUB) | ISBN
     9780772679444 (Kindle) | ISBN 9780772672988 (PDF)
Subjects: LCSH: Tod Inlet (B.C.)—History. | LCSH: Tod Inlet Region (B.C.)—History. | LCSH:
     Tod Inlet (B.C.)—Social life and customs. | LCSH: Tod Inlet Region (B.C.)—Social life
     and customs. | LCSH: Tod Inlet (B.C.)—Social conditions. | LCSH: Tod Inlet Region
     (B.C.)—Social conditions.
Classification: LCC FC3845.T63 G73 2020 | DDC 971.1/2—dc23

10 9 8 7 6 5 4 3 2 1

Printed in Canada by Friesens.

To **DERRICK MALLARD**, who dedicated his later years to the establishment of the park at Tod Inlet, and to **TSARTLIP ELDER JOHN SAMPSON**, who was born the day after me, and shared the same delight in exploring Tod Inlet, and shared our dreams and knowledge of the inlet, with regret that he died too soon.

CONTENTS

A Sikh cremation ceremony in 1907. See p. 86.

Foreword

Tod Inlet and its surrounding area has long been a place of intense interest for many of us. It represents layers of history, layers of human presence, a home place for myriad plants, animals and fungi, a convergence of marine and terrestrial habitats, and a convergence of nature, industry and horticultural beauty. Its SENĆOŦEN name, SṈIDȻEȽ, translates as "Place of the Blue Grouse," reflecting the human–nature interface of this remarkable place.

This book presents a story of immense complexity about a relatively small place, at once special and typical, told with clarity and authority by one who knows it intimately. David Gray, with his background as wildlife biologist and heritage consultant, understands what research entails, and has had the imagination and insights to bring together diverse information drawn from human history and natural history into this compelling and fascinating narrative. Who would have thought, when David and his brother, Jamie, uncovered some pig skulls at Tod Inlet as young boys, that their discovery would initiate a lifelong quest to better know and understand this place, its environmental features and its historical richness? His book is a result of that quest, that curiosity ignited all those years ago and brought to fruition over half a century later.

We have known David over most of that time (in Nancy's case, as fellow members of the Victoria Junior Natural History group since the early 1960s; for Robert, as friends and fellow students at the University of Victoria), and we are both delighted to see the results of his meticulous search for knowledge and understanding of this unique place. This book, begun as a questioning spark so many years ago, is a perfect gift to Canadians and world citizens of the 2020s. At a time when the knowledge and history of Indigenous peoples are finally being recognized in mainstream society—when "reconciliation" is a household word across Canada—and when the histories of those of Asian heritage, including labourers and immigrants, are gaining wider attention, recognition and appreciation, this book about Tod Inlet is right on target.

David chronicles the deep and enduring relationships of the Tsartlip and other W̱SÁNEĆ peoples with the inlet and its surrounding lands and waters, which have been their territory since time immemorial. Starting with the archaeological sites—evidence of ancient reliance on the resources of Tod Inlet—he then describes more recent occupation and use by the Tsartlip people, and follows with documentation of the surveys and geological assessments that gave rise to the establishment of the industrial cement works and the associated influx of newcomers. The rise and decline of the cement works and nearby settlements, the associated shipping and other transportation, geological and chemical features of cement, links to diverse places and historical events, fishing and hunting activities, and personal experiences are all described in detail, culminating in the replacement of the cement works by the world-famous Butchart Gardens, the establishment of a superb, ecologically diverse provincial park of nearly 3,200 acres, and the revisiting of the long-standing claims of the Tsartlip to their traditional lands.

In his careful and respectful search for information and understanding, along with his own on-the-ground investigations, David interviewed and read letters and accounts from dozens of individuals, not only from the developers and owners of the cement plants and related industries that dominated the area for decades, but from historians, ethnographers and residents and their relatives. One treasure trove of information was a "scattering of wet and mouldy papers in the old cement company office in the late 1960s." In particular, he describes the experiences of those who lived in crowded substandard housing and laboured in the quarries, in the factory buildings and on the docks, digging limestone, carrying heavy sacks of

cement, making the best out of difficult, perhaps lonely circumstances. Chinese labourers and, later, Sikhs from Punjab and other regions of India, were drawn to the opportunities for earning wages. Some of them stayed for substantial periods, while others moved on quickly, but in the end, the cement plants closed down and most left for good. David's narrative brings the human side of this fascinating story to life. No longer can anyone think of the workers or their families as faceless statistics; now they have personality and each has a separate story to tell.

It is entirely appropriate that the Royal BC Museum should publish this book, because it integrates the broad spectrum of what makes up BC's heritage, both social and natural, and covers all the areas of research and exhibition encompassed at the museum. Not only is Tod Inlet itself a fascinating place of enduring interest, but, in a sense, this place and its history represents a history of "everyplace." It is a microcosm of historical and ecological interactions that could be chronicled for dozens of small communities across Canada and beyond. Reading it, you will not only be informed about Tod Inlet, but moved by the humanity and beauty that are so much a part of this engaging story.

Nancy J. Turner CM, OBC, PhD, FRSC
Distinguished Professor Emeritus,
University of Victoria

Robert D. Turner MS, FRCGS
Curator Emeritus, Royal BC Museum

Preface

My interest in the history of Tod Inlet began with pig teeth. As a young boy in the 1940s and '50s, when our family boat, *Squakquoi*, was moored in Tod Inlet, I spent hours exploring the inlet's shores and venturing up Tod Creek. It was along the steep banks of the creek, under the decaying leaves of bigleaf maples, that my brother, Jamie, and I first found the buried treasures that led to a lifetime of discoveries.

Pig skulls were our first trophies. As we dug into the loose soil to find more of the curving tusks in earth-stained jawbones—the *real* prize, we thought then—we discovered old bottles, broken pottery and chopsticks, and then beautifully glazed jugs, pots and rice bowls. Back at the anchorage, our questions to the old-timers led to faint vague memories of a long-deserted Chinese village connected to the abandoned cement plant at Tod Inlet. That's when I became hooked on history.

From time to time over the years, as a schoolboy and later as a high school student, I returned to Tod Creek to poke through the crumbling remains of the village. Bricks and corrugated tin roofing revealed the location of some buildings. And down the steep slope of the creek bank, my friend David Neilson and I found a trove of discarded objects—a Chinese midden. Dozens of nail-studded workboots with weathered soles suggested this was a working man's community, as did the hundreds of beer bottles—some from local sources, others from breweries around the world.

The discoveries fuelled my curiosity about the Chinese workers and eventually led me, as a student at the University of Victoria, to search the provincial archives of British Columbia. But I found no official records of the Chinese community at Tod Inlet, though one Vancouver Island directory mentioned 200 "Orientals" who had lived there 50 years before. Hidden in the forest parkland were the remains of a forgotten immigrant community, and hidden in the mists of history were the stories of the people who lived there.

Although two Chinese workers still lived in the abandoned community until the mid-1960s, in the only house still standing, I didn't meet them when I was exploring in the area. It was through background information in official government reports on the

Vancouver Portland Cement Company operations at Tod Inlet that I began to form a picture of the industry and of the labourers' lives.

The old cement plant itself yielded more fascinating details. One winter day in the mid-1960s, while I was exploring the abandoned, windowless office building, I found remnants of some company files from 1911 and 1912 scattered on the floor: torn, wet, mouldy and priceless. Priceless because they contained details of the everyday life of the company, the ships and the workers, available nowhere else.

It wasn't until after I moved to Ottawa in 1973 that I finally learned another of Tod Inlet's secrets: the Chinese had not been the only immigrant workers there. The exciting discovery of a single photograph in Canada's national archives depicting a Sikh cremation ceremony at Tod Inlet not only opened a whole new chapter of the story for me, it also changed my life, bringing both history and filmmaking into my career.

Shortly after finding the 1907 photograph, I was delighted to discover a trove of personal stories of life at the inlet. They had been written by Mary Parsell, wife of James Parsell, one of the cement company's first engineers.

My picture of the Tod Inlet community sharpened further when, in 1978, I began corresponding with Mary's son, Norman Parsell. Norman had grown up at Tod Inlet, had worked there for the cement company as a teenager

and lived nearby until his death in 1987. After I interviewed him at his home in 1979, I also tracked down a number of other local "old-timers." These men and women, who had grown up in the community or worked in the cement plant, taught me even more.

Desmond "Dem" Carrier, who grew up at Tod Inlet, and former gardener and cement plant worker Pat van Adrichem both shared their memories of Tod Inlet, especially of the Chinese workers they knew, during several fascinating rambles with me through the site of the old village and shantytown.

I talked with several Elders from the Tsartlip First Nation in 2001 and again in 2010 about their knowledge of Tod Inlet and its importance to their culture and history. I also interviewed the descendants of the Chinese and Sikh workers at Tod Inlet between 2007 and 2010 while researching my documentary films on the inlet's history.

In the spring of 1989 I introduced my own children to the wharfs, shorelines and old cement plant ruins of Tod Inlet. At the wharf, we met two men who kept their boats at Tod Inlet, enjoying a peaceful day in the quiet surroundings. Tod Inlet's future was then in doubt due to proposed commercial and housing developments, and I asked the two boat owners for their thoughts on it. One of them looked around at the quiet shores and the dark forests climbing up to the horizon, and said, "Nothing will change for a long time to come."

Teco at Tod Inlet, 1935. See p. 125.

Tod Inlet, 1982. See p. 187.

Introduction

Today, when visitors cruise the sheltered waters of Tod Inlet, walk the tranquil trails of Gowlland Tod Provincial Park or view the floral landscapes at the world-famous Butchart Gardens, few understand the vast wealth of the human and natural history of this special place.

Tod Inlet is a southward extension of Brentwood Bay, a small part of the body of water known as Saanich Inlet, which separates the main part of southern Vancouver Island from the Saanich Peninsula, just north of Victoria. A long, thin passage rapidly narrows a short distance inside the entrance, then winds to the south and southeast for more than a kilometre. In one place, the passage is less than 190 metres wide, but the depth is at least 11 metres throughout. The inlet then widens as it curves to the east. Only at the end, or head, of the inlet does the depth decrease, at the tidal flats that form around the mouth of Tod Creek. The creek comes down into the inlet over several sets of small falls, audible from the water: a sort of *wha cha cha, wha cha cha* sound. As Tsawout Elder Earl Claxton Sr. described for me, this is the origin of the ẈSÁNEĆ (Saanich) name of Tod Creek: in SENĆOŦEN, the name is "ẈEĆEĆE."

The inlet's western and southern shores are steep and wooded; the northern shores are terraced and more open. Most of the shoreline is rocky, but there are a few small beaches. Looking across the inlet from the former village and cement plant site, the forests rise up the slopes to the height of land called the Partridge Hills. From the viewpoint at the Butchart Gardens' famous Sunken Garden, the Partridge Hills are the only part of Tod Inlet that a visitor can see. The hills are also the only part of the Tod Inlet area that has not been reshaped by the forces of history.

To the Tsartlip First Nation, now based just north of Tod Inlet at Brentwood Bay, the area around Tod Inlet is known as SṈIDȻEȽ (pronounced like "sneek-with"), or Place of the Blue Grouse. The area is of significant spiritual and practical importance to the Tsartlip people. Several archaeological sites around the inlet, marked by layers of clamshells at the shoreline, attest to thousands of years of traditional occupation and use. Tod Inlet has continued to be used, but not lived in, by the Tsartlip people for the last 200 years.

The entire area was once known by the official geographical name of Tod Creek, given in 1858 to honour John Tod, an employee of the Hudson's Bay Company and a member of the 1851 council of government for the Vancouver Island colony.

Within the last 110 years, Tod Inlet has also existed as an industrial town, a town that has seen great changes. Houses built by the cement company for the white families at Tod Inlet were occupied into the late 1950s, then abandoned, and finally destroyed. All that remains today of the community and cement factory's structures are one small storehouse, one tall chimney and a few crumbling foundations and scattered artifacts.

From the early 1970s, area citizens urged governments to establish a park at Tod Inlet—a more suitable land use, they said, than the hotel-resort complex or housing developments proposed by the new landowners after the cement company was sold. The new development proposals were the stimulus for a long campaign to make Tod Inlet a protected place. In 1995, after 25 years of efforts by environmental groups and the Tsartlip First Nation, this area, where Indigenous people had lived for thousands of years and where immigrant workers had toiled, was finally preserved in the new Gowlland Tod Provincial Park.

Tod Inlet itself is still suffering from the ravages of industrial activities associated with the cement plant, industrial and agricultural pollution from a dump near the headwaters of Tod Creek, and

logging and log-booming operations from the 1950s. Efforts to ecologically restore the inlet, led by the SeaChange Marine Conservation Society, are ongoing.

The world-famous Butchart Gardens have been designated a National Historic Site, and Tod Inlet is now officially recognized as a Historic Place of Canada. These designations recognize Tod Inlet's connections to the local community, the province of British Columbia, Canada, North America, and the world.

Today, Tod Inlet and Gowlland Tod Provincial Park receive many visitors, who come by boat, by car, on horseback or on foot, many on a daily basis. They love the trails, the forest, the inlet and the history. To some, this is a sacred and healing place. This book is meant to help those visitors, and others who can only visit vicariously, know the history of this rich and fascinating place.

(*left*) The Gray family at the Vancouver Portland Cement Company plant ruins in 1987. David R. Gray photograph.

(*right*) The Gray family on the shoreline of Tod Inlet, north of the wharf, with metal debris from cement plant ruins, 1987. David R. Gray photograph.

(*overleaf*) Aerial view of Tod Inlet, 1930. See p. 147.

1

SN̲IDȻEⱢ: Place of the Blue Grouse

For hundreds and thousands of years, the W̱SÁNEĆ (Saanich) people have lived in the area surrounding Tod Inlet. Once referred to as the "Saanich tribe," the W̱SÁNEĆ First Nations—Tsartlip, Tsawout (East Saanich), Pauquachin, Tseycum and Malahat—are Straits Salish peoples. Since time immemorial they have occupied an area that extends from Saanich Arm in the west to the San Juan Islands in the east and from Mount Douglas north to Satellite Channel, as well as lands in the neighbouring Gulf Islands. A part of the larger group of Coast Salish peoples, they have lent their name to three of Greater Victoria's municipalities and to the Saanich Peninsula itself.

Leaders of the Tsartlip and Tseycum First Nations. See p. 14.

PLACE OF REFUGE: ⱢÁU,WELN̲EW̱

ⱢÁU,WELN̲EW̱, renamed Mount Newton by settlers, means "place of refuge" in SENĆOŦEN.

The following version of the W̱SÁNEĆ creation story was written by Philip Kevin Paul of the Tsartlip First Nation in a paper for the Institute of Ocean Sciences in Sidney, BC:

> Long before the first white man arrived on the shores of Vancouver Island, in a time when my people shared the Earth with all that is living, the people who lived here were given a name. This is the story of the Saanich People:
>
> Once, long ago, the ocean's power was shown to an unsuspecting people. The tides began rising higher than even the oldest people

could remember. It became clear to these people that there was something very different and very dangerous about this tide.

An elder amongst the people brought everyone together and told them they would no longer be safe in their homeland, that they would have to move up into the mountains where they would be safe. He told them that they would have to gather together their canoes and all the rope that they could carry. He told his people that he did not know how long the tide would continue to rise, and that for this reason they would have to leave. So the people of this small village took some food, their canoes and all the rope they could carry and moved to the nearest mountain.

The sea waters continued to rise for several days. Eventually the people needed their canoes. They tied all of their rope together and then to themselves. One end of the rope was tied to an arbutus tree at the top of the mountain and when the water stopped rising, the people were left floating in their canoes above the mountain.

It was the raven who appeared to tell them that the flood would soon be over. When the flood waters were going down, a small child noticed the raven circling in the distance. The child began to jump around and cry out in excitement, "NI QENNET TŦE"—"Look what is emerging!" Below where the raven had been circling, a piece of land had begun to emerge. The old man pointed down to that place and said, "That is our new home, W̱SÁNEC, and from now on we will be known as the W̱SÁNEC people." The old man also declared, on that day, that the mountain which had offered them protection would be treated with great care and respect, the same respect given to their greatest elders and it was to be known as ȽÁU,WEL,N̲EW̱—"The place of refuge." Also, arbutus trees would no longer be used for firewood.

"That is our new home, W̱SÁNEC, and from now on we will be known as the W̱SÁNEC people."

Paul comments on the important symbols within the W̱SÁNEĆ story of the flood: the arbutus tree, the raven, the mountain and the emergence of the W̱SÁNEĆ people. He emphasizes the importance of each symbol to his people and how the story is "a reminder of our relation to the animals, represented by the raven; to the plants, represented by the arbutus tree; to the Earth, symbolized by the

mountain; and to the Creator (or God), shown by the emergence of W̱SÁNEĆ Saanich and by the rising flood waters."[1]

Tod Inlet is a significant part of the Tsartlip First Nation's traditional territory. The Tsartlip people have not lived on the inlet itself for about 200 years, though traditional use of the area as a harvest camping site and for spiritual purposes has been virtually continuous.

First Nations people bake clams at Cordova Bay, north of Victoria, about 1900. Henry Muskett photograph. RBCM G-04231.

ARCHAEOLOGY

To better understand the people who the legends and oral histories introduce, it is helpful to visit, investigate and explore the places where they lived over the past millennia. Tod Inlet itself gives us clues to their lives. Walking the inlet's shoreline, across the water from where hikers walk today, takes us back to a time when people lived in and depended on the natural environment in a direct, personal and daily way.

In 1998, I walked and scrambled around the shoreline of Tod Inlet to see for myself the places where archaeologists had found evidence

The eroding shell midden near the water's edge on the north bank of Tod Creek. David R. Gray photographs.

of people living long before the first contact with European explorers and settlers.

The present-day signs of those long-ago people are not obvious or dramatic. There are only half a dozen places along the shore where we can see certain evidence of their story. Clamshells—thousands of clamshells, in places forming a thick layer in the exposed banks at the high water level of the shore, and still slowly eroding out onto the lower beach—echo the story. These ancient banks of shells are known as middens, and they are prehistoric refuse piles, marking the places where people lived.

It is not difficult to imagine the people waiting for the low tides, carrying their handwoven cedar baskets down to dig for clams, their feet sinking into the soft, cool mud—and then gathering together as families, as a community, to bake the clams, preserve them and feast on them, casting aside the shells, an unthought gift to a future understanding.

The largest archaeological site in Tod Inlet is a shell midden some 180 metres long and 20 metres wide, on the north side of Tod Creek, extending from the creek mouth along the terraced shore of the inlet. Part of the site is covered by the cement foundation of a much more recent house. The midden is easily noticed from the water at low tide, though, as the shells are eroding out of the bank and are spread over the near shore. Among the shells found here are littleneck clam, butter clam, mussel and native (or Olympia) oyster. Based on the large area of the site, the massive accumulation of shells and fire-broken rock, and the variety of shellfish and other animal remains eroding from the site, archaeologist Grant Keddie suggested that the site might have once supported a permanent village.[2] The only artifact found here during the

archaeological studies in 1975 was a hand maul, a
type of striking tool that functions as a hammer.
This hand maul is of the nipple-topped type, a tool
typical of the culture known to archaeologists as
the Marpole Culture, named for the location of an
important archaeological site in Vancouver. Based
on the hand maul and in the absence of other
artifacts, archaeologists suggest that people lived
at this site at least 2,500 years ago.

I visited another site on the south bank of the
mouth of Tod Creek that is also marked by shells
visible on the surface and eroding from the banks
of the creek. At most of the site, the shells are
intact, and they include butter clamshells, littleneck
clamshells and cockle shells. On the beach the shells
are broken, probably due to recent traffic related
to the nearby log dump from the 1950s. Just north
of this site, in 1996, a team of archaeologists led by
Duncan McLaren found a flat-top hand maul in the
stream's sandy-mud deposits. Flat-top mauls are
associated with the Gulf of Georgia Culture, the
culture that followed the Marpole Culture. This
suggests that people continued to live at this site in
the period from 1,200 to about 200 years ago.

Hand mauls are a type of stone hammer used in cutting down trees,
splitting planks from cedar logs with wedges, driving pegs and even
caulking cracks in hulls of canoes. Finding two mauls in this small area
suggests that it may have been a place important for felling trees in
order to build houses or canoes.

My own archaeological excursions never brought me to a third
important site, located in a bay on the northwest side of Tod Inlet,
opposite Butchart Cove. This large site shows evidence of canoe runs,
areas where large rocks were cleared away so that canoes could be
hauled up onto the shore. Logging operations in the 1950s caused
extensive damage here, but there are small, intact areas at both the

Sketch of a flat-top hand maul
found at Tod Creek.
Watercolour by David R. Gray.

south and the north ends of the site where parts of a larger midden remain, between half and three-quarters of a metre deep. The original midden extended about 110 metres along the shore and 12 metres inland. Archaeologists speculated that it may be the remnant of another village fortified against raiders from the north.

The number of people living at the Tod Inlet sites at any given time is difficult to assess. It seems likely that there would have been several extended families, probably living in a few large houses made of cedar logs and planks.

ABANDONMENT

After visiting these sites, the obvious questions are when and why did people abandon them? Local biologist, fishing guide, teacher and amateur archaeologist Jim Gilbert, who had visited some of these sites in the 1970s, suggested two potential reasons for abandonment: changes in the environment and warfare. Gilbert thought the abandonment could be related to variability in climate, such as cumulative El Niño effects. He pondered the clues offered by archaeology and history that pointed to the possibility of warm water coming north, leading to a collapse in the dynamics of the marine life within Tod Inlet and Saanich Inlet. Perhaps there was no herring run in some years, no salmon or no lingcod. Could ecological change have prompted the move? Based on talking with Tsartlip Elders and his knowledge of the local oral history, Gilbert also pondered another explanation: raids by northern peoples.[3]

Dave Elliott Sr., Tsartlip Elder and author, described this warfare in his book *Saltwater People* (1983, revised in 1990): "We used to fight with the northerners. They used to come down and attack our homes, our villages. Many serious wars were fought with the Haidas and the Kwagulths [Kwakwa̱ka̱'wakw]. They used to take slaves when they would raid our villages. We also took slaves, if we took prisoners. This is the way it was before."

Tsartlip Elder Tom Sampson also recalled for me, from oral traditions that had been passed on to him, how in the early times, hundreds of years ago, when the Kwakwa̱ka̱'wakw and Haida came, the men would send their families way up into the hills for safety.[4]

The number of people living at the Tod Inlet sites at any given time is difficult to assess. It seems likely that there would have been several extended families, probably living in a few large houses made of cedar logs and planks.

Anthropologist Diamond Jenness recorded in 1935 that Tsartlip Elders David Latasse and his wife—Jenness never refers to David Latasse's wife by name, but the 1911 census lists her as Genevieve—attributed the destruction of their old village at the mouth of Tod Inlet (he called it Brentwood Bay) in about 1850 to either Kʼómoks or Kwakwa̲ka̲ʼwakw raiders, who attacked the settlement and burned its three long, shed-roofed houses along with several smaller ones.

THE SALTWATER PEOPLE

In *Saltwater People*, Dave Elliott Sr. described his family's connection to early Tsartlip history. His great-great-great-grandmother SEX̱SOX̱ELWET lost her husband and brother to northern raiders while she hid in the woods. They lived in a place now called Tsawout, on the east side of the Saanich Peninsula. In her shock and grief she wandered for many hours and came upon a beautiful meadow divided by four streams. Each stream had a name in her language. "This is where I will raise my son to be a man," she thought, and later persuaded some of her people to move away from the place of grief to a place of hope. They established a village there called W̱JOȽEȽP, now called Tsartlip. Her son, ȻELOW̱EṈTET, became a strong and tough leader in his tribe, but he too, in old age, was killed by northern raiders. He left many sons, among them the

(*top*) The house belonging to Tsartlip chief David Latasse, left on the waterfront, on the Tsartlip Reserve in 1922. RBCM PN11740.

(*bottom*) Tsartlip chief David Latasse on the Tsartlip Reserve in 1922.
RBCM PN6165.

Tommy Paul (*left*) and Chief David Latasse of the Tsartlip First Nation and Chief Edward Jim of the Tseycum First Nation (*right*) in 1922. RBCM PN11743.

ancestors of Dave Elliott Sr. The original name of the Tsartlip people is ȻESESIṈSEȽ, meaning "the people that are growing themselves up."

Dave Elliott Sr. lived with a sadness that the "beautiful way of life" had become only a story in history. Born in 1910 on the Tsartlip Reserve in Saanich, he grew up in two worlds, watching his old world of the canoe gradually transform into the wider world of international travel and space-age technology. He remembered the reef-net fishing from cedar canoes and the smell of woodsmoke from cooking fires of his childhood, and the traditional names for the geographical features of Saanich. He devoted his later years to teaching young people of his nation their own story.[5]

Most of the following information about the significance of Tod Inlet to the Tsartlip people over the last 100 years or so was shared with me in interviews with Elders of the Tsartlip in September and October 2001.

Tsawout Elder Earl Claxton Sr. remembered his uncles Dave Elliott Sr. and Tsartlip Elder Philip Paul, talking about Tod Inlet as an ideal place for fishing—in particular for spring salmon, because of the shallow sand bottom. In the evening they could always catch springs on the sandbar.

Philip Paul himself said to ethnobotanists Nancy Turner and Richard Hebda that his grandfather Thomas Paul (1864–1950) took the family to Tod Inlet for clams and seabirds. When hunting birds, one canoe would go into the inlet and scare the birds, which would then fly out low over the water up the narrows where the hunters would be waiting in their canoes.[6]

In an interview in 2002, Stella Wright from Tsartlip remembered the importance of fishing at Tod Inlet to her people in the days before the cement plant came: "In the spring when the herring spawned, the Tsartlip people used to go up to Tod Inlet. They would take a big cedar branch down to the beach and tow it behind a canoe to Tod Inlet. They would anchor it there, and when the herring spawned, the eggs [roe] would cling to the branches. They would later take it home and clean the roe off the branches. That seasonal delicacy was something the people used to talk about; getting ready for the herring, towing and anchoring the big branches. Different families would do it. They would row back and forth to keep an eye on the branches. As the boats started coming in and there was more traffic, the herring stopped coming in. For fishing, every young man owned a dugout canoe—no one owned a launch in those days. In early spring when the grilse [one-year-old salmon] came in, everybody went out fishing by canoe. Eventually gas boats took over. They did fish in Tod Inlet. Tod Inlet has always been a nice little place for fishing with a canoe."

A First Nations canoe, adapted for rowing, on the west coast of Vancouver Island, about 1910. Bonnycastle Dale photograph. Courtesy of Kim Walker.

As a young boy, Ivan Morris of the Tsartlip Reserve watched the men and women in canoes, rowing, as they came home from Tod Inlet with their catch: "Our people went out there fishing for fish that they needed to survive." At times, he recalled, they caught enough fish that they could sell some to get money to buy sugar.

The Tsartlip people used Tod Inlet for many practical purposes, but it also had a profound significance as a spiritual place. It was a place where spirit dancers went to complete their initiations and where young men and young women went to spend time alone, bathing in the cold waters and seeking spiritual insight and support.

As Dave Elliott Sr. put it, "We knew there was an intelligence, a strength, a power, far beyond ourselves. We knew that everything here didn't just happen by accident. We believed there was a reason for it being here. There was a force, a strength, a power somewhere that was responsible for it. . . . Our people lived on whales, seals, porpoises, and all the different kinds of fish, clams, oysters, crab. This was all the food of our people. This is how much we had. We were well nourished from that great food supply that was put here by the Creator, the Great Spirit."[7]

Tod Inlet was still an important spiritual place for Tsartlip Elder Tom Sampson and his family in the 20th century. "It was sort of forbidden because it was where a lot of spiritual people went." Tom's great-grandmother Lucy Sampson told him that Tod Inlet was "a good place, but not until you were ready. . . . People went up into the hills to prepare for spiritual quests and stayed for days. They would take food: clams and fish and deer. That is why there are some middens at the top of the mountains."[8]

Ivan Morris remembered Elder Louis Charlie telling of people going to Tod Inlet for new dances—longhouse dances. "I heard a lot about our people going over to Tod Inlet and living there for the winter, eating fish and clams." In the spring, Elders always told them, they came back from Tod Inlet, walking home to the Tsartlip Reserve.

The Tsartlip people used Tod Inlet for many practical purposes, but it also had a profound significance as a spiritual place.

THE YEARLY ROUND OF THE TSARTLIP FIRST NATION AT TOD INLET

The stories told by the artifacts and structures found at the archaeological sites around Tod Inlet, when put together with the knowledge and memories related and recorded by Tsartlip Elders such as David Latasse and Dave Elliott Sr., offer at least a glimpse into the lives of the people who lived at Tod Inlet for countless generations before colonization changed things.

The following yearly round of activities of the Saanich people is based on information from *Saltwater People* (1990 edition), *The Saanich Year* by Earl Claxton and John Elliott (1993) and Diamond Jenness's 1935 notes based on interviews with Tsartlip Elders David and Genevieve Latasse, and Tommy Paul, as published in the 2016 book *The W̱SÁNEĆ and Their Neighbours: Diamond Jenness on the Coast Salish of Vancouver Island, 1935*, edited by Barnett Richling. The information comes from both West Saanich (Tsartlip) and East Saanich (Tsawout) people.

We don't know just how closely this rendering of a year's possible activities represents the lives of the people who lived at Tod Inlet a thousand years ago or more, but the environment and the plants and animals of a century ago, which some of these memories reflect, would have been similar. Rather than starting the year in mid-winter, with the European tradition, I start this account in the spring, with the spawning run of the herring, an important event in the lives of the Tsartlip and in the natural cycle of life in Tod Inlet. The names of the months or seasons used by Elliott (1990 edition), Claxton and Elliott (1993) and Latasse in 1935 (as recorded by Jenness) are not identical, so I have included the variations.

Diamond Jenness and "the Indians of Canada"

New Zealand–born and Oxford-educated anthropologist Diamond Jenness (1886–1969) became the foremost of Canadian anthropologists. His first visit to Victoria was in 1913, when he joined the Canadian Arctic Expedition of 1913–1918 as it was launched from the city. During his three years with the expedition, he studied the Copper Inuit, little known to anthropologists, of the Coronation Gulf region of the Arctic. From August 1914 Jenness spent two years visiting, trading, travelling and living with the Copper Inuit. His experiences and the knowledge he gained were documented not only in five volumes of expedition reports, but also in two still-popular books for general readers (*The People of the Twilight* and *Dawn in Arctic Alaska*). Jenness collected a huge variety of ethnological materials: from clothing and hunting tools to stories, games and sound recordings of dance songs. On his return from the expedition, Jenness enlisted in the Canadian Army and served overseas for two years as a gun spotter. In 1935 Jenness spent several months interviewing Elders of the W̱SÁNEĆ (Saanich) people and recording their way of life, stories and legends.[9] During World War II he was Deputy-Director of Intelligence in Ottawa. His experiences with Canada's Indigenous peoples from coast to coast while working for the National Museum of Canada resulted in a major work, *The Indians of Canada*, published in 1932.

Blue camas flowers. Grant Keddie photograph.

SX̱ÁNEȽ (bullhead) / le.mas (crane)—April
The spring run of herring, which spawn in this month, was an important component of this season of fishing. At sea the men also caught cod, grilse, spring salmon and halibut. They hunted deer and elk on land.

PENAW̱EN̲ (harvest seaweed) / q'woiatstan (fawn embryo?)—May
Hunting seals and ducks, and fishing for spring salmon, cod and grilse occupied the men in May, while the women began the annual harvest of blue camas bulbs, spring gold (or wild carrots) and rushes for making mats.

ĆENȾEKI (sockeye returns to the earth) / panxweman (camas time) / k'wilkwak.en (time of hard ground)—June
During the three-week camas season, W̱SÁNEĆ people left their villages and camped on San Juan Island near their camas harvesting grounds. They also fished for halibut in the deep waters of the Gulf Islands. This was also a time for visiting neighbouring villages and occasionally holding potlatches.

ĆENHENEN (humpback returns to earth) / hanane'n (humpback salmon)—July
The people of the Tsartlip village left for Point Roberts on the mainland to begin two months of fishing, first for sockeye and then for humpback (or pink) salmon. The women gathered berries and dried the seeds of the consumption plant (wild celery) for flavouring fish and meat.

ĆENȾÁWEN (coho salmon returns to earth) / sowantan (coho salmon)—August
In this month the men took on the additional activities of building and repairing canoes, and sometimes a trip to the coastal mountains of the mainland to hunt mountain goats. These were added to the regular fishing, hunting and gathering of berries.

ĆENQOLEW̱ (dog salmon returns to earth) / skeye'n (sockeye salmon) / sakai (sockeye salmon)—September

The Tsartlip people returned to their village early in the month and prepared their houses, graveyards and wood supplies for the coming winter. Some men went hunting for seals, sea lions and sea otters by canoe, out among the islands. Late in September they would begin harvesting chum salmon as they approached the Goldstream River spawning grounds.

PEKELÁN̲EW̱ (first frost, leaves turn white) / pakalenuk (leaves)—October

The months of September and October saw more travel between villages, as this was an important time for potlatches. During the month of the "shaker of the leaves" or "winds and falling leaves" (W̱ESELÁN̲EW̱), it was a good time to hunt deer and elk, and to catch ducks using aerial nets suspended between trees over a bay or inlet. Other nets were floated on top of the water to catch diving ducks as they came up to the surface.

    The people moved back to their home villages on the Saanich Peninsula from their summer and fall travels to the Gulf Islands. The newly caught food would be safely stored for winter.

W̱ESELÁN̲EW̱ (winds and falling leaves) / hwesalenuk (falling leaves)—November

As the people settled down for winter, travel by the men was limited to hunting and fishing close to home, and by women only to gather fern roots and clams.

ŚJELȻÁSEN̲ (putting your paddles away) / tcilxomatsan (frosty month) / stilq'wesun (puts paddles away)—November–December

The month of ŚJELȻÁSEN̲ was a time of winter storms and sometimes snow, a time to be at home in warm and comfortable houses. This was the time for winter dances, visiting and storytelling. It was also a time for important work: For the women, a time to make baskets, mats and blankets. For the men, a time for making tools and utensils, carving, finishing lumber for houses and working on canoes.

(*top*) Salmon spawning grounds of Goldstream River, October 2018.
David R. Gray photograph.

(*bottom*) Tod Inlet in winter.
David R. Gray photograph.

"Salish dog" at Tsawout in November 1935. This 14-year-old dog had been shorn each year for its wool. Diamond Jenness photograph. Canadian Museum of History Archives 79346.

SISET (Elder)—December

The long winter moon is called SISET, meaning "old one," and was a time of continuing storytelling, winter dances, visiting and feasting—a time of legends and family histories.

From December to February people generally remained in the village. When the weather was good, the men fished offshore for cod or grilse, or hunted ducks. The women gathered clams and seaweed, but it was the dried fish and berries, and other plants gathered during the summer, that formed their main winter diet.

NINENE (offspring or young ones)—January

NINENE is the month of "offspring" or "young ones." During the last moon of winter, the people continued with the regular annual indoor work of carving and making baskets and other necessities of life. It could also be a time for the first duck hunting, but only close to the village. As the tides changed, the people knew the herring would soon arrive, and the busy seasons with them. This is the season that deer fawns are born, and so the end of deer hunting.

WEXES (FROG) / waxlis (frog) / nenana (East Saanich, young one)—February–March

The hunting of seals and catching of spring salmon, cod and grilse supplied fresh food in March. This month marked the end of winter spirit dances, but also the holding of ceremonies by the secret Black Dance society. The society dancers painted their faces black or wore wooden masks representing the thunderbird, the wolf, and Skwanelets, the fish spirit. Tom Paul remembered that his father owned a large wolf mask with a mouth that could be opened and closed.

PEXSISEN (blossoming)—March

During this moon the people hunted brant geese, harvested clams, oysters and mussels, and harvested strips of cedar bark. Before the days of raising sheep, people used dog and mountain goat hair for spinning yarn to make clothing. The local breed of a small white woolly dog shed at this time as the weather warmed.

EUROPEAN EXPLORATION AND SETTLEMENT

The first recorded European sighting of Tod Inlet dates from the British Royal Navy's exploratory voyages of the mid-1800s. Captain (later Admiral) George Henry Richards surveyed several parts of the BC coast in the steam sloop HMS *Plumper* between 1857 and 1859 and in HMS *Hecate* in 1862. During a survey of Saanich Inlet in 1858 he gave the name "Tod Creek" to the whole area now known as Brentwood Bay and Tod Inlet.

Sketch of HMS *Plumper* in BC waters from the *Illustrated London News*, 1862. Note the Indigenous canoe. Author's collection.

The "Tod" refers to John Tod (1794–1882), an employee of the Hudson's Bay Company who later became a member of the council of government for the Vancouver Island colony in 1851, and of the later Legislative Council. As both were living at Victoria in 1857, it is likely that Captain Richards and John Tod knew each other socially, as well as professionally.

Captain George Henry Richards and the Cool Arctic Connection

Before Captain Richards explored Saanich Inlet and Tod Inlet, he served in the Arctic on one of the expeditions searching for Sir John Franklin. During the British Naval Franklin Search Expedition of 1852–1854, George Henry Richards was captain of HMS *Assistance* under Sir Edward Belcher. In 1852 Richards and Belcher sailed up Wellington Channel and wintered at Northumberland Sound on the northwestern peninsula of Devon Island. In the late winter and spring of 1853, Richards and his men sledged along the north coast of Bathurst Island to Melville Island and back, a return journey of 1,300 kilometres. This small party was one of the first to explore north of Bathurst Island, now the site of one of Canada's newest national parks. Bathurst Island was also the site of the High Arctic Research Station, where I spent many years studying muskoxen and other arctic wildlife. I love the connection that Captain Richards was among the first Europeans to see Tod Inlet and also among the first Europeans to explore Bathurst Island, the two places in the world that I have spent the most time "exploring"!

But why was an inlet called Tod "Creek"? In British English, the word "creek" refers to "a narrow recess or inlet in the coastline of the sea, or the tidal estuary of a river; [or] an armlet of the sea which runs inland in a comparatively narrow channel"[10] and offers facilities for harbouring and unloading smaller ships. All of these describe Tod Inlet perfectly. The use of "creek" to describe a small stream or tributary of a river is a North American peculiarity.

Based on Richards's survey, the 1864 publication *The Vancouver Island Pilot* gives the following description of Tod Creek: "Tod Creek is 2 miles southward of Cole bay. Senanus Island, a small wooded islet, 150 feet high, lies off its entrance with deep water on either side of it. There is anchorage in the outer part of the creek in 15 fathoms. A short distance within it narrows rapidly and winds to the southward and south-east for three-quarters of a mile, with a breadth of less than a cable, carrying 6 fathoms nearly to its head."[11]

By 1936 the *British Columbia Pilot* had applied the name "Tod Inlet" to what had been called Tod Creek, and maps now showed the name Tod Creek applied only to the stream as we know it today.

THE DOUGLAS TREATIES

The earliest European visitors viewed lands on the Saanich Peninsula, once referred to simply as North and South Saanich, as productive lands suitable for agriculture. In his book *Four Years in British Columbia and Vancouver Island* (1862), Richard Mayne describes the northern part of the Saanich Peninsula as "some of the best agricultural land in Vancouver Island. The coast here . . . is fringed with pine [Douglas fir]; but in the centre it is clear prairie or oak-land, most of it now under cultivation."[12]

In a somewhat underhanded arrangement, Sir James Douglas had "purchased" the land from its Indigenous stewards in February 1852. The Tsartlip people were not properly informed of the content and meaning of the agreement, nor were they actually paid anything other than blankets, and the "X" marks that were considered signatures all looked the same, according to Elder Dave Elliott Sr.[13] The treaties Douglas signed reserved to the First Nations the "liberty to hunt over the unoccupied lands, and to carry on our fisheries as formerly" in the vast treaty area, which included Tod Inlet.

Following the first survey of 1858, 18,000 acres were marked off for pre-emption by settlers, in allotments of 100 acres for single men and 200 acres for married men. Pre-emption is the "purchase, or right of purchase, of public land by its occupant, (usually at a nominal price), on condition of his or her improving it."[14]

The Pemberton map of Saanich Peninsula in 1859 shows no features at Tod Inlet. In the South Saanich District the only locations identified near Tod Inlet were "Senanus I.," "Chawhilp Inds.," and "Stelly's."

FIRST SETTLERS

When the electoral district of Saanich, which included Tod Inlet, was created in 1858, only 21 names were on the voters' list, and only eight represented residents of Saanich District. William Sellick (who was not actually a resident of Saanich District at that time) first pre-empted the land on the north side of Tod Inlet in 1859, then forfeited and sold it at auction to Bishop George Hills in 1861. The Right Reverend Bishop Hills, bishop of British Columbia, who arrived in Victoria in 1860, was particularly interested in land in North Saanich, and he purchased several hundred acres, including part of the present site of Sidney—probably as speculation on behalf of the Anglican church. The land the bishop purchased at Tod Inlet was sold in 1866 to a Thomas Pritchard. The land changed hands again that same year, this time going to farmer George

Saanich Inlet and Tod Creek. Part of *Haro Strait and Middle Channel*, an 1862 map based on the surveys by Captain Richards and the officers of HMS *Plumper*. Engraved by J&C Walker. City of Vancouver Archives AM1594-: Map 839.

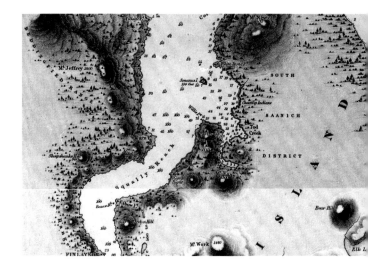

Albert Thomas. Thomas and his wife, Elizabeth (née Watson), lived in Saanich until their deaths in 1909 and 1916.

Other early farmers in the area included Peter C. Fernie, German immigrant William A. Pitzer, John Sluggett, and Peter Bartleman, a farmer and blacksmith. Bartleman's wife, Janet, was from the Tsartlip First Nation. Their sons, Issac and Gabe, later made a significant impact on the Tsartlip community.

The land on the west and south sides of Tod Inlet was in what was originally called the Lake District because of the many lakes to the south. One of the largest landowners in that area was the Victoria Water Works.

In the 1850s, as wooden buildings were replaced by larger buildings of brick or stone, a need for lime to make mortar and plaster developed. Though farmers had long used lime for fertilizer, the use of lime as a building material increased demand for it and led to a flourishing of small lime kilns. The 1887 British Columbia Directory notes that "an excellent quality of lime is obtained in [Saanich and the Lake District], which . . . finds a ready market in Victoria and Vancouver."[15] Tod Inlet became an important locality for this new enterprise of lime burning.

John Greig, born in Burness, Orkney Islands, in 1825, arrived in Victoria in 1854 after working for the Hudson's Bay Company. He bought land at Parson's Bridge, near View Royal, built a lime kiln and went into business as a lime burner. As the limestone there was of not of good quality, "he went scouting about and discovered Tod Inlet."[16] In 1869 Greig purchased 219 acres of land there, and in 1870 he became the area's first lime burner. He moved to Tod Inlet, built a log cabin and a lime kiln, and continued to produce lime with the help of his several sons.

In a 1904 photograph (12 years after Greig died), we can see some details of this early lime kiln. As this type of kiln was fed from the top, and the lime extracted from the bottom, these kilns were often built against a hill or rock outcrop. Greig's kiln was on level ground, so there was a ramp leading to the top, up which the raw limestone was carried to be dumped into the body of the kiln. The side wings probably offered shelter and storage space for the lime.

Greig also farmed, and his property at Tod Inlet was called Burness Farm after his birthplace in Scotland. Priscilla Bethell, Greig's great-

The early Greig/Wriglesworth lime kiln at Tod Inlet, about 1904. The small building to the right was probably the office building for the Saanich Lime Company. BC Archives G-06193.

An aerial view of Tod Inlet in 1930 showing the Fernie farm buildings.

National Air Photo Library.

great-granddaughter, recalled John saying that he sold the property to his second-oldest son, Robert, for "$10 and a Stetson Hat" when the Hudson's Bay Company began buying lime from San Juan Island rather than Tod Inlet.[17] This source of competition, which hampered Greig's business, was one of the earliest large-scale lime kilns on the Pacific coast. It was located at Roche Harbor on San Juan Island, just 25 kilometres northeast of Victoria across the American border. Greig and his wife, Margaret, lived out the remaining years of their lives at Tod Inlet. He died in 1892.

Peter Fernie, Tod Inlet's second lime burner, is listed in the 1890 city directory as a lime burner at the Lake District. Fernie owned and farmed 60 acres on the east side of Tod Inlet, north of the main body of the inlet. The Fernie house had a foundation of rock and lime, and the farm well was a beautiful one, lined with brick.

Peter Fernie burned lime in a beehive-type kiln for use by local farmers. According to the Canada census of 1891, he employed a total of nine men, including an American named C. Kane as a lime burner and three Chinese men as wood choppers, at his lime kiln. Though Fernie died in 1892, the 1901 Canada census described him as "Head" of the family, with a servant, James Gray. Peter is listed as a farmer, James as a farm labourer.

The third of the lime burners was an Englishman, Joseph Wriglesworth, born in Yorkshire in 1840. Wriglesworth was a water diviner, a volunteer fireman and a member of the Odd Fellows fraternity. He was also a lime merchant and a lime burner at Tod Inlet between about 1892 and 1904. Wriglesworth came to Canada from England in 1862, travelling across the Isthmus of Panama. After a brief and unsuccessful foray into the Cariboo goldfields, he returned to Victoria, built the London Hotel on Johnson Street and became a businessman and politician. By 1881, at the age of 38, Wriglesworth was married with five children and living on Yates Street in Victoria.

In the May 1, 1885, *Daily Colonist*, there is an ad under the heading "Home Productions" that reads, "Saanich Lime and San Juan, Roche Harbor Lime for sale by J. Wriglesworth, corner of Yates and Blanchard streets." His storefront advertised "Lime, Plaster, Hair, Cement &c." (The hair was probably horsehair, used as a binding material in mortar and plaster.)

He served on the Victoria city council for many years, and in 1886 he ran for election to the provincial legislature. During a speech before his potential electors, he received cheers for his comment that he had no axe to grind and would take particular notice that he turned no stone to grind other candidates' axes.

It seems that Wriglesworth prospered in his lime business, and he was described as an "extensive lime burner." An advertisement in the Victoria *Daily Colonist* in 1887 offered wholesale lime from the Saanich Lime Company, in what seems to be a joint venture by Wriglesworth, Caleb Pike's operation in the Highlands (southwest of Tod Inlet), the Raymond lime kiln near Esquimalt Harbour and Greig's Tod Inlet kiln. Wriglesworth's company, J. Wriglesworth & Co., was associated with the US-based San Juan Lime Company in 1889, and a year later with the Saanich Lime Company.

Joseph Wriglesworth was a lime merchant and lime burner at Tod Inlet between about 1892 and 1904.

The Saanich Lime Company was incorporated in 1890, with Joseph Wriglesworth, William Fernie and Peter Fernie as trustees. The company was formed "to acquire by purchase, operate and carry on, and extend the lime-kilns on Tod Creek and Highland district, now being carried on at the above-named places." The company office was at 127 Yates Street, Wriglesworth's store and home.

Wriglesworth's store on Yates Street in Victoria, in the 1870s. BC Archives A-03469.

The *Victoria Daily Times* of September 1, 1890, reported that the steamer *Rainbow* had brought 205 barrels of lime from Saanich to Victoria. The report is one of the earliest records of a large ship entering Tod Inlet for commercial purposes. *Rainbow* was a 108-foot, 150-ton steam-powered wooden schooner. After delivering the lime to Victoria, she headed to Texada Island, north of Nanaimo, to carry 436 barrels of lime to Vancouver on their way to a final destination of Seattle, Washington.

In November 1890, the *Times* noted that Vancouver Island lime was beginning to find a good market on the BC mainland, and that shipments from Saanich were being made quite frequently. The article, entitled "Lime Shipments," also recorded that the paddlewheel steamer *R.P. Rithet* had brought over a large number of empty barrels and was leaving "for the kiln to unload the barrels and take on 800 more barrels of lime headed for New Westminster. . . . This shows that the people of Vancouver Island are beginning to use their lime which so long laid untouched, while San Juan Island reaped the benefit."[18]

The Saanich Lime Company described their assets in the Victoria *Daily Colonist* in 1891 as part of a proposal to form a joint stock company to expand their works: "The property of the company is situated on Tod Creek, Saanich Arm, about eleven miles from Victoria, the creek being well sheltered and deep watered, the land comprising 435 acres. . . . On the land in question there are two draw-kilns of the latest pattern, and capable of burning 130 barrels of lime per day; the quarries are close to the kilns and reached by good macadamized roads, which can be used by tramways. There is also a substantial wharf, with 14 feet of water. . . . The buildings, outhouses, stables, and other structures are of the best material and most improved workmanship."[19] The company also had a wooden warehouse in Victoria capable of holding 600 barrels of lime.

It seems that Wriglesworth eventually bought the Greig property at Tod Inlet from Robert Greig, the son of John Greig, sometime after John's death in 1892.[20] It is not clear whether Wriglesworth bought the property for himself or on behalf of the Saanich Lime Company.

By 1892 Wriglesworth & Co. owned 225 acres of land along the north shore of Tod Inlet and Tod Creek. In 1893, the Saanich Lime Company announced that Wriglesworth had been "appointed sole agent for the sale of our Lime." Wriglesworth sent a sample of the limestone to England for testing, and when the sample showed good potential, he tried, unsuccessfully, to interest Victoria businessmen in developing a new industry— probably the making of cement.

An 1895 map of the "South Eastern District" of Vancouver Island is the earliest map I could find that shows Lime Kiln Road—now Benvenuto Avenue. The road appears on this map as an extension of Butler Cross Road, leading west from West Saanich Road towards, but not all the way to, the shores of Tod Inlet. The next east-west roads to the north are Sluggett Road and Stelly's Cross Road.

FROM LIME TO CEMENT

The Vancouver City Directory for 1896 lists Joseph Wriglesworth of Victoria, the CPR Cement Works of Vancouver, and four others under the heading of "Lime, Plaster & Cement Dealers."

The Canadian Pacific Railway Company had decided to build a factory in Vancouver to produce cement for their construction work in Western Canada in the early 1890s. They built a factory on the shores of False Creek and began making cement. The quality of the cement was not up to expectations, so in 1894 they hired an experienced British cement worker. Within a short time the quality had improved enough to match any cement produced in Britain or Germany.

The Geology of Limestone

Limestone has great quantities of calcite, a common carbonate mineral and a rock-forming material. Calcite and dolomite, and the rocks containing them, are valuable sources of calcium and magnesium carbonates, which are used in the cement industry (in making Portland cement) as well as in the iron and steel refining process (as a flux in blast furnaces). Limestone is an organic sediment, derived from animal fragments compacted into rock layers. Organic limestones are formed when coral reef builders inhabiting warm, shallow seas secrete calcium carbonate. (Sedimentary limestone rock becomes marble when metamorphosed.)

Local journalist Robert Connell described the origin of the Tod Inlet limestone rock formation as "reefs girding the volcanic islands of the warm Jurassic or Triassic sea, and when the countless swarms of coral animals built them as their many-patterned homes out of the lime of the waves. And since then, in the strange transmutation of things, the contents of this quarry has passed into the walls of human habitations." [21]

The Vancouver *Province* and the *Victoria Daily Times* reported in August 1896 that a new company, the Pacific Coast Portland Cement Company, had applied for incorporation to take over both the Saanich Lime Company's location on Tod Inlet and the Canadian Pacific Railway Company's cement works on False Creek. The Vancouver-based company was to carry on business as a manufacturer of Portland cement and lime. But the plan apparently never materialized. Tod Inlet was to remain a quiet backwater for the time being.

Through the first few years of the 20th century, there were no new developments at Tod Inlet. An article in the *Victoria Daily Times* on July 22, 1905, describes what a "Victoria sportsman" would have encountered at Tod Inlet at the beginning of 1904.

> He… followed what is still known as the Limekiln Road, until, descending a long grade, he saw the blue waters of Todd [sic] Inlet through the foliage which grew thickly on its shores. No sign of life, or of human occupation marked the scene, excepting the scamper of a band of deer which hurried up the precipitous banks across the bay as he dropped his canoe in the water. A tumbledown wharf, a deserted lime kiln, and the almost unused road leading to them, alone marked where the hand of industry had left its impress on the spot, only to be withdrawn as if the futility of a fight with the forces of nature had been recognized.[22]

2

A New Enterprise—a New Community (1904-1910)

When the president of the British Columbia Board of Trade made
an announcement in December 1900 that a new cement works was to
be established at Tod Inlet, it was heralded as the beginning of a new
enterprise for British Columbia that would have a "profound impact on
the economic future of the Province."[23] Was this going to be another
announcement with no practical follow-up, as had happened at the
incorporation of Pacific Coast Portland Cement four years previous?
Or would the "hand of industry" once again join battle with the "forces
of nature" at Tod Inlet? It seemed promising for the latter.

W.A. Ward told the meeting of the board of trade in Victoria that a
property had been purchased by a man called James Keith-Fisher, and
that assays showed that the materials available at the site were suitable
for the manufacture of cement. So who was this new man on the scene,
and what was he up to?

James Keith-Fisher was an English businessman from New York
who had come to Vancouver in July 1898. By February the next year he
was a newly elected member of the Vancouver Board of Trade, and in
October he was listed as the general manager of the British Columbia
Portland Cement Company.

In 1899, the new British Columbia Portland Cement Company
leased and then purchased the cement works of the CPR at False
Creek in early February. By late February the company had announced
plans to bring in some five railway carloads of new machinery from
Copenhagen and New York. Keith-Fisher had had the cement tested

in Montreal, and the results showed a tensile strength "of rare quality" and an "exceedingly good" fineness.

In the *Victoria Daily Times* of February 1900, the purchasing agent for the City of Victoria requested tenders for 2,000 barrels "of White's Portland Cement, or any other brand of Portland Cement of equal quality in strength to White's." White's Portland Cement was a "celebrated" brand produced in Great Britain by the Associated Portland Cement Manufacturers and available in British Columbia. Until cement production began in Western Canada, cement had to be ordered from British cement companies and shipped by the barrel around Cape Horn. In the United States, no cement companies operated on the Pacific coast until about 1900. Before that, institutions, governments and industries had ordered cement from Germany.

Keith-Fisher was in New York in November 1900 and in Montreal in December. The "Personal Intelligence" column of the *Montreal Gazette* of December 1900 listed J. Keith-Fisher (and, incidentally, Winston Spencer Churchill) as guests at the Hotel Place Viger in Montreal. Keith-Fisher was making the rounds . . . and undoubtedly talking about Portland Cement.

Portland cement is a finely ground manufactured mineral product resulting from combining the raw materials of crushed limestone and clay at a high temperature. When mixed with water and sand or gravel, the powdered cement solidifies to form the solid building material called concrete.

An English inventor, Joseph Aspdin, came up with this idea in 1824. He tried mixing burned ground limestone and clay to produce an "artificial cement" that would be stronger than that produced using plain crushed limestone. His idea worked. Aspdin named this new product "Portland cement" because it produced a light grey-brown concrete, similar in colour to the building limestone found on the Isle of Portland, on the south coast of England. (The best-known use of Portland limestone was in the rebuilding of St. Paul's Cathedral after the Great Fire of London in 1666.)

Until the early 1900s, relatively small amounts of cement had been manufactured in North America. Wood and stone had met all

The Parsell family. See p. 71.

Until cement production began in Western Canada, cement had to be ordered from British cement companies and shipped by the barrel around Cape Horn.

1522 – CEMENT WORKS, COLTON, CALIFORNIA.

The Colton Portland Cement Company, near San Bernardino, California.

Postcard in author's collection.

building requirements, and few people envisioned any widespread use for cement. However, as cement plants multiplied, the new material became more available, and the use of cement soared. Cement was used in the foundations of brick buildings, in construction of bridges and in paving of sidewalks.

The first two companies to produce cement in the American West were both in California. The Colton Portland Cement Company began producing cement near San Bernardino, about 100 kilometres east of Los Angeles, in about 1900. The town that arose near the plant was actually named Cement. The Pacific Portland Cement Company started production soon after at Suisun Bay, about 60 kilometres northeast of San Francisco.

Other than the small cement plant in Vancouver, built by the Canadian Pacific Railway Company in about 1890 to manufacture Portland cement for the railway's own use, the only cement plant in Western Canada was a small, short-lived one erected near Princeton, BC.

At about the same time in Eastern Canada, businessman Robert Pim Butchart had joined other investors in developing a proposition

The letterhead of the Vancouver Portland Cement Company, showing a portrait of Captain George Vancouver. From the Butchart Gardens historical display, 2016; presented with permission of the Butchart Gardens. David R. Gray photograph.

to make Portland cement at Shallow Lake, near Owen Sound, Ontario. This was a new venture for Canada, and notable even for the continent. Butchart, born in Owen Sound in 1856, had inherited his family's hardware and ship chandlery business. Knowing that a local cement plant could successfully compete with cement imported from England, he launched into cement production. This first venture at Shallow Lake was a failure. The bricks lining the kilns were unable to withstand the high temperatures needed to burn the limestone in the kilns. After consulting with a distant relative in the cement business in England, Butchart tried a different type of kiln and went on to build and operate two successful cement plants in Owen Sound and Lakefield, Ontario.[24]

Sensing a profitable new market, Butchart then turned his attention to the west. His interest in the western market led to the cement plant that he is best known for—the first large successful cement plant in British Columbia.

Butchart and his wife travelled to BC in 1902 to investigate the prospect of establishing a cement factory on the West Coast. He was undoubtedly aware of the lime-burning industry in British Columbia,

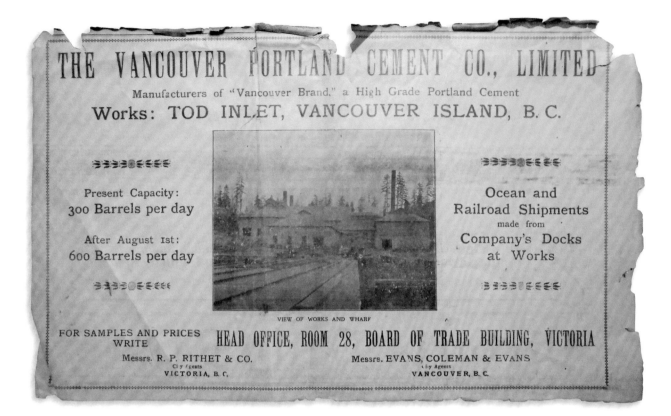

Vancouver Portland Cement Company
newspaper advertisement, 1904.

Author's collection.

and as an astute businessman, he would have been following the
movement towards the manufacture of cement in Western Canada.
Although I have found no record of such a meeting, I suspect that
Butchart would have met with James Keith-Fisher and Joseph
Wriglesworth. His investigation complete, Butchart returned to
Ontario and set the wheels in motion to purchase land at Tod Inlet
and establish the Vancouver Portland Cement Company Limited.

The new company was incorporated under the Dominion of Canada
Companies Act in 1902. Its official purposes and objectives were
"to search for, make merchantable, manufacture, use, produce, adapt,
prepare, buy, sell, and deal in Portland cement and all kinds of natural
and other cements and products into which cement enters either as a
part or as a whole, and all kinds of building materials, and to dig, mine,
dredge, or otherwise procure earth, marl, clay, stone, artificial stone,

shale, slate, clay granite or other materials necessary to the manufacture of cements, building materials and other products aforesaid."

The property the company purchased for the new cement works was the land that had been previously owned by John Greig and later, at the time of purchase, by Joseph Wriglesworth's company. This was the area along the north sides of Tod Inlet and Tod Creek. (The land was subdivided into "sections" within "ranges"; in this case the property was in Section 15, Range 2w, where "w" means west.) The purchase included the lime kiln and quarry formerly operated by the lime burners.

The purchase of the old lime-burner property was complex. Property records show that by 1901, the old Wriglesworth property—once John Greig's—belonged to James Edward Murphy of Meaford, Ontario. Butchart's new company purchased 246 acres from Murphy in 1903. And who was Murphy? He was a colleague of Butchart's and a vice-president of the Vancouver Portland Cement Company, of which Butchart was the managing director. Keith-Fisher, who was said to have purchased this property in 1900, never appears in the ownership records, and soon disappears from the scene. It seems that he went back to England, though his name still appears occasionally in newspapers as he travelled between Europe and the US.

At first the new cement company's head office was on Toronto's King Street. But by the time the plant was under construction, the company had set up a new headquarters on Bastion Street in Victoria.

A 1903 letter from Robert Butchart to William E. Losee, then manager of the Lakefield cement plant in Ontario, confirmed the decision to proceed with the cement plant at Tod Inlet. Construction began in June 1904. It was an early step at the beginning of a new industry in BC, and it would bring a new prosperity, and a promising new community, to the Saanich Peninsula.

CONSTRUCTION OF THE CEMENT PLANT

The Vancouver Portland Cement Company brought in experienced personnel from Ontario to oversee the construction of the plant and to manage the production of cement. Two men, Robert Vincent and Charles Carney, came to Tod Inlet from the cement plant at Shallow

> At first the new cement company's head office was on Toronto's King Street. But by the time the plant was under construction, the company had set up a new headquarters on Bastion Street in Victoria.

Lake to help build the new plant. William Losee, from the Lakefield plant, was engaged as plant superintendent.

One of the first priorities for the building of the cement plant was the construction of a substantial wharf suitable for receiving shipments of building supplies and the machinery needed for the mill. The old wooden wharf belonging to the Saanich Lime Company was undoubtedly useful at first, but a larger, stronger structure was needed.

The first wharf was constructed of wood early in 1904 so that equipment for the plant could be unloaded and moved into the building before construction was completed. It was about 11 metres wide and 60 metres long.

Designed to accept scows or barges on both sides, the end of the wharf was at just the right height so that loaded railway cars could be pulled from a barge onto one of three sets of tracks on the wharf. These tracks in turn led right into the plant building. The kilns, dryers and other machinery for the growing plant were all brought to the site on barges towed by tugs.

From the earliest photographs of the plant, we know that Chinese workers were involved in construction of the first buildings. Among them may have been some of the men whom Peter Fernie had employed at his nearby lime-burning operation.

There is no official record of the Chinese members of the community at Tod Inlet until the Canada census of 1911. This is not unusual for early non-white communities in British Columbia. It is typical of the province at the time that for as long as the village of Tod Inlet existed, the directories for Vancouver Island's communities listed the names and occupations of the white male inhabitants, but never listed any of the Asian immigrants, and seldom listed women. For Tod Inlet the existence of the Asian immigrants is mentioned in directories only once, in the Vancouver Island Directory for 1909: "Nearly 200 Orientals located here."

Little is known of how the 200 or so Chinese workers originally came to Tod Inlet. The large number of them suggests they were probably hired through one of the companies specializing in bringing Chinese workers to British Columbia for various building projects, including the Canadian Pacific Railway.

As well as workers from Ontario and China, some local inhabitants were also hired. Wilfred Butler, who ran the store at the corner of V&S (now Veyaness) Road and Keating Cross Road, had the first contract to haul freight down to Tod Inlet. He used a big old wagon as a stagecoach to run supplies and people from the Keating Station of the Victoria & Sidney Railway to Tod Inlet. His first job was delivering a load of sand to the site, undoubtedly for mixing with cement as the buildings were constructed.

Little is known of how the 200 or so Chinese workers originally came to Tod Inlet.

A First Nations dugout canoe on the wharf of the partially constructed cement plant, 1904. BC Archives I-56386.

The Vancouver Island Directory for 1909, the first to list the new community at Tod Inlet, gives an idea of the range of jobs performed by the men at the new cement plant. The most numerous were for the labourers at the plant (jobs taken by the "200 Orientals"). The 15 other jobs listed included oiler (there were 6), miller (3), then blacksmith, engineer, kiln burner, machinist and teamster (2 each), plus a manager, superintendent, chief engineer, chemist, clerk, coal grinder, carpenter and boilermaker.

As the plant went up, the new community of Tod Inlet began to grow, first with the builders, then the workers, and eventually with some families. The immigrant workers, however, didn't enjoy the "privilege" of families at that time. There is no official record of men from the Tsartlip First Nation working at the plant, although an early photograph of the plant under construction does show a First Nations dugout canoe on the wharf.

THE FIRST BUILDINGS

The actual construction of the cement plant began in June 1904, with a large number of employees working double shifts. The factory was built on level ground between the shore of the inlet and the new quarry. In its first phase the cement plant consisted of five lime-concrete buildings grouped together, some sharing a common wall. The lime for these buildings was burned in the old lime kiln built by the former owners. The concrete walls were about six metres high, and in those buildings where the process created much dust, the walls were surmounted by a wooden framework about two and a half metres high. This open space, between the concrete wall below and the horizontal beam or wall plate above, was filled with wooden lattice work, allowing ample light and ventilation. The five buildings of the plant's first phase were the coal house, the mill (including the kilns and grinding mills), the engine room, the boiler room and the stock house.

It seems that at least some of the cement used in building the plant itself may have been imported. In photographs, Chinese workers can be seen mixing and spreading cement from the standard 350-pound barrels that imported cement traditionally came in at that time.

Robert James Parsell, an engineer, was hired to help install machinery in the plant. Parsell was the son of an engineer, and his father worked on the Great Lakes steamship *Chicora*. The Parsell family had arrived in Vancouver by train from Toronto in 1901 and made their way to Victoria on the CPR steamer *Charmer*. Parsell worked as an engineer on Victoria's Outer Wharf. But when he heard of the plant being built at Tod Inlet, he joined up as a fitter and an engineer. Parsell left Victoria on March 3, 1905, on the Victoria & Sidney Railway's train. He covered the last five kilometres to the plant on foot, because there was then no transportation from the Keating railway station to Tod Inlet.

Mary Parsell, James's wife, was one of the first women to live in the village of Tod Inlet. Her memoirs, though written in 1958, are an important first-hand source of information on the people and early growth of the new community.

(*above*) The cement plant under construction, looking east from the ridge, pictured in the *Victoria Daily Times*, 1905. Author's collection.

(*below*) The CPR SS *Charmer* at Tod Inlet, about 1905. BC Archives.

(*top*) Drilling in a limestone quarry, possibly at the Bamberton cement works. Still from the film *The Manufacture of "Elk" Portland Cement* (BC Archives AAAA6718, 1963), presented with permission of the Lehigh Hanson Cement Company.

(*bottom*) Positioning dynamite in the quarry. Still from *The Manufacture of "Elk" Portland Cement*. See above.

(*opposite*) Chinese workers mining limestone in the quarry. Courtesy of the Butchart Gardens.

THE QUARRIES

While the plant buildings were going up, the new quarry was being prepared for the extraction of limestone. The Tod Inlet limestone deposit was a ridge running parallel to the inlet only about 300 metres from the shore, behind the new buildings. The new quarry was the second to be developed in the deposit. The first quarry was the one worked in 1869 by John Greig, then sold to Wriglesworth's Saanich Lime Company. Although it was part of the lands purchased by the Vancouver Portland Cement Company, it had little suitable limestone left and was not used.

To expose the raw material, the labourers had to strip off the forest growth and the surface soil, which was less than a metre deep. The men drove an open cut 60 metres long and 6 metres deep through the overlying clay between the plant and the limestone, and two men opened up the new quarry with a steam drill along a 12-metre face. Their main technique for removing limestone was drilling followed by blasting.

After blasting, the Chinese labourers excavated the raw limestone by hand. It seems likely that the quarry workers would have also broken up the larger chunks of limestone after the blasting, before loading it into steel tram carts that they pushed downhill on the track to the storage bins at the plant.

Although there were more than 200 Chinese labourers at Tod Inlet, discovering their personal stories has been more than difficult. After some 50 years of off-and-on searching, I still know only the stories of just three men out of the hundreds, and only a small part of those.

The earliest personal story from the Tod Inlet Chinese community is that of Chow Dom Ching. Lorelei Lew, Chow's granddaughter (whom I only met in 2017), has recorded her grandfather's history. He worked at Tod Inlet between about 1903 and 1906 and had paid the Chinese head tax, which was a fortune at that time, to enter Canada. "Grandfather Chow was one of the Chinese supervisors at the Butchart's limestone quarry and was very well paid. He helped hire Chinese workers for the quarry."

Victoria architect and former mayor Alan Lowe told me of his grandfather, who also worked in the limestone quarry at Tod Inlet:

The Chinese Head Tax and the Exclusion Act

Many Chinese workers were in Canada just to make enough money to escape a life of poverty at home. When they had earned enough, they would return to China. For this and other reasons, few brought families with them. Also, fearing massive immigration from China, the Canadian government had passed the Chinese Immigration Act in 1885. This act established a head tax of $50 for each Chinese immigrant. At this time there was widespread opposition to Chinese workers coming to Canada, with the often-expressed fear that they would take jobs from settlers and immigrants from Europe, primarily Great Britain. The imposed tax was increased to $100 in 1900 and $500 in 1903, making it increasingly difficult for immigrants to bring their families. This resulted in a disproportionately male immigrant population.

For example, in 1902 Vancouver's Chinese community was composed of 2,053 men and only 27 women, all of whom were married. For Vancouver Island's Nanaimo District, which included Saanich and Tod Inlet, the 1911 census listed 2,889 men and 45 women who were born in China. Many of these men were employed in the coal mines in Nanaimo and Wellington.

"My grandfather's name was Lowe Sai. They used to have our surname first, so his name was Lowe Sai. . . . My grandfather was born in 1888 in China. Initially, because of the Exclusion Act, he was unable to bring any family members over. And when my grandfather arrived in Canada, he paid the $500 head tax. . . . He came to Canada to look for prosperity . . . to look for a place so that his family could have a better life. He worked with the . . . cement factory back then, working as labourer. . . . That was probably in the early 1900s. He was probably not more than 20 years old. He went back to China to get married. He probably went back two other times, and he had two sons, one of them being my father. My father did not get to come to Canada until the Exclusion Act was lifted . . . so it was many, many years that my grandfather was away from China. He became a gardener for the well-heeled Caucasian families in the Uplands in the Oak Bay area."

Although most of the Chinese workers remain unknown and nameless, the story of Yat Tong, who worked at Tod Inlet for over 50 years, is well remembered by the people who grew up at Tod Inlet and by his former colleagues. Tong came to Canada in the early 1900s on one of what he called the "slave ships" from China. He worked on the railways until he became alarmed at the number of fatal accidents, then left to work at the cement plant in about 1912.

PLANT OPENING

By the end of March 1905, the cement plant buildings and equipment were ready and the necessary personnel hired to start the manufacture of cement, just 10 months after beginning construction. Within another month, after testing, adjusting and likely more testing, quality cement was being produced.

The newspapers of Victoria and the province made no announcement of the plant being completed, nor of the first cement being bagged. We can imagine the community gathering, waiting to hear the machinery start up, making an occasion of it. But was there an official opening ceremony? Did Robert Butchart invite the company directors or shareholders to an event? Did the mayor or the premier attend? It seems not. The only announcements made were of the first shipment of cement from Tod Inlet in April 1905: the Victoria *Daily Times* tells us this first shipment was on board the barge *Alexander*, towed by the tug *Albion*.

So this major development in a large and promising new industry for British Columbia seems to have passed almost unnoticed. This is not really surprising, as the average citizen had little experience of cement and limited understanding of how it might be used.

One of the first recipients of the new cement from Tod Inlet, sold as "Vancouver Brand" in honour of Captain George Vancouver, was the city of Victoria. As part of a new street improvement project, Yates and Johnson Streets were to receive cement sidewalks—cement from Tod Inlet![25] A few months later, probably after people began to walk on the new cement sidewalks, interest increased to the point that there were excursions by boat to Tod Inlet and tours of the plant. Cement became a product people wanted to learn about.

In 1902 Robert Butchart had bought 19 acres of land north of the shores of Tod Inlet from Peter Fernie, the local farmer and former lime burner. The purchase included the Fernie farm and the Fernies' small wood-frame house.

Fernie built a new house close to Tod Inlet, and the Butcharts lived in the Fernie cottage during the summer while they planned and built a stately new house closer to the cement plant. With his wife, Jennie, and their two daughters, Jennie and Mary, Butchart settled there permanently once their house was completed.

Soon after their house was built, Jennie began to organize a series of topical gardens around the house. It wasn't long before the tours

One of the first recipients of the new cement from Tod Inlet, sold as "Vancouver Brand" in honour of Captain George Vancouver, was the city of Victoria.

from Victoria, which came to visit the cement plant and learn about the process, also came to enjoy beautiful Tod Inlet.

One of the first records of formal tourist excursions to Tod Inlet dates from 1905. In July of that year an advertisement in the *Daily Colonist* announced an "Excursion to Tod's Inlet on Saturday, August 5, including Inspection of Cement Works." The excursion, organized by St. John's Church, also included a "sail through the islands" and a "concert on board" the steamship *City of Nanaimo*, all for the price of 75 cents for adults and 50 cents for children.

The Tod Plant had been only open for four months when Robert Butchart, the managing director, was off on another business venture. In August 1905, the *Victoria Daily Times* reported that an R.P. Butchart had decided to begin the manufacture of Portland cement at Calgary, then still part of the Northwest Territories, to meet the demands of the prairie towns for cement. He had spent six weeks in the territories looking for an appropriate location and the right combination of natural materials. "The new works will not require Mr. Butchart's direct attention for some time. He will, therefore, be in a position to give the Tod creek works his immediate supervision."

Robert Butchart's business interests were varied and numerous: timber, steamship lines, hardware, and firebrick and fireclay companies, not to mention cement. He served on boards as adviser or director, and he was also becoming known as a philanthropist. Butchart also loved fast cars and elegant yachts. He had joined what was to become the new Victoria Automobile Club in March 1905, a time when there were still very few automobiles in British Columbia, and was elected to two of the club committees. Butchart's yachts were among the first pleasure craft in Tod Inlet.

EXPLOITATION IN THE QUARRY?

After the Tod Inlet plant was finished, the Chinese labourers were mainly employed in excavating the raw limestone from the limestone quarry—by hand, as this was before the advent of the steam shovel. In those early days, safety precautions were few, and accidents were all too frequent. A tragic and fatal incident in the quarry was remembered by many because it was characterized by sacrifice.

One of the first records of formal tourist excursions to Tod Inlet dates from 1905.

Former cement worker and gardener Pat van Adrichem heard the story from his Chinese colleagues when they worked together in that same quarry. He shared that story with me in an interview in 2007: "In wintertime they used to heat the dynamite in a pail over the fire. Then they would stuff it in a hole. . . . It would go pretty quick-like. . . . One time this guy waited too long. One of what they call the straw boss, which was Chinese, he seen what was happening, so he grabbed the pail and ran with it, but it blew before he could get rid of it."

Mary Parsell recalled the same incident: "Sing, boss of the Chinese crew, noticed that the explosive which had been placed by the fire to warm was becoming too hot. He grabbed the explosive up in his arms and started to run but before he had gone far it exploded blowing him to bits. Undoubtedly he saved the lives of many others at the expense of his own." [26]

The *Victoria Daily Times* also published the news of the death of a man named Sing—perhaps the same incident—in September 1908: "Kop Sing, a Chinaman, was yesterday taken to St. Joseph's hospital suffering from the result of injuries received at the Tod Inlet cement works. He died about 5 o'clock." [27]

Mike Rice spent time at Tod Inlet with friends as a youth, and he lived and worked there in the 1950s. He was impressed by the "endless" lines of Chinese workers as they walked in single file from the plant up to their village at lunchtime. Rice was still upset, some 70 years after the fact, by the way the Chinese workers had been exploited. In an interview for the Sidney *Review* in 1987, he noted that for their high-risk work in the quarries, including the use of dynamite, the Chinese were paid roughly half what Canadian employees were, which was typical of the times. They were also forced to pay a part of their wages to the "bossman," an interpreter and foreman for the Chinese crew. The Chinese never had any key position apart from this bossman. "Some worked night shifts. There was a greater number of Chinese than white folk working there. And a lot of the Chinese became very skilled. But they weren't treated the same as us—not by any stretch of the imagination." [28]

"There was a greater number of Chinese than white folk working there. And a lot of the Chinese became very skilled. But they weren't treated the same as us—not by any stretch of the imagination."

The labourers at the cement plant were paid 10 cents an hour for both straight time and overtime. They worked 10 hours a day, six days a week, and were paid out once a month.

Norman Parsell, Mary's son, also remembered Chinese funeral processions. When the hearse took the deceased away, the mourners scattered thin rice paper along the road, each piece with many holes punched in it. Norman was told that these holes made it difficult for the devil to reach the dead man, since he had to pass through each hole first.

SEARCHING FOR THE SIKHS

It was through the discovery of a single photograph in Canada's national archives in 1978 that I first learned the Chinese were not the only immigrant workers at Tod Inlet. The photo of a Sikh cremation ceremony at Tod Inlet in 1907 opened a whole new chapter of the story for me.

From Mary Parsell's memoirs I learned of the arrival of 40 "Hindu" workers at Tod Inlet in 1906, and the effect of this new cultural contact: "To us they were a strange looking company of men with their long beards and their strange head coverings. They used to stare at the women as if we too were something quite different being without veils.

The Sikh cremation at Tod Inlet, 1907, as it appeared in the *Canadian Courier* magazine. Bonnycastle Dale photograph.

A Hindoo Cremation.

More than a month ago, there died a Hindoo labourer, employed at the Tod Creek Cement Works, near Victoria, B. C. The body was cremated in the adjacent woods, and two of the bones were sent back to the family in India, while the rest of the ashes was strewn in the waters of Tod Creek.

In the evenings they used to gather in the field at the back of our house and sing sad and mournful songs." [29] What Mary was hearing was the Sikh devotional and communal singing called "kirtan." Normally sung in the Sikh temple or gurdwara, these songs are not necessarily sad or mournful. Kirtan can be done anywhere Sikhs may gather when there is no gurdwara.

At this time in Canada, all immigrants from India were called "Hindu," regardless of their religion. This was not just common practice but official policy: in a 1907 amendment to the Provincial Elections Act, the legislative assembly of the province of British Columbia declared that "the expression 'Hindu' shall mean any native of India not born of Anglo-Saxon parents and shall include any person whether a British subject or not." In fact, many of the men described were of the Sikh faith.

The discovery of the one photograph was tantalizing, but initially led me nowhere. I could find no other reference to the Sikhs and there were no personal names. Hoping to learn more, I ventured to the Victoria gurdwara on Topaz Avenue. There the Granthi—the reader of the Holy Book—directed me to the elders' house, where I met Amrik Singh Dhillon. He recalled for me the stories of friends of his father who worked at the cement plant, and gave me the names of their descendants.

Meeting Amrik was the beginning of a long search that slowly and steadily brought to life the story of this unique group of immigrants. He told me about the two ships that brought South Asian immigrants to Victoria and Vancouver in 1906. The people remembered the ships they arrived in not by the ships' names, but by the number of South Asians on board: they called them "the 700 boat" and "the 800 boat." These ships were the CPR trans-Pacific steamers *Monteagle* and *Tartar*.

Records at the gurdwara show that the *Tartar* brought a large number of people from Jandiala village (in the Jullundar district of Punjab), including Hurdit Singh Johl, Sadhu Singh Johal, his uncle Diwan Singh Johal, Partap Singh Johal and Takhar Singh Johal. All of these men worked at least briefly at the Vancouver Portland Cement Company plant at Tod Inlet. [30]

In this group also were Hardit Singh and Gurdit Singh (Dheensaw), from the village of Moron in the Punjab. Hardit and Gurdit Singh originally used Moron, the name of their village, as an identifying name. This was changed to Dheensaw at the request of their children when the meaning of the word in English was pointed out. (It was only in the 1940s and 1950s that the use of Singh as a last name, a traditional Sikh practice, began to be replaced by using the name of their home village and keeping Singh as a middle name.)

Jeet Dheensaw, son of Hardit Singh, shared with me, in an interview in 2007, the stories of their travels he had heard from his mother: "Why my father and my uncle left India . . . to get a better life, which they didn't know they were going to get. They were very frightened and scared. They had heard stories of a vast land, open spaces, and just opportunities to do something . . . more than just living in the village, just tilling your own little farm, year after year and just surviving. Sikhs are quite industrious and adventurous . . . get itchy feet I guess, that's what they had in them."

Sometime before August 1906, the first group of Sikhs came to work at Tod Inlet, primarily as labourers, some likely as stokers and firemen for the plant's furnaces and kilns. The *Nanaimo Free Press* of September 4, 1906, reported, "Hindus are now employed at the cement works at Tod inlet. If their immigration is allowed to proceed with, it will not be long before they become as serious a competitor as the Chinaman."

The only first-hand account of the arrival of a group of Sikhs that I have found comes from a 1960 radio interview with Gurdit Singh Bilga, recorded by Laurence Nowry and held in the archives of the Canadian Museum of History.[31]

In 1906, when Gurdit Singh Bilga was only 18 years old, he heard about this new country called Canada, which was open to people from India. When he heard that you could earn a dollar a day, equivalent to three rupees, a great daily earning in India, he decided to make the trip. When he arrived in Victoria in October 1906, there were more than a thousand people from the Punjab already in Canada, and many were unemployed. The job situation was particularly bad in Vancouver and Victoria. He described his visit to Tod Inlet: "When we landed in Victoria, I heard there is a cement mill about 20 miles from Victoria. There is one of our friends, who is come from our village, he was a foreman over there. So we, about 30 or 40 people, go to that cement mill." They learned that people working there were getting a dollar and a quarter a day for 10 hours of work. "So . . . my friend tried to the mill owner, if they could hire some more people. But unfortunately, is another foreman beside my friend, and some his friends coming the same ship as we coming. They went to the mill owner, they offer, they can supply the man for dollar a day. So he get the job, we been refused."

The second group of Indian immigrants, mostly Sikhs, came from Jandiala in the fall of 1906. Among them was Gurditta Mal Pallan, a letter writer. He came straight from India with five or six people, male friends who travelled together on a ship from Calcutta (Kolkata) to Hong Kong. There they changed to a CPR ship headed to Victoria and Vancouver.

Mukund (Max) Pallan told me about his family history in a series of interviews in 2007 and 2008: "And my father, Gurditta Mal Pallan, came to Canada in 1906 with a group of people from the same village, Jandiala, where he used to live. Actually five people started together. They decided to come to Canada because a few of their friends, they were already here—they wrote back and said, 'Come on over. It's a big country, lots of jobs, and you will be happy here.'"

Victoria businessman Mony Jawl told me about his grandfather: "Well, my grandfather Thakar Singh emigrated from the village of Jandiala in the state of Punjab, in India, to Canada in 1906. He came with a group of others who were asked to come out to provide labour at the lime quarry at Tod Inlet. My understanding is that there were at least 10 or 12 people that were required and they were recruited from the village where my grandfather lived. They came to this country together, to work there."

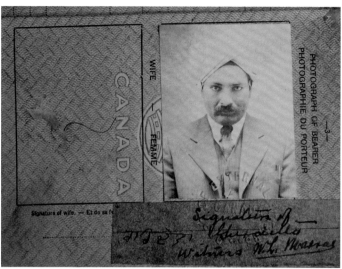

Gurditta Mal Pallan, from his passport.
Courtesy of Rupee Pallan.

Jawl's sister, Jeto Sengara, of Vancouver, also shared stories of Singh's arrival in Victoria: "I remember when my grandfather Thakar used to tell us stories . . . about when he first came to Canada. They didn't know where to live and there was no place to go. There was no temple at the time, so they pitched tents right where the Empress Hotel now is. And the group of men that had immigrated with my grandfather, they pitched tents there. There were mud flats there, and that's where they lived and slept . . . My grandfather walked all the way up to the cement plant by Butchart Gardens."

When G.L. Milne, medical inspector and immigration agent, was making inquiries in 1907 of some firms that had employed "Hindoos," he contacted the Vancouver Portland Cement Company. He reported

Why They Came: The Story of Davichand

Some of the men who came to Canada from the Punjab after 1904 were recruited by Canadian Pacific Railway agents in Hong Kong and Calcutta (Kolkata). Others were encouraged by individuals who may have seen immigration as a means of increasing their own incomes, such as Dr. Kaishoram Davichand. He was a Hindu Brahman doctor who had come to Canada in about 1904, with his young son and his wife, then said to be the only Hindu woman living in Canada. At an exhibition in Seattle, Washington, in 1905, Davichand and his son were offering "eastern palm reading" to visitors.

By 1907 he was encouraging immigration from his home country. He seems to have had an arrangement with several sawmills in the Vancouver area to supply men to work in the mills. As well

as writing to villages where he was known or had relatives, he also sent tickets to men in these villages to encourage them to emigrate.

In July 1906 the *Vancouver Daily World* reported that Davichand had gone to Victoria in response to a letter from the Vancouver Portland Cement Company who wanted him to get "a number of Hindoos to work for them."[32]

With encouragement from both individuals such as Davichand and companies like Canadian Pacific, immigration from India expanded until there were some 5,000 Sikhs in Canada by 1908. Most of them came in 1906 and 1907. The people who immigrated were mostly Sikh farmers and landowners, all from the same area of Punjab. In fact, many came in groups from the same villages.

that the company "spoke rather favourably of them as they were a competitor with the Chinese who were inclined to strike for higher wages at times, and by their presence kept the wages at the usual rate of $1.50 per day."[33] Milne also referred to "another peculiarity of the Hindoo, they are divided into numberless 'Casts' which is a great hindrance to their being employed in numbers."

But Milne was not well informed about the Sikh and the Hindu religions. His conclusion that "the Emigration of a large number of Hindoos into this country would not be desirable" was based on a lack of understanding of Sikhs and of the Indian caste system and was illogical at best. Sikhs, of course, have no caste system; even if they had, it is hard to see how this would have affected their usefulness as workers. Those who employed them described them as hard workers of good character. That good character, and the ability to withstand hard work and long hours, would be necessary in the harsh conditions inside the cement plant.

INSIDE THE CEMENT PLANT

At the beginning, the cement plant at Tod Inlet had a powerhouse attached to the mill room with a battery of five tubular boilers fired partly by wood and partly by slack coal, which generated the steam necessary to run the plant machinery. "Slack coal" refers to small or inferior pieces of coal that burn at a high temperature, suitable for use in burning limestone—especially in cement factory kilns that process limestone.

Norman Parsell remembered that in the early days of the plant, before the switch to electrical power, the plant used steam engines of various sizes, some very large. "They had a large block of coal-fired return tubular boilers and the firemen and stokers were mostly East Indians." When the plant was operating at full capacity, there were 11 engines to keep in order. A large Corliss steam engine drove the main power belt that operated the mill. There were smaller engines for individual phases of cement making. Norman's father, engineer James Parsell, would move from one to the next, checking them when on duty.

Mary Parsell told a story in her memoir of a potentially fatal accident in the mill: "One night when my husband was on duty in the engine room, he was walking around to the various machines to see that each

Norman Parsell remembered that in the early days of the plant, before the switch to electrical power, the plant used steam engines of various sizes, some very large.

Workers inside the powerhouse.
Author's collection, from BCCC photo album.

one was functioning properly . . . As he walked past the door opening into the mill he saw Fred Chubb standing pale and dazed looking, clad only in a suit of underwear. Upon enquiry as to what was the matter, Fred pointed to the huge fly wheel spinning around and around and said, 'I have just been around on that.' He had caught his sweater sleeve on a set screw and in a second he was caught up and whirled around. I do not know how many times he was carried about on that wheel but I know that his sweater was almost reduced to its original yarn and his new overalls were in ribbons. It was a miracle that he survived. Yet, with the exception of a few bruises and scratches, he was unhurt. Recently he was telling my son about this incident and he said that my husband took off his coveralls and gave them to him to wear."[34]

John Hilliard Lewis wasn't so lucky. Working in the mill room on a mould for the cement piers, he ducked under a moving belt while going down into an excavation. He was struck on the head by the bolts holding the ends of the belt together. He died the next day from a fractured skull, according to the *Victoria Daily Times* for December 4, 1905.

The largest and most complicated building in the cement plant was the mill room, where the large cylindrical crushers, rollers and kilns transformed the raw limestone and clay into cement.

When the men in the limestone quarry had finished loading the tram carts, they pushed them down the rails to the mill room, the first of the plant buildings. The tram-lines ran over a line of separate storage bins for raw clay and limestone, and into the crushing plant. The clay and limestone were carried separately on the tram-line and went on different paths into the plant.

The rough limestone rock was sent first into a crushing plant known as a Gates crusher. From there the crushed limestone was discharged into a rotary dryer, a hollow, wrought-iron cylindrical shell 1.5 metres in diameter and 13 metres long. The dryer rotated on tires, with a slight inclination down from the feeding end. It was heated in part by hot waste gases that were fed back from the kiln into the dryer. These gases passed into the lower end of the dryer, meeting the crushed material and drying it, then passed out the upper end into a separate brick chimney stack that was 19 metres high. As the cylinder revolved, the crushed material travelled through the dryer and was discharged automatically.

The crushed and dried limestone then passed from the rotary dryer into a screw conveyor, which carried it horizontally to a bucket-elevator. The elevator fed the partially crushed limestone into the Krupp ball mill, a horizontally revolving iron shell about two metres in diameter and two metres long. In the mill, which was lined with a heavy chilled-iron screen, were round steel "cannonballs." As the mill revolved, the cannonballs rolled over and through the crushed limestone, grinding it to a fine texture. From the Krupp mill another screw-gear raised the fine limestone and deposited it into a storage bin capable of holding 50 tons.

The clay arrived at the plant over the same tram-line as the limestone, but went directly into a Potts disintegrator, where a pair of rollers with revolving knife-like teeth disintegrated the clay. From there it passed into the same dryer into which the limestone was fed. The dryer was used alternately for limestone or clay, as required. The clay, already fine enough and needing no further grinding in the Krupp mill, went

(*top*) The dryers in the plant.
Still from *The Manufacture of "Elk"*
Portland Cement. See p. 44.

(*bottom*) The ball mill.
Still from *The Manufacture of "Elk"*
Portland Cement. See p. 44.

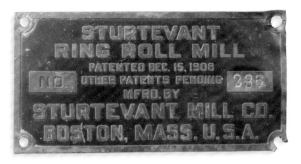

(*above*) Manufacturer's plate from a 1908 roll mill at Tod Inlet. David R. Gray photograph.

(*below left*) The kilns at the Tod Inlet plant. Still from *The Manufacture of "Elk" Portland Cement.* See p. 44.

(*below right*) Looking through the kiln door. Still from *The Manufacture of "Elk" Portland Cement.* See p. 44.

directly from the dryer to the ground-clay stock bin, located beside the ground limestone bin.

At this point the materials, which until this point had been treated and handled separately, were mixed. The men weighed the desired amount of both limestone and clay and gradually discharged the materials into a horizontally placed screw conveyor, which thoroughly mixed the two ingredients. From an elevated hopper bin, the mixed materials were fed down into two tube mills for further mixing and grinding.

The tube mills were iron tubes about 1.5 metres in diameter and 7 metres long, lined with hard flint stones embedded in cement. When the tube was rotating, larger round flint pebbles would roll over and through the ground limestone and clay, thoroughly mixing and grinding the materials. Next, the materials were fed into the rotary kiln, a horizontal iron tube mounted on rollers, 2 metres in diameter and 22 metres in length.

The noise in the plant must have been deafening. A contemporary account of a visit to a cement mill described the noise as the material was fed into the rotary kiln as "a rattle and din much resembling the discharge of musketry." Difficulty with hearing, if not outright deafness, must have been a constant risk for the many workers who spent 10 hours a day, if not longer, in the mill.

The kiln, lined with firebrick, was heated to a temperature of 2,700°F (1,482°C) by the burning of fine, dry coal dust. As the kiln rotated, the crushed limestone and clay slowly passed through and were fused

together by the heat, forming the "cement clinker" that when pulverized would become cement.

To break up large clumps of clinker without entering the kiln, workers fired a large kiln gun through the open door. The additional noise, as well as the heat the workers would endure with the kiln door even briefly open, is almost unimaginable.

The hot gases from the kiln were directed to the large central chimney stack. The first main stack at Tod Inlet was made of brick and stood 26 metres tall. Some of the hot gases were conducted back to the rotary dryer, providing enough heat to dry the incoming clay and limestone, and probably heating the building beyond comfort as well.

Next, the red-hot clinker went into the rotary cooler, another revolving iron cylinder about 1.5 metres in diameter and 15 metres long. The rotary cooler was set on an incline, and as cool air was let in,

The cement plant showing the first brick chimneys, about 1906.

Author's collection, from BCCC photo album.

the clinker cooled as it moved down the tube. When the clinker was cool enough to permit handling, it was mainly the Chinese and Sikh labourers who screened out any large clinkers and broke them up with sledgehammers.

Jeet Dheensaw relates his family memories of the work: "It was hard, dusty, breaking rocks, like breaking rocks and stuff, nothing by machinery. . . . They never had any machinery there."

After the cement left the cooler, the workers added gypsum to the mix. Gypsum was a necessary ingredient that acted to slow the setting time of the cement. The company had to bring gypsum in from various sources: Vancouver, Alaska, California, even France.

After being broken up by hand, the combined material was fed into a Bonnet ball mill, 1.5 by 2.5 metres in size, where it was partially crushed. From the Bonnet mill a screw conveyor took the material to another tube mill for final crushing to the level of fineness required for the finished product.

From the tube mill the cement went into storage bins in the adjoining stock house to await sacking. From the bins, men poured the cement into 87.5-pound (39.7-kilogram) sacks for storage or shipment. A bag warehouse and sack cleaner room provided more storage and workspace

(*top*) Looking into the kiln at the lumps of forming cement as they tumble with the rotation of the kiln. Still from *The Manufacture of "Elk" Portland Cement.* See p. 44.

(*bottom*) Adding gypsum to the imestone powder. Still from *The Manufacture of "Elk" Portland Cement.* See p. 44.

Gypsum

Gypsum is a sedimentary rock formed from the evaporation of salt water. It is found in large deposits worldwide at sites where there has been evaporation of sea water. A mineral containing sulphur and oxygen, in its massive or solid form it is called alabaster. As well as being important for making quick-setting building cement, gypsum is also used in the manufacture of plasters (including plaster of Paris) and plasterboard. Some of the gypsum brought to Tod Inlet from Alaska probably came from the Pacific Coast Gypsum mine, on Chichagof Island, Alaska, near Juneau in the Alaska panhandle.

Loading bags of cement on the wharf at Tod Inlet in 1907. Bonnycastle Dale photograph. Courtesy of Kim Walker.

for handling the sacks. The new method of shipping 87.5 pounds of cement in burlap sacks was based on the old barrel system: four 87.5-pound sacks weighed 350 pounds—the same as the old "barrel" of cement.

HEALTH AND SAFETY: THE DANGERS OF DUST AND HEAT

Gurditta Mal Pallan's first job at Tod Inlet was to fill the 87.5-pound bags with cement powder and carry them half a block to a waiting scow. He was a strong man and could handle the heavy work easily, but the dust compromised his lungs, so he looked for another job. By Christmas of 1906 he had moved to downtown Victoria and found work with BC Electric installing streetcar tracks, working 10-hour shifts for 10 cents an hour.

One of the newspaper reports relating to the Sikhs of Tod Inlet was a somewhat sensational article that appeared in the *Victoria Daily Times* in August 1906.

Under the headings of "Hindus are in Great Distress" and "Being Cared for by City Until Decision is Reached as to Their Disposal," the article starts with "Hindu Invaders have struck Victoria." The writer describes how 15 Sikhs had left the employment of the Vancouver Portland Cement works at Tod Inlet, walked to Victoria and camped on Fourth Street without tents or food. When concerned citizens appealed to the mayor of Victoria, police constables brought the Sikhs to the

The writer describes how 15 Sikhs had left the employment of the Vancouver Portland Cement works at Tod Inlet, walked to Victoria and camped on Fourth Street without tents or food.

Sikhs at the Tod Inlet wharf with scarves around their necks to combat the cement dust, 1907. Bonnycastle Dale photograph. Courtesy of Kim Walker.

patrol shed at city hall. The reporter gives us one of the few written descriptions of the early immigrant Sikhs and their belongings: "Heavy brass basins here and there and a large black pot of rice are the only evidences of food. . . . Only one speaks even imperfect English. He is an old man, a former member of one of the Sikh regiments and bears on his breast an imperial medal for one of the Chinese campaigns. . . . They attempted to work at Tod Inlet, but could not stand the dust. Complaints of bronchitis and throat troubles seem to be the chief cause of their quitting."[35]

Gurditta Mal Pallan told his son Max about how the people at Tod Inlet did indeed get sick: everyone, he said, was coughing from the coal and cement dust. No precautions were taken officially, but the Sikhs tied extra clothes around their necks to cover their mouths and noses. It was mostly the Chinese workers who unloaded the coal. The resultant silicosis was especially fatal in combination with tuberculosis.

A May 1909 story in the *Victoria Daily Times* headlined "Chinese Fireman Dies Suddenly" describes the fate of fireman Joe Do Yen, who suffered a heart attack while working in the boiler room and collapsed on a pile of coal. He was found by his friends but was beyond medical help. His body was taken to Victoria, where he was to be buried in the Chinese Cemetery at Harling Point, between Gonzales Bay and McNeill Bay.

The special firebricks used to line the kilns were of different sizes, shapes and places of manufacture and were imported both from Vancouver and Scotland. They had to be replaced periodically as they became worn out or broken. Pat van Adrichem, who worked in the kilns at the Bamberton cement works, described for me the process of replacing the firebricks. The men working with the kilns watched for red areas on the outside metal of the kiln where heat was coming through, indicating faulty bricks. When such areas were spotted, workers were sent into the kiln to pull out and replace the bricks. The only bricks sometimes retained were the larger bricks at the end of the kiln. Although they waited until the kiln cooled down before entering, it was still hot enough in the kiln that the workers would get blisters on their feet, even through their boots. Workers used picks, bars and mattocks to remove the hot bricks, which were all keyed in together. As they cleared one side out, the operator would revolve the kiln slightly to allow loose bricks to fall and the men to get at another area. At Tod Inlet they loaded the loose bricks into wheelbarrows to get them out of the kiln and dumped them at the shore or used them as fill.

Firebrick made by Clayburn (a Vancouver company) discarded from the kiln, at the shore of Tod Inlet near the wharf. Glenboig and Snowball from Scotland are other brands of brick you can find there.

David R. Gray photograph.

The Tod Inlet wharf with barge and tugboat unloading machinery for the cement plant, 1906–1907.

Author's collection, from BCCC photo album.

THE CEMENT PLANT COMPLEX

By 1905, the company was making cement piles to support the structure of the wharf where equipment and supplies were unloaded. These giant piles were pointed at one end, with a metal pile-shoe to facilitate driving them into the seabed with a piledriver. When the wharf was extended, sometime after 1907, these new, long-lasting piles were driven into the sea floor in a long L-shaped pattern.

The coal to power the cement mill was unloaded from barges and carried directly up to the coal house on a conveyor belt from the wharf. The coal house was situated directly beside the mill room on the west side.

Beyond the coal house and slightly apart from the mill were the other major company buildings—the blacksmith shop, the machine shop and the office building.

Inside the blacksmith shop in 1965.
David R. Gray photograph.

The forge and bellows in the blacksmith shop, 1965. David R. Gray photograph.

The blacksmith shop was a one-storey concrete building east of the mill house. There the blacksmith and his assistants created the ironwork needed for the plant and took care of tools, machines and even horses. Bill Ledingham was the first man in charge of the blacksmith shop, followed by Douglas J. Scafe. The equipment in the shop included a large forge and a round bellows made of wood and leather.

To the east of the main plant outbuildings were four other smaller buildings—the laboratory, the cookhouse, the larder and small storage shed—and the larger two-storey bunkhouse.

The small wood-frame chemistry laboratory stood between the plant and the cookhouse. It was in use by July 1905. The first chemist was Mr. Highberg; the second, Adolph Neu, later took up residence in Tod Inlet with his family. The chemist took samples from the kilns, slurry tanks and ball mills several times daily to ensure the quality of the cement. The large kilns had lidded holes through which samples could be taken. Because the raw limestone was of varying quality in the quarry, the finished cement also varied in quality depending on its internal chemistry. As the test results were received, adjustments could be made in the mixing process.

Adolph Neu had been the head chemist at the cement plant at Colton, California, in 1903. In May he was demonstrating the apparatus for testing the tensile strength of cement at a street fair in

Exterior of the company laboratory in the early 1900s. BC Archives A-09160.

Taking a sample of the cement. Still from the film *The Manufacture of "Elk" Portland Cement* (BC Archives AAAA6718, 1963), presented with permission of the Lehigh Hanson Cement Company.

The cement testing machine. Still from *The Manufacture of "Elk" Portland Cement*. See left.

The briquette breaking in the testing machine. Still from *The Manufacture of "Elk" Portland Cement*. See left.

San Bernardino. In October he had been issued a patent for a new oil burner that produced a higher and steadier heat than those used previously. In June 1904, he left the Colton plant to accept a position with the Hudson Cement works in Hudson, New York. One wonders if perhaps Butchart, searching for an excellent chemist, had found him at a competitor's laboratory.

Mary Parsell noted that "each batch of cement was always very carefully tested in order to retain the high standard required." [36] Jennie Butchart and her two teenage daughters sometimes assisted Mr. Highberg in the testing of the cement at the laboratory.

The cement was tested in two ways: the sand test and the tensile test. The sand test required that 95 per cent of the cement powder pass through a mesh with 10,000 perforations per square inch. In the tensile test, a square inch of cement had to withstand a force equal to 450 pounds.

Cement samples were moulded into briquettes shaped like a solid figure eight or a short dog bone, three inches long, one inch thick and an inch wide at the narrowest point, and were stamped with a date or number for identification. These were kept underwater for five weeks before testing. The rounded ends of the briquette were clamped to the cement tester, and a small pail on the beam end was slowly filled with

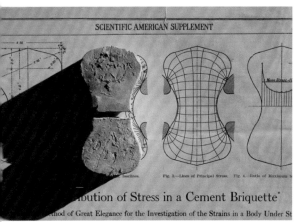

(*top to bottom*) Older, cookie-style cement briquettes from the shore of Tod Inlet. David R. Gray photograph.

A newer cement briquette from Tod Inlet, on top of an illustration in *Scientific American Supplement*, 1913. David R. Gray photograph.

Broken cement test briquettes on the shore. David R. Gray photograph.

lead shot until the sample broke. Tests in 1905 showed that the Tod Inlet cement could withstand a strain of 950 pounds, much higher than the industry standard. Other apparently handmade briquettes found on the shore of Tod Inlet near the plant, shaped like a cookie or sand dollar, 7.5 centimetres in diameter, with numbers inscribed by hand, were probably used for the first rounds of testing as the plant was coming into operation.

The cookhouse was where the single men who lived in the bunkhouse had their meals. Several Chinese men worked for the company as cooks, either on the company ships or in the company cookhouse. The cooks grew vegetables and raised livestock, mainly pigs. Pat van Adrichem, a former gardener at Tod Inlet, remembers seeing corrugated tin used in the village to keep the pigs enclosed, and pig skulls were certainly numerous in the old Chinese midden above Tod Creek.

When Mary Parsell first arrived at Tod Inlet, she had some difficulty getting used to the necessity of ordering food once a month to come in on the company boat. When they ran short, the "Chinese cook would sell us one loaf of bread but he never looked too pleased when we asked for it. After all, he had a large gang of men to feed and both he and his helpers worked hard."[37]

The company built a large two-storey concrete bunkhouse for the single men, halfway between the plant and the village of wooden company homes where the married men lived with their families. When the men's bunkhouse was built, it included a large room at one end that the company allowed the villagers to use for recreation, including card games and parties.

A dam was constructed on Tod Creek in 1904 or 1905 to create a reservoir from which to pipe water to the cement plant and village. The chairman of the Victoria Fish and Game Club spoke to Robert Butchart in 1905 about the dam obstructing fish from reaching Prospect Lake from Tod Inlet.[38] At the time, Butchart promised to construct a fish ladder, but if it was built at all, it did not last long and it was never effective.

Once the mill began operations, large quantities of coal were burned in the boiler room, creating huge amounts of ash and cinders. The ash and cinder residue was initially used for surfacing on the roads and paths that led from the mill to Lime Kiln Road. Some was also used in the construction of the plant buildings. With his team of horses and dump cart, the company teamster, Billy Greig, the son of the former lime burner, carried the excess to the shore in front of the bunkhouse. There he dumped it over the banks of the inlet, extending both the steep banks and the shoreline below. The company horses were kept in the concrete stable that stood between the family houses and the Chinese village.

The post office for the new village of Tod Inlet was located in the two-storey company office building, just east of the cement plant. In 1904, local businessman Wilfred Butler's offer to deliver mail to Tod Inlet was accepted by the postmaster general, and the community had received its official name. Mail service to the Tod Inlet Post Office began on May 1, 1905. Butler's job was to collect mail at the Keating

(*top*) Oil painting of horses in the
company barn at Tod Inlet, 1924,
by Joseph Carrier (1850–1939).
Carrier family collection. David R. Gray photograph.

(*bottom*) The cement barn in the 1960s.
David R. Gray photograph.

Station of the Victoria & Sidney Railway each morning (except Sunday) and deliver it to the new post office "with dispatch." He was then required to get the return mail from Tod Inlet to the Keating Station by 5:54 p.m. to catch the Victoria-bound train.

The post office opened in the office building on the same day mail service began, with H.A. Ross, treasurer of the Vancouver Portland Cement Company, as postmaster. When the first directory entry for Tod Inlet appeared in the Vancouver Island Directory for 1909, it listed an assistant postmaster: W.E. Losee, superintendent of the cement plant.

The postal service wasn't the only way of communicating. The city directories for Victoria from 1910 on describe the Tod Inlet connections to the telegraph system by road: "Stage connects twice daily with V. & S. Ry. at Keating which is the nearest telegraph office distant 2½ miles." [39] The first telephone in Tod Inlet was not installed until 1910.

The local maps of 1905 show Lime Kiln Road reaching the shore of Tod Inlet at the site of the new village. Maps based on topographical work done in 1909 show both the road leading to Tod Inlet and other smaller roads leading to Butchart Cove and the Fernie farm, as well as a loop through the cement plant, and a longer road across Tod Creek to the southeast. This road leading east from the Tod Inlet community and south across Tod Creek towards Durrance Lake first appears on a 1909 map, and it is also shown in 1911 and 1921. (The lake itself is man-made, designed as a source of water for the industrial works at Tod Inlet.) A house marked between the hills is probably the house known locally as the Beetlestone cabin, owned by John Beetlestone, an early farmer of the area. The 1911 census also mentions Lime Kiln Road, under the name of Cement Works Road.

Gus Sivertz, a local columnist in Victoria, described what it was like to travel to Tod Inlet down Lime Kiln Road in the early 1900s: "One reached Tod Inlet by the simple expedient of boarding the old V & S railway at Victoria, riding its dusty and swaying carriages to Keatings and transferring to a stage coach—really! It was a wonderful ride in strawberry time and if one was reasonably fast afoot he could jump down at a hill, leap a fence and snatch a handful of sun-ripe

"One reached Tod Inlet by the simple expedient of boarding the old V & S railway at Victoria, riding its dusty and swaying carriages to Keatings and transferring to a stage coach—really!"

strawberries and race ahead to catch the stage before the horses started to trot down the next slope. At Tod Inlet the driver held his team hard and his foot was pressed down on the brake as the stage seemed to want to override the horses on the last steep incline." [40]

THE SETTLEMENT OF TOD INLET

Tod Inlet quickly became a thriving community. As the plant was built and the beginning of production loomed, the arrival of new personnel and their families and the hiring of large numbers of labourers began to create a rugged pioneer community.

In May 1905 Mary Parsell and her three children took the Victoria & Sidney Railway to Keating Station, where they were met by a man driving a horse-drawn buggy. On their way to Tod Inlet they passed just four houses along Keating Cross Road. The Lime Kiln Road down to Tod Inlet ran through dense bush and then down a long, steep hill. "I felt extremely nervous as we continued going down and down. At last we reached home, a tent twelve feet by twenty feet with board floor and boarded sides two feet high." [41] Wilfred Butler II, who ran the stagecoach

The Parsell family at their old house-tent in 1906. Courtesy of Norman Parsell.

The Parsell family at their new house
in 1906. Courtesy of Norman Parsell.

as a teenager as soon as he was able to handle the horses, found it
a challenge holding the brakes on the long hill down to Tod Inlet.

The tent, the Parsells' first shelter, was the former home of
superintendent Losee's family and included a leaky lean-to kitchen
with a cookstove. The tent was close to the active quarry, and before
each round of limestone blasting, quarry boss James Thompson or one
of his men would warn Mary to take her children a safe distance away.
The small pieces of flying rock that frequently hit the tent did little
damage, but "one day a huge rock landed just beside our dwelling and
if it had been a direct hit, there would have been plenty trouble." [42]

In the fall of 1905, the Parsells were able to move into one of the newly built houses along the road leading to the Chinese quarters. Within a year there were seven more houses, all built by Thomas Tubman, a local carpenter and builder contracted by the cement company. After their tent dwelling, a newly built house in the village seemed deluxe to Mary Parsell. It was also significant to the community. In 1910, during the construction of a new cement plant on the west shore of Saanich Inlet, the manager of the British Columbia Telephone Company came to Tod Inlet looking for a suitable place for a telephone to be installed. The most suitable place turned out to be in the Parsell house.

While living in the village, Norman Parsell and his sister Ella walked to the West Saanich School in what is now Brentwood, "a long walk for six-year-olds, especially in the rain." In those days much of their route was just bush. The distance was about three and a half kilometres, and it would have taken the children close to an hour to walk. The original school had been built in 1880 at the corner of Sluggett and West Saanich Roads. A new school, still only one room with a pot-bellied stove and outhouses, opened in 1908 and operated until 1952. There were lots of children in the village, and all went to West Saanich School.

The Parsell family moved to a second house at the top of the upper row of houses, by the gate, to get away from the aerial tram-line that often spilled limestone from the overhead buckets. They stayed there until 1912. In that year they bought six acres about a kilometre and a half up Lime Kiln Road from the village, beside the Pitzer family property, and built a new house. The Pitzers were farmers, a large and friendly family who had lived there since 1891. As Norman Parsell put it, "a nicer family would be hard to find."

The Vancouver Island Directory for 1909 lists 31 residents of Tod Inlet. As usual, the immigrant labourers were not listed, though their presence was recognized: "nearly 200 Orientals located here." Peter Fernie, retired, and John Beetlestone, farmer, are the only two men listed who were not associated with the cement industry. By 1910 the

The Parsells were able to move into one of the newly built houses along the road leading to the Chinese quarters.

cement plant was described as employing 250 men, of whom only 32 were listed in the directory. The Canada census of 1911 lists 368 employees of the plant: 239 workers living in the Chinese camp, 63 in the "Hindu Camp," 56 in the bunkhouse and 10 men as heads of families in the village.

Henderson's 1913 directory only lists 25 men, 21 of whom were employed by the cement plant—mostly the married men of the village.

The others were Herbert Hemmings and Frederick Simpson, farmers; Hugh Lindsay, a gardener for the Butchart family; and Robert Hunter, keeper of the small store at the top end of the village.

The social life at Tod Inlet was created from within, mostly by the wives and children of the cement company employees. It was an important part of life in the isolated community, keeping morale high in families and giving a sense of community belonging.

Dances and card parties were held in the cookhouse dining room, with permission from the plant manager, William Losee. Everyone attended these events. The cook would make a large cake as a contribution. Mary Parsell remembered Billy Greig, the company teamster, taking a dozen or so residents to dances at the Saanichton Agricultural Hall in the hay wagon.

Although there has never been a church in Tod Inlet, Sunday services were held in the community for about a year and a half, beginning about 1909. The church services and Sabbath school took place in the kitchen of the Parsell home, with the Reverend Frederick Letts as minister. When the West Saanich Hall was built in 1911, the Tod Inlet residents held services there. They then moved to the new Sluggett Memorial Church the next year in what is now the village of Brentwood Bay.

The Chinese labourers lived apart from the other workers in a group of roughly built dwellings above Tod Creek. The road to the Chinese quarters passed between the rows of new houses that were constructed in 1906–1907 for the white employees and their families. The Chinese labourers mostly built their own houses. To Norman Parsell, the houses always looked makeshift, but they seemed to withstand the elements. Most of them had few windows, and they always seemed to be dark inside. There were no wives or families in that part of the village.

Dances and card parties were held in the cookhouse dining room, with permission from the plant manager, William Losee. Everyone attended these events.

Four to six men lived in each house, but they ate together in one large building. Gardener Alf Shiner remembered them using a large communal pot. Dem Carrier, who grew up at the inlet, used to take fresh cod up to the village to sell. He remembers most vividly the smell of incense and the clutter in the houses; the village was "pretty ramshackle, pretty poor living structures: low, dark, dingy. Terrible place to live, really."

The Parsell family often had Chinese friends come to their house in small groups for lessons in English. Norman remembered the names Wong, Fong, Sam and Wing among them.

At Lunar New Year, the Parsells visited the men who worked for James in the furnace room and were given gifts of firecrackers, ginger and lychees—and always Chinese lilies for Mary, whose friendship they particularly appreciated. She felt a real sense of trust between them.

It is unfortunate that we have no accounts of life at Tod Inlet from the Chinese workers themselves. Those who do tell the stories of the relations among the races at Tod Inlet from a white perspective remember them as excellent, even as anti-Chinese riots were taking place nearby in Vancouver. Chinese labourers were not popular then in Canada, and in some areas of British Columbia, anti-Asian racism was rampant—and at times vicious.

Another impact of the poor working conditions, along with the laws and regulations that prevented family from joining the immigrant workers, may have been the use of alcohol and opium by the overworked and lonely men. After the Chinese village was abandoned, the area where it had stood was identifiable by the abundance of various liquor bottles: rice wine, gin, whisky and beer from around the world. Also conspicuous were the tiny, fragile glass bottles or vials known as opium bottles, and the ceramic bowls of opium pipes. Several stores in Victoria's Chinatown were still legally selling opium in 1905: Shon Yuen & Co., at 33 "Fisguard" Street, and Tai Yeu & Co. were listed

Opium pipe bowls found at Tod Inlet in the 1960s. P. van Adrichem collection. David R. Gray photograph.

in Henderson's Directory for Victoria as "opium dealers," and Lee Yune & Co. as "opium manufacturers." The use of opium was not banned until 1907. As opium poppies grow well in Victoria, it seems that some workers chose to grow their own rather than buying from the sources in Victoria.

When Dem and I walked through the old Tod Inlet village area in 2007, we stopped at a circular cement ring with a hole in the middle, in front of the old bunkhouse foundation. "The flagpole was in the centre here, where you see the hole in the ground. The whole garden was raised up, it was full of poppies, which we always assumed to be opium poppies. . . . Our parents told us to stay away, don't handle them, but of course we did. We used to take the heads off, get the milky substance all over our hands. . . . I'm sure they were opium poppies, and obviously grown by Chinese people."

Max Pallan also remembered stories about the use of opium from his dad, Gurditta Mal Pallan. "The Chinese loved opium. It helped them work, gives them stamina and strength. My dad tried it too, but then he got sick. He threw the tin away: 'I'm not going to use it.'"

The Sikhs at Tod Inlet had a separate kitchen and bunkhouse from the Chinese workers. In 1907 the Sikh bunkhouse was described as "a small one-storey bunk house, some seventy feet by forty." [43]

Jeet Dheensaw, son of Hardit Singh, who arrived in 1906, remembered his mother's stories of the Sikhs living in shacks with dirt floors, using cardboard for insulation and flour sacks as blankets. Material possessions were virtually non-existent. There were few houses, and the men slept four or five in one room. She said the men had no raincoats at first, and they got used to working in the rain, as they did not want to spend their wages on new clothing. They preferred to use "old stuff" left behind by others over spending money on new things.

Jeet remembers, "My dad and my uncle, that group of people, used to just have shacks there, working and staying in shacks, making their own food and living on dirt floors. In winter it got bitter, so they used to put planks down, but that's all. They survived. When something fell down, they just added up another board or something and stuffed newspapers, whatever they could get their hands on, if nothing else

The "Hindu Town" at Tod Inlet, showing the living conditions of the Sikhs at the plant. In other archives the photo is titled *An East Indian Farm, Tod Inlet, Saanich*. The two-storey Chinese bunkhouse is just visible in the background on the right.
BC Archives A-09159.

The Sikh brick ovens at Tod Inlet in 1968
(*left*) and 1979 (*right*). Alex D. Gray (*left*) and
David R. Gray (*right*) photographs.

mud even, just to keep the elements away. There was nothing, no beds,
no tables and chairs."

One man was assigned to do the communal cooking for the Sikh
community, and each worker gave one day's wages to the cook each
month. One of the men who prepared the food in exchange for money
was named Katar. Katar Singh was a blood relative of Hardit and
Gurdit Singh, known as "Uncle" to Jeet Dheensaw and remembered
as very strong. The Sikhs at Tod Inlet apparently followed the tradition
of using two cooking fires side by side: one for cooking lentils and
vegetables, the other for cooking chapati (flatbread) on a steel plate
griddle. Norman Parsell and the other young boys living at Tod Inlet
often watched the Sikhs cooking their chapati on an iron plate over
an outdoor fire and were often invited to join the meal.

Lorna Pugh (née Thomson) told me a story of her father, Lorne
Thomson, and Claude Butler Sr., hunting up in the Partridge Hills
above the inlet in about 1910 and being caught by the darkness. They
decided to stay the night up there rather than run the risk of going
over one of the cliffs in the dark. When they came down at dawn the
next day, they came out of the woods opposite the Sikh village: "After
crossing Tod Creek they approached the Hindu campsite, where the
Hindu employees of the cement company lived. The cook offered them
tea, for which they were very grateful. The water was heated in a large

brick trough, and the cook dipped his finger . . . into the trough to test the temperature of the water before giving them their tea. . . . It was hot and helped them to continue on their way home."

There are remnants of two brick structures near the trail that branches off from the main trail in what was the Chinese village. These are typical of Indian cooking ovens and are the only physical evidence of the Sikh community that remains there today.

Amrik Singh Dhillon of Victoria heard stories from his father, Bachan Singh, about the details of the life of his friends, Gurdit and Hardit Singh (Jeet Dheensaw's father), both workers at Tod Inlet. They ate mostly beans, dal or roti, though they also made pancakes, and drank tea. They used lids from food cans as cups, and made serving utensils from a can on a stick. At that time, a 50-pound sack of flour cost one dollar, butter was 25 cents a pound, and beans 5 cents a pound. The men chewed the ends of willow tree branches to make improvised brushes for cleaning their teeth.

Gurditta Mal Pallan told his son Max how the Sikhs at Tod Inlet walked six kilometres up to the Prospect Lake Store to buy groceries. Two men would go every two weeks or so by turn. He said they carried the food, clothes, socks and dollar bottles of whisky back in a kind of tub on their heads. They also walked to the nearby farm to buy chickens and eggs. The Sikhs carried water from the creek in two large buckets, each at the end of a pole carried over the shoulder. Baths were taken only once a week. A committee arranged the finances for purchase of food and supplies and computed each man's share at the end of the month. In general, anyone visiting from India and hoping for a job was fed free for a month. For newcomers, after the first month, expenses were paid by a sponsor until they got a job.

Max Pallan also recalled his father's memories of their day of rest from the early days of the cement works in 1906: "Every Sunday, just about every Sunday, Mrs. Butchart, she used to have a, just like open house, all the workers from the cement mill, and she used to serve tea. They made a special trip to go to the Butcharts' residence and look around in her garden, which was very small at that time . . . but still Mrs. Butchart came out herself and greeted everybody and said 'Hello,'

In general, anyone visiting from India and hoping for a job was fed free for a month. For newcomers, after the first month, expenses were paid by a sponsor until they got a job.

The Butchart residence and surrounding garden, 1930s.
Postcard in author's collection.

and served tea there in the garden. My dad and other friends who came from India were very excited that a rich lady like that was giving that much time to the workers and to the foreigners."

In 1907 there was a very serious outbreak of typhoid fever at Tod Inlet. Tod Creek, which provided the community's drinking water, flowed through miles of open ditch on its way from Prospect Lake, and during the summer became seriously polluted. The company soon switched to drawing drinking water from a spring located just east of the houses at Tod Inlet. Water from the creek was still used for the cement plant and for irrigation, and the use was heavy enough that no surplus came over the dam at what is now Wallace Drive.

LOADING AND SHIPPING CEMENT

For its first few years of operation, the Tod Inlet plant steadily increased production of cement, and its capacity rapidly doubled.

As well as working in the quarries and in the plant itself, the Chinese and Sikh workers also loaded cement for export. In the very early days they may have unloaded and loaded large barrels of cement onto barges or scows. Later they would have been involved in pouring the cement into sacks for shipping, carrying the 87.5-pound bags of cement onto the barges or ships for export and unloading the various incoming cargoes, including the gypsum from the United States and elsewhere needed in the cement-making process.

Victoria physician and Sikh historian Dr. Manmohan Wirk shared with me what he had learned about the working environment of the Sikhs of Tod Inlet from his patients (and his wife, whose father, Gurdit Singh, worked there): "Their job was to unload the supply ships. . . . And then they had to load the cement in bags onto the barges, which then took off to distribute them elsewhere. But they described it as very dirty work—their beards were always white with cement. That's the way they put it. When you hit their beard, cement flew off."

The SS *Alexander* in her former days as a side-wheel tug, ca. 1886.
BC Archives B-00687.

Max Pallan also described for me what he knew about his father's work: "It was just common labour. He worked as a common labourer, loading the scows. They used to carry bags on their backs, or when the ship or the scow wasn't there, then they were just filling the bags, and getting ready for the shipment when it came. It was common labour."

Among the reasons noted by the Department of Mines for Robert Butchart establishing the cement plant at Tod Inlet was the suitability of the inlet for marine transport. Tod Inlet is a natural harbour, deep enough for large ships to load cement directly for transport up and down the Pacific coast. It is also sheltered enough to allow the use of scows or barges towed by tugs.

Among the reasons noted by the Department of Mines for Robert Butchart establishing the cement plant at Tod Inlet was the suitability of the inlet for marine transport.

There was only one hazard to navigating Tod Inlet: a rock outcrop on the channel bed near the narrow mouth of the inlet. A black can buoy was moored at the spot to mark the potential danger.

When the first outward shipment of cement from Tod Inlet was made in April 1905, it was carried by the barge *Alexander* and towed by the tug *Albion*. The *Alexander* was built in 1875 as a side-wheel paddle steam tug and had a storied but short career in British Columbia waters. The tug was ahead of her time, too large and expensive to operate profitably. With her engines removed she was converted to a barge. The first shipment from Tod Inlet consisted of 5,000 barrels of cement in sacks to Victoria and Vancouver.

Butchart's first ship purchase for the cement company, also made in April 1905, was the former sealing schooner *Beatrice*, built in Vancouver in 1891. At the time of purchase she was being used to carry gunpowder to ships at the naval yard in Esquimalt. Butchart bought *Beatrice* for $625, and it was said at the time that the copper sheathing her sound hull was itself worth more than that. The company purchased three scows at the same time, all four to be used either to stockpile cement or to carry it while pulled by tugboats.

Cement from Tod Inlet was first used in such projects as the BC Electric Railway Bridge in Vancouver, and for sidewalk construction in both Vancouver and Victoria. By 1906, cement from Tod Inlet had been used by the cities of Vancouver, Victoria and Nelson, and by such companies as the West Kootenay Power and Light Company, the Crow's Nest Pass Coal Company, the Western Fuel Company of Nanaimo, the Britannia Smelting Company and the British Columbia General Contract Company.

When the City of Victoria asked for tenders for cement for use in building city sidewalks in 1909, the R.P. Rithet company offered Vancouver-brand Portland cement at $2.40 per barrel of four sacks and an alternative tender "of 10,000 barrels, Tod Inlet manufactured cement, at $2.55 per 350 pounds, delivered." Unreturned sacks would be charged at 10 cents each.[44]

The cost of a single 87.5-pound sack of cement in 1909 was 64 cents, about $14.60 in 2020 dollars. In 2020, the cost of a 40-kilogram bag of Portland cement is still about $16.

From 1906 to 1910 several small coastal steamships, not owned by the cement company, carried cement from the wharf at Tod Inlet to various ports on the coast. The demand for cement was so great that the ships could not keep up. In those days, newspapers still carried "shipping news," announcing the comings and goings of both passenger and freighting vessels. Two examples from many in the *Vancouver*

Cement from Tod Inlet was first used in such projects as the BC Electric Railway Bridge in Vancouver, and for sidewalk construction in both Vancouver and Victoria.

31564

Daily World refer to Tod Inlet cement: "The freighter *Belfast* is at No. 4 shed today, discharging a cargo of Vancouver Island cement from Tod Inlet" (February 21, 1906); "The *Henriette* had 250 tons cement from Tod Inlet" (November 18, 1907).

Belfast carried 700 barrels of cement from Tod Inlet to New Westminster in 1907. *Trader* was also carrying cement in 1907—one of her loads of 4,000 sacks got wet and was therefore unusable. It had to be returned to the plant as the damage could not be assessed properly on the ship. In 1909 she made several trips with cement destined for the BC Electric Railway Bridge. *Cascade* carried 4,000 sacks of cement to Vancouver in May 1907 and February 1909. *Belfast* and *Trader* both carried cement in 1910, as well.

The loading of cement was not without its hazards. When the steamer *Vadso* was at Tod Inlet loading cement in September 1909, a deckhand who was helping to close the hatch accidently fell into the hold and died from a broken neck.[45]

228 Larkin St.(Left) City Hall.(Center) Market St.(Right) San Francisco,Cal.

San Francisco after the earthquake
of April 1906. Postcard in author's collection.

As well as carrying cement out, the different ships also brought in raw materials. The Tod Inlet cement boats often returned from delivering cement with cargoes of gypsum from Alaska or San Francisco or elsewhere.

With three kilns operating and capable of producing up to 1,000 barrels a day, Butchart decided to install a new kiln and associated dryers in 1906. He wanted to be in a position to stockpile cement and thus to supply it to any new project requiring large quantities. At the time, the plant was already storing the bulk of their daily output, but also shipping cement to Puget Sound, Washington State, where there was a local shortage.[46]

After the major earthquake and subsequent fires in San Francisco in April 1906, there was a high demand and a serious shortage of Portland cement on the Pacific coast. Robert Butchart told the *Victoria Daily Times* that he had no intention of taking advantage of the shortage and consequent higher prices. He would meet the local demands first before sending cement to the United States.[47]

The new larger kiln was installed at Tod Inlet in 1906–1907 along with associated machinery. Teams of Chinese labourers hauled railcars loaded with heavy equipment by hand from the scows onto the wharf. The plant had been planned so that all heavy shipments could be shipped on railcars loaded onto a barge. Once the tug had positioned the barge, the workers could pull the cars straight onto the wharf and into the plant, then off-load the equipment onto a platform the same height as the railway cars.

After the major earthquake and subsequent fires in San Francisco in April 1906, there was a high demand and a serious shortage of Portland cement on the Pacific coast.

Chinese workers pulling loaded freight cars from the barge up the Tod Inlet wharf, 1906–1907.
Author's collection, from BCCC photo album.

THE CREMATION OF TAR GOOL SINGH

In April 1907, when Tar Gool Singh, one of the Sikh labourers, died, probably of tuberculosis, his cremation sparked much interest among the residents of Tod Inlet and Victoria. Although it was not the first Sikh cremation in Canada, it was certainly the best documented at the time. Articles in the *Victoria Daily Times* on April 12 and April 20 provided detail on the cremation ceremony.

In the *Times* articles, titled "Weird Ceremony at Tod Inlet" and "The Sepulture of Tar Gool Singh," we learn for the first time the names of four additional Sikhs who lived at Tod Inlet: Tar Gool Singh himself; Bishua Singh, his brother; Malooh Singh, "the Priest"; and Sundah Singh, described as the headman or leader of the Sikhs.

Dr. Manmohan Wirk commented on the typical Sikh cremation ceremony, in reference to the Tod Inlet cremation photo, in his book on the history of the Sikhs of Victoria. "After the body has been washed and dressed in new clothes, a platform of dried wood is erected. The

Although it was not the first Sikh cremation in Canada, it was certainly the best documented at the time.

Sikhs in prayer (ardas) prior to the lighting of the funeral pyre at the cremation of Tar Gool Singh, April 1907. Note the layers of wood. Bonnycastle Dale photograph. Courtesy of Kim Walker.

body rests on this bier, and after accelerants (clarified butter) are spread, the funeral pyre is lit by the eldest son, while prayers for the deceased are recited. . . . At the cremation ground, before the wood pyre was lit, the Sikh ardas and a liturgical text . . . were recited for the peace of the departed soul." [48]

In the first photograph, the men standing with their hands folded in front are saying the Sikh prayer, the ardas. Ardas is a prayer said during many Sikh ceremonies and in everyday circumstances. During a funeral service, ardas is said as the body is being taken away, while the body is being consigned to the fire and when the pyre is completely aflame.

The cremation was an event unusual enough to warrant national coverage. The *Canadian Courier* of Toronto (June 15, 1907) published a photograph and commented, "More than a month ago, there died a Hindoo labourer, employed at the Tod Creek Cement Works, near

Victoria, B.C. The body was cremated in the adjacent woods, and two of the bones were sent back to the family in India, while the rest of the ashes was strewn in the waters of Tod Creek." [49]

The published photograph was not credited, but it was almost certainly taken by Bonnycastle Dale, an author, naturalist and photographer from Ontario (born in 1861) who lived and travelled in British Columbia between about 1907 and 1912.

The editor of the *Canadian Courier* magazine described Dale as "the lover of nature, who writes and photographs in a most wonderful way. He has no superior in this field." Dale moved to BC in 1907, living first in Vancouver, then in Victoria, and then in Sooke. He travelled up the west coast of Vancouver Island as far as Ucluelet, and through the San Juan Islands and south to Seattle. He wrote and illustrated many articles about BC, commenting on the wildlife, Indigenous peoples and historic buildings. He left BC in about 1912 and spent time in Ontario, especially at Rice Lake, before returning to the Maritimes, where he died in 1936 at Middle Clyde River, Nova Scotia.

Prints of two of the photographs of the cremation are held in various BC archives. Dale had his negatives printed in Victoria and probably gave the prints to people who were at the cremation. Some of the photos that have ended up in local archives may have originated with storekeeper Wilfred Butler's family. The caption accompanying one of the photos at the Saanich Pioneer Museum reads, "East Indians cremating body on site of Butchart Gardens. Wilfred Butler in white shirt can be seen through the smoke." Butler witnessed the Sikh cremation at Tod Inlet, and his grandson

Photographer Bonnycastle Dale

Although I first found one of the cremation photographs in the national archives in 1978, it was not until 2006 that I finally tracked down the photographer. Searching through all the 1907 issues of the *Canadian Courier* magazine, I discovered a series of articles on British Columbia by photographer and writer Bonnycastle Dale.

I eventually located Dale's original notebooks and negatives in a private collection in Nova Scotia. In one of his notebooks I found a list of the photographs he had taken at Tod Inlet in April 1907, confirming that he was the photographer at the cremation ceremony. Unfortunately, all the negatives of his Tod Inlet photographs were lost in a house fire many years ago.

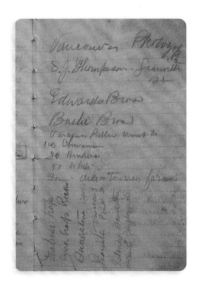

A page about Tod Inlet from one of Bonnycastle Dale's notebooks. Courtesy of Kim Walker. David R. Gray photograph.

(*above*) The cremation after the funeral pyre was lit, 1907. The man in the white shirt behind the smoke is said to be Wilfred Butler. Bonnycastle Dale photograph. Courtesy of Kim Walker.

(*below*) A page about Tod Inlet from one of Bonnycastle Dale's notebooks. Courtesy of Kim Walker. David R. Gray photograph.

Bud Butler remembered seeing the photograph at home as a child: "He had this picture in his living room of this funeral pyre with this East Indian. . . . I always remember him telling me about how they had all this cordwood, and that piled up, and he was given the honour of torching it off."

Although Bonnycastle Dale's notebook for April 1907 has only a reporter's shorthand abbreviation of what he learned about the Sikhs of Tod Inlet, it does give us a rare outsider's glimpse into the origin of a community that has no official written history: "Hindoos—Sikh—Native police—Hong Kong good men—told good times now man send letters back and no more come—try new country—speak poor English—gentlemanly—many very dirty—some Mad men write say come. CPR say no more ticket—many Mutiny men . . . Afghanistan medal not mutiny—A leader is first sent out to new countries and his report decide the men." On the back page of his notebook, he recorded that there were "120 Chinamen, 40 Hindous, and 50 Whites" working at the cement plant.

Indian War Canoe Race in the Inner Harbour, Victoria, B. C.

Annual First Nations canoe races
in Victoria Harbour, about 1908.

Postcard in author's collection.

ON THE WATER: CANOES, ROWBOATS AND YACHTS

Bonnycastle Dale also photographed the traditional canoe races
held annually in Victoria in 1907. His article on the canoe racing was
published in the same *Canadian Courier* issue as the Sikh cremation
photograph. And there was a connection. In the 1900s, the people from
Tsartlip paddled to Tod Inlet during their practice for the annual "War
Canoe" (ẊELXEȻEL in SENĆOŦEN, the Saanich language) races. The use of
Tod Inlet for training canoe teams is likely a long-standing tradition, as
the inlet is similar in narrowness to Victoria's Gorge Waterway. Canoe
racing had become a popular part of the annual May Day celebrations
in Victoria by at least 1886, only some 25 years after the war canoes
were last used for less friendly purposes: raiding between southern
and northern neighbours. The races were held annually on the Gorge
Waterway between Victoria's Inner Harbour and the Gorge Bridge.

The following description is Bonnycastle Dale's description of the
1907 canoe races:

> Now through the throng of white men's boats these long swift craft
> creep, ten paddlers and a big [man] in the stern to guide it. Not a
> word from these silent shoremen, but the West Saanich [Tsartlip]
> men knew that the Valdez had been victors of late and tribe feeling

(*left*) Men's canoe race on the Gorge Waterway, Victoria, in 1907. Saanich and Valdez canoes. Bonnycastle Dale photograph. Courtesy of Kim Walker.

(*centre*) Start of men's canoe race on the Gorge Waterway, in 1907, with Saanich and Valdez canoes. Bonnycastle Dale photograph. Courtesy of Kim Walker.

(*right*) Women's canoe race on the Gorge Waterway, in 1907. Bonnycastle Dale photograph. Courtesy of Kim Walker.

coursed hotly… Saanich strained on their paddles like hounds in leash. At the signal, both crews drew their paddles back as though each canoe were a great bird with strong, short wings, then the lifting forward motion, the paddle's splash—and the race was on.… Away up the course they go, clinging to one another like two giant centipedes afloat, the rhythm of rise and fall, the increasing but steady stroke a beautiful sight… now they appear returning, side by side like catamarans, each fringe of paddles rising and falling as regularly as the wing-beats of a bird, as splashless as swift paddling in heavy canoes can be done. Now the Valdez let out a bit. The Saanich respond nobly. Again the Valdez spurt. This time they hold the lead and, working like demons, keep it, crossing the line in a mad dash a scant length ahead.

Boating for pleasure became an important activity early on at Tod Inlet. In the early 1900s, someone from Tsartlip began building rowboats and had no trouble selling them. Elder Earl Claxton Sr. suggested that it was likely Etienne Smith who was building boats. In 1906 the Parsell family purchased a large rowboat, formerly a ship's lifeboat, named the *Maunaloa* and used it for family outings. It was the second pleasure boat

Boating for pleasure became an important activity early on at Tod Inlet. In the early 1900s, someone from Tsartlip began building rowboats and had no trouble selling them.

in the inlet. "Many happy and pleasant hours were enjoyed as we fished or picnicked on the Saanich Arm," said Mary Parsell.

When her husband, engineer James Parsell, was working 12-hour shifts at the cement plant in 1908, Mary used to take the children out in the family rowboat often to allow James to sleep during the day. On one of those excursions, James got more quiet time than either of them planned for. Mary and her four children set off in a rowboat with a large party—Daisy Scafe and her daughter, Lillie; Ruby and Roxy Caine; Manny Simpson; and a house guest from Australia—on an excursion to the beach below the Malahat. The boat was 18 feet long and very seaworthy, being a former lifeboat; it was co-owned by the Caine family. On the beach below the old Elford lime kiln, they had their picnic. When the wind started to blow, they got the children aboard and headed out into Saanich Arm, back towards Tod Inlet. As the wind strengthened, they realized that they could not row directly home, into the wind, and so headed for Senanus Island, hoping to shelter there. After a brief pause they set out again, but were forced back to shore. They set off once more but soon faced rough water again, with even larger waves, and had to bail continuously as they tried to get back to Senanus. The rowers were exhausted when they reached the shelter of the island.

The Parsell family in their rowboat with banks of clinker and the cement plant behind, about 1910. Courtesy of Norman Parsell.

In the meantime James had alerted the plant manager of the missing expedition and two boats were sent out, but both had to turn back. Finally, the fast and powerful launch owned by Mr. Rogers (of the BC Sugar Refining Company) motored out from Tod Inlet, reached the rowers and towed them back to Tod Inlet and safety.[50]

Later, "Old Harry" (probably Marshall Harry) from Tsartlip, who used to bring fish to the Parsells, told Mary that he and others from the reserve had been watching their progress, worried that they were not going to make it. Alice Pratt, the Australian, refused to go out in the boat again, and Mary confessed, "I never enjoyed those outings later, particularly if a breeze was blowing."[51]

In 1908 Butchart was invited by John S. McMillin, president and general manager of the Tacoma and Roche Harbor Lime Company on nearby San Juan Island, to join a month-long hunting and fishing excursion on his 50-foot yacht *Calcite*. The ship's name is uniquely appropriate, as calcite is the name for the native carbonate of lime. This pleasant excursion may have precipitated Butchart's purchase of his own yacht just a year later.

In 1909 Butchart purchased *Iloilo*, a 60-foot yacht built in Seattle in 1905. The yacht was described as "one of the trimmest and most handsomely appointed launches." His new yacht had berths for 15 people, and Butchart used the ship frequently to entertain visitors.

CANADA CEMENT

Butchart decided to temporarily close the Tod Inlet plant in 1908 because of oversupply and a stagnant market. The *Daily Colonist* of May 7, 1908, reported that the closure might last "from six weeks to three months."

It may have been at this time that Chow Dom Ching left Tod Inlet, moving on to work at the James Island explosives plant before going back to China. His granddaughter Lorelei Lew, of Victoria, recounted that "Chow Dom Ching went back to China very early, as he had made enough money and wanted to be with his family. Because of the discriminatory immigration laws in Canada at that time, he could

Butchart decided to temporarily close the Tod Inlet plant in 1908 because of oversupply and a stagnant market.

not bring his family over. Grandfather Chow bought land with his hard-earned money to pass out among his descendants."

In 1909, most of the operating cement plants in Canada amalgamated into a single enterprise, the Canada Cement Company. All of the cement companies Butchart had been involved with, including Shallow Lake, Lakefield and Calgary, became part of this new company, with the sole exception being the Vancouver Portland Cement Company at Tod Inlet.

Butchart's reasons for retaining control of the Tod Inlet plant were personal. By 1909, Jennie Butchart had embarked on a project to create gardens around their wonderful new home. Robert Butchart had a new yacht and a great location for boating excursions. He had multiple interests, both in business and for pleasure, and their location at Tod Inlet was perfect for this stage of their lives.

3

Expansion, Competition, Excursions and War (1911–1921)

THE CANADA CENSUS OF 1911

When I first looked at the 1911 Canada census records for Tod Inlet, in about 1973, I was disappointed to find that the census of the village of Tod Inlet did not include the Chinese or Sikh workers—but not really surprised. The Canada census, taken every 10 years, provides a wealth of information on the history of a town or city, but the page for Tod Inlet only listed the 10 white families living in the company village, the Butcharts and their staff (including four Chinese helpers), and other families living on Lime Kiln Road. Asian immigrants, especially those who lived at a work site, were not always counted in an official census of Canada, so my disappointment wasn't unusual.

Many years later, when searching the online census records for the names of men who worked at the plant in 1911 but were not listed in the census of the company village, I discovered something amazing: the census actually did record the Chinese and Sikh workers of Tod Inlet, along with the men who lived in the bunkhouse. I had missed these men initially because their information was recorded on a different day, 13 days later, and so listed 10 pages further along in the records. The census was taken in late June, and the census taker was George Sluggett, a local man who would have known many of the people at Tod Inlet.

In the Canada census of 1911, Sluggett recorded 239 men living in Tod Inlet in the "Chinese Camp," 63 men in the "Hindu Camp," 56 men

Slurry tanks. See p. 102.

(5 of them married) in the company bunkhouse, and 10 families living in the "white" company village: 10 men, 11 women (one a "domestic") and 17 children, giving the total population of Tod Inlet as 396 people.

The 1911 census, the first census to include Tod Inlet, records 22 different jobs in the cement plant. The most numerous were labourers (309), carpenters (9), engineers (8), boiler makers (5), machinists (5), oilers (5), teamsters (4) and blacksmiths (4).

Though the jobs of the white men in the village and in the bunkhouse are indicated on the census, the "Hindu" workers are all listed simply as "labourers," as are all of the Chinese men. Sluggett wrote on the bottom of the first of six pages listing the Chinese men, "No information obtained concerning these people." However, for both the Chinese and Sikh workers, Sluggett did record their age and date of coming to Canada.

Of the 63 Sikhs listed, all with the surname "Singh," over half were between 20 and 30 years old, and only 10 were between 40 and 60, with 60 being the oldest. Just over half of the Sikhs had arrived in Canada in 1907; 20 arrived in 1905 and 1906, and 10 in 1908.

Other than the men from India and China, the "Race or Tribal" origin of the cement company workers was European: 31 of English background, 18 Scottish, 8 Irish, 4 French, 2 Danish and one each from Italy, Austria and Germany. Eight men were born in Ontario, 2 in the US, and 1 each in Quebec and British Columbia. The women of the village were born in England (5), Ontario (2), Scotland (1), British Columbia (1), the US (1) and India (1).

The 1911 census gives no indication of anyone from Tsartlip working at the cement plant. The occupation of all the Tsartlip men listed is either farming or fishing. However, a 1911 report by W.R. Robertson, Indian agent at the Cowichan Agency, refers to the occupations of people from the Saanich Nations, including Malahat, Tseykum, Pauquachin, Tsartlip and Tsawout. The report states, "These Indians are chiefly engaged in farming, fishing, hop-picking, and working in the cement works and mines." Tsartlip Elder Manny Cooper, though, didn't know of any Tsartlip people working at the cement plant. He said the Tsartlip people were pretty "strict with the cement," avoiding it because the cement dust would stick in the windpipe.

Other than the men from India and China, the "Race or Tribal" origin of the cement company workers was European.

THE SIKH COMMUNITY RETREATS

Sikh immigration to Western Canada was just beginning in the early 1900s. Seven years after the first Sikhs arrived, the 1911 Canada census reported 89 people of "Hindu" origin living in Saanich, 85 in the city of Victoria, and 2,289 in British Columbia. In the Nanaimo District of Vancouver Island, which included Saanich and Tod Inlet, there were 192 men and 37 women who were born in India, but there is no indication of how many of these people were actually of British descent. The census also reported 1,730 people in British Columbia whose religion was classified as Sikh or Hindu.

There were many challenges affecting the Sikhs in British Columbia at this time: new immigration regulations, increasing discrimination and racism, and the developing nationalist independence movement in India. As a result, between 1908 and the beginning of World War I, the population of Sikhs in British Columbia dropped from about 5,000 to 2,500. Many Sikhs left Canada: some crossed into the United States, some continued on to Mexico and some went back to India.

Cross-border travel at the time was not easy. According to "Hindu Immigration" files (from Library and Archives Canada), when one of the Sikh workers at Tod Inlet, "an old Hindoo named Nama Moran," tried to get back into Canada in 1910, the official response was that he was "to be admitted if can prove previous domicile in Canada and is identified to satisfaction of agent at Victoria." H.A. Ross, treasurer of the cement company, successfully requested his readmission.

These issues had an impact on many of the Sikhs at Tod Inlet. With the recent expansion of the cement plant, things were looking good for the company. Markets were increasing, and as a result, so was production. From the outside the plant looked prosperous, and it was. But on the inside, the workers were unhappy. The Sikhs were well regarded for their good work ethic, so when they became dissatisfied with conditions at Tod Inlet, it was not because of the hard work. It was that their work was also unhealthy.

When Inda Singh died in Victoria under somewhat mysterious conditions in August 1911, the coroner's jury brought in a verdict that his death had been caused by an unknown drug. Singh had lost

There were many challenges affecting the Sikhs in British Columbia at this time: new immigration regulations, increasing discrimination and racism, and the developing nationalist independence movement in India.

his position at the Tod Inlet cement works the previous week. One wonders if he was unable to work because of poor health brought on by the working conditions. He had been found in a stupor, was given an antidote without effect and died in the Jubilee Hospital.[52]

Amrik Singh Dhillon's father told him about the poor working conditions experienced by the Sikhs at the mill. Amrik told me that his father's friends, Gurdit and Hardit Singh, had regarded their work as a hard and dirty job that included packing heavy sacks of cement onto the ships while lime dust flew about, coating their beards and turbans.

Dr. Manmohan Wirk's research in the community records at the Victoria gurdwara showed that the people from India thought it was better to leave this unhealthy place. Some of the Sikhs had spent two to three months in the Chinese bunkhouse at Tod Inlet, where there had been a severe outbreak of pulmonary tuberculosis. Suddenly people became scared. Men were dying of tuberculosis in the Chinese community. Tod Inlet had become a "place of breeding death" because of tuberculosis, made worse by the cement and coal dust, and typhus from the polluted stream that ran through the community.

A few of the Sikh men stayed on at Tod Inlet and continued to work for the Butcharts as their gardens were developing.

Dr. Wirk described the situation to me. "They noticed a very heavy rate of death among the Chinese workers, and this was secondary to an outbreak of tuberculosis. So they held an emergency meeting of the group—there were 40 of them—and decided they hadn't come to Canada to die of tuberculosis here. So they moved from here."[53] Documents at the gurdwara, in the Gurmukhi language, show that the Sikhs decided to all leave Tod Inlet together: "We came to work, not to die." The time of their leaving was said to be around 1910, but the 1911 census shows that the Sikhs must have left Tod Inlet after late June 1911.

A few of the Sikh men stayed on at Tod Inlet and continued to work for the Butcharts as their gardens were developing. Jeet Dheensaw, Hardit's son, remembered his mother telling him that when his father finished at the cement plant, he went to work at the Butchart Gardens, but as a labourer, not a gardener. However, most of the group, including Hurdit Singh Johl and Diwan Singh Johal, went to Golden, BC, to work in the sawmill there, and returned together to Victoria in 1930. Others went to Ocean Falls or Vancouver to work in other sawmills.

The sawmill at Golden, BC, depicted on a postcard stamped June 30, 1912.

Author's collection.

Still others stayed on Vancouver Island, to work in Victoria or in the sawmills up-island.

Dr. Davichand, the Brahman doctor who had encouraged immigration from India in the early 1900s, also went to Ocean Falls, where he was employed at the sawmill as a doctor for the Sikh mill hands.

The short time for which the Sikhs were at Tod Inlet, and the relative poverty of their lives there, helps to explain why no artifacts of obvious Indian origin, except the brick ovens, have yet been found or identified at the site.

The Sikhs now disappear from the core of the Tod Inlet story, but their presence at Tod Inlet foreshadowed their great impact on the British Columbia economy. This little Sikh community also had an important and a continuing impact on my life as a researcher: telling of the story of the Sikhs at Tod Inlet brought me into a new career as a filmmaker.

> The Sikhs now disappear from the core of the Tod Inlet story, but their presence at Tod Inlet foreshadowed their great impact on the British Columbia economy.

THE CEMENT PLANT EXPANDS

At the time when the Sikhs left Tod Inlet, the quality limestone of the second lower quarry was almost depleted, only six years since the opening of the quarry. The company soon began work on a new quarry about one kilometre north. Here there was another outcropping of the

(*above top*) One of the wooden towers that supported the cable system, 1967. Alex D. Gray photograph.

(*above bottom*) A metal sheave from the cable system, found on the route of the cable system in 1998. David R. Gray photograph.

(*below*) A metal bucket from the cable system at the Butchart Gardens. David R. Gray photograph.

same limestone rock, on the north side of the wagon road leading south to Victoria, now called Wallace Drive.

Bringing the raw limestone and clay to the plant from the new quarry required a new system of transport and substantial changes to the plant structure. Also, by this time, the plant needed to expand again to meet the increasing demand for cement. Just as in the first few years of operation, the production of cement at the Tod Inlet plant had steadily increased, and the plant's capacity had doubled again since 1908. Orders for cement had begun to come in so fast that Butchart decided to install a sixth kiln.

In the new upper quarry, about 80 Chinese workers excavated the limestone by hand after blasting, did the initial crushing of the limestone and loaded the crushed limestone into large buckets for transport to the plant.

Rising to the challenge of finding new technology to transport the limestone, Butchart and his staff and planners came up with a plan to carry it using an aerial tramway: a new system of cables supported by large wooden towers. Known as a telpher line or telpherage, this new system had been in use in Britain since 1885, when the Sussex Portland Cement Company first used it to carry clay from a clay pit to a railway station.

The aerial support cable was of two thicknesses: the heavier cable was used on the way down to the plant, and the lighter to return the empty buckets on the way back up. The large metal buckets hung on sheaves—grooved wheels within a pulley for the cable to run on. As the force of gravity moved the limestone-filled buckets downhill, they provided the power to send the empty buckets back up. Whenever the clutch slipped, the buckets bumped into each other, causing rock to spill out. This rock spill and the cables can still be seen along the route of the tramway today. I found one of the large sheaves near the remains of a wooden tower near Wallace Drive; it was 16 inches (41 centimetres) in diameter and marked "Pat'd Mar 26 1895, 9-1911."

At the plant, the burst of activity must have been dramatic, as the engineers and builders installed the new kiln and constructed a new terminal for the aerial cable system, a new mill to crush the limestone,

Metal buckets from the cable system at the old plant.
David R. Gray photograph.

two slurry mixers, a new stock house, three new concrete chimneys and a bag-packing facility.

When the company expanded the plant, they also converted it from the previous "dry" process of making cement to the "wet" process, where the materials were fed into the kilns as a wet mixture known as "slurry." The slurry was mixed in two circular tanks—huge open concrete pans 29 metres wide and about 1.2 metres deep. They were at slightly different elevations, and the slurry flowed from one to another to obtain exactly the desired proportion of ingredients. Huge paddles, revolving about a central column in the middle of each pan, constantly stirred the liquid. From the pans the slurry was pumped to the drying kilns. The kiln cylinder was rotated slowly by powerful new electric motors. The liquid entered the chimney end of the cylinder and slowly flowed down to the searing jet of flame. It gradually thickened and hardened to become cement clinker. From this point the cement-making process was the same as for the dry method used earlier.

(*left*) The new slurry tanks at Tod Inlet.
BC Archives J-05136.

(*right*) One of the slurry tanks in 1979.
David R. Gray photograph.

Along with the new kiln came the need for new chimney stacks. The building of the new stacks was overseen by an experienced American who brought his own crew for the job. There were three new concrete chimneys built; one old brick chimney was retained.

Tragedy struck during the final stages of construction for the last of three new chimneys, when Charles Luce of Omaha, Nebraska, fell 130 metres to his death. On June 14, 1911, the *Nanaimo Free Press* reported that Luce "was engaged in lifting a bundle of staves with which to encase the inside of the chimney while the brick work was being erected and the last stage of the chimney was just in the course of erection when the rope hauling up the staves broke. Luce was standing on the interior scaffolding when the bundle of staves fell, striking the scaffolding on which he was standing, breaking it and sending him to his death."

Mary Parsell recounts that "the boss of the stack crew was so upset by this accident that he said he would never build another stack even though he had been in that business for eighteen years."[54]

An article in the *Victoria Daily Times* of February 1, 1911, describes yet another accident, in which Joe Sing, the Chinese foreman of the quarry workers, was killed in the quarry by an explosion of dynamite, and two Chinese workers were seriously injured.

As the company doubled the capacity of the plant, they also installed electric power to replace what the steam boilers had provided, and they introduced many labour-saving devices. The *Vancouver Daily World* for September 10, 1912, mentioned an important shipment: "Stowed away in the holds of the Maple Leaf liner Frankmount, which is due at Victoria today from New York, . . . is the first shipment of electrical machinery for the new Tod Inlet Cement Works plant . . . 100 tons of machinery." [55]

By 1913 the plant was fully equipped. It operated largely on electric power from the BC Electric Company plant at what is now Brentwood, but it also maintained an auxiliary steam plant. With the conversion to electric power, the old boiler room became a storage room for machinery.

When the director of the British Columbia Electric Railway Company had met with Butchart as manager director of the cement works back in 1907, Butchart had told him that if a proposed new water power plant were to be constructed, the cement plant "would gladly

(*above*) Plate from the Tod Inlet powerhouse: "Starting compensator . . . for induction motor. Canadian General Electric Co. Limited. Toronto–Peterboro."
David R. Gray photograph.

(*below*) Undated map of the new power line to Tod Inlet, an offshoot of the main line at the BC Electric Railway.
Author's collection.

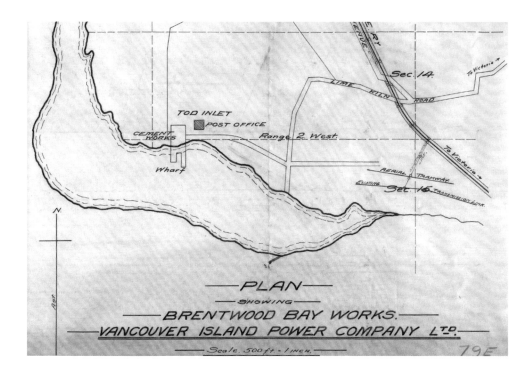

(*top*) The electric locomotive—
Tod Inlet's "Toonerville Trolley."
Author's collection, from BCCC photo album.

(*bottom*) Brake wheel from the electric
locomotive (Toonerville Trolley) found
in the gulch. David R. Gray photograph.

take 1,500 horsepower of current."[56] Now the plant had that power, enough to serve the entire plant operations.

In addition to the aerial tramway to carry the limestone from the new quarry down to the plant, the company engineers also devised a new system to carry clay, and to remove the rock spoil—the inferior quality limestone—from the quarry.

They devised a small narrow-gauge railway to run south from the new quarry about a kilometre along Tod Creek to a new clay mill, halfway between the quarry and the village. While the upper quarry was in operation, a small electric-powered "train" on the narrow-gauge track carried both rock spoil and clay. The locomotive used on this railway was known to the children of Tod Inlet as the "Toonerville Trolley," after a popular cartoon of the day.

At the northern end of the railway they blasted and dug out a gully so that the track could be laid at a level below the clay pit and with a moderate grade down to the clay mill. At the new clay pit opposite the

(*left*) Aerial photograph of the upper quarry, rail line and clay mill system, 1926. National Air Photo Library.

(*below top*) The bed of the electric railway running from the upper quarry to the clay mill, 2019. David R. Gray photograph.

(*below bottom*) The foundation of the switch house where the railway splits near the clay mill, 2019. David R. Gray photograph.

quarry, a power shovel with a clamshell (double) bucket dug out the clay and loaded it into the small railcars. A large metal skip, probably also used to excavate and load the clay, still sits in the woods near the clay pit. At the southern end, the rail line was gradually built up with rock spoil from the quarry, and extended and split into two branch lines at a small switching station. The western track ran to the clay mill, where the clay was mixed with water and pumped down to the cement plant in a large pipe. The eastern track extended over the road running down to the village, and then over to Tod Creek, where rock spoil from the upper quarry was dumped over the bank of the creek, partially damming it.

The raised railbeds are still visible, and the former position of the now-rotted wooden ties can be seen in the irregular surface of the track bed. Though the rails were removed, a few pieces of rail are still found in the area, and the cement pad of the switching station is still evident. In the wet winter season a small creek, an overflow from the flooded quarry, still runs south through the gully at its northern end.

When the new quarry opened, two Chinese men cut wood nearby, on the south side of Tod Creek, to fuel the steam shovels working in the new quarry among other needs. They lived in a small cabin opposite the dam on the creek. Norman Parsell remembered the Chinese woodcutters as "wiry and strong and they cut thousands of cords of wood in our area from virgin timber. They . . . would pull a cross-cut saw all day at a steady pace and that is hard monotonous work."[57]

A strange article in the *Vancouver Daily World* entitled "In a Logging Camp" describes the conditions at a camp "at Tod Inlet" in 1913. The article quotes an anonymous letter-writing logger who wanted a reporter to visit the camp. He describes the camp as "a menace to health, where intelligent white men who have left comfortable homes, are fed and housed worse than negroes were in slavery days, where all the laws of hygiene are ignored, where nearly three hundred men live without the chance of having a bath, except in the cold sea."[58] It is an interesting description that may refer to the cement company operations, but I have found no other confirmation that such a situation really existed.

PAPER TREASURE

In the absence of company records for the Vancouver Portland Cement Company in any archive, it is difficult to understand the daily workings of the cement plant, the quarry, and the production and shipping of the cement. So when I found a scattering of wet and mouldy papers in the old cement company office in the mid-1960s, it was like discovering a lost treasure. This unlikely but exciting trove was part of a file that was dropped and forgotten when the plant offices were vacated some 40 years before. These few abandoned papers represent a variety of company activities, but only for limited parts of the years 1911 and 1912.

Inside the cement company office building where I found the papers.
David R. Gray photograph.

They would have soon rotted away to nothing had I not been trespassing that day. Ironically, they seem to be the only Vancouver Portland Cement Company records that have survived.

As well as grocery orders and work orders for the blacksmith and machine shops, the old files included a few workers' time sheets for July and September 1911. Half of them were illegible, but a few give us new insight into the lives of a blacksmith and other mill workers at Tod Inlet, and the interesting variety in their jobs. Another window opened.

Douglas Scafe was a blacksmith
at the cement plant. He lived with
his wife, Daisy, and daughter,
Lilian, in the company village.
In 1911 he was 38 years old. On
23 days in September 1911 Scafe
worked a full 10 hours. Most
of his time was spent on jobs
relating to the mill, the quarry,
the powerhouse and the kilns.
Smaller jobs included work for the
coal house, the new quarry and

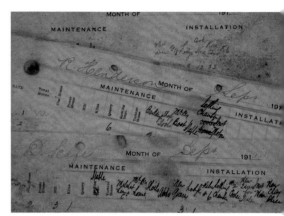

the new clay dryer. In addition, he spent a few hours a month on some
less expected extra jobs: four hours for the Malahat Lime Company,
three hours on Mr. Butchart's house, and two hours on Butchart's
yacht *Iloilo*. William Love, 21 years old, who lived outside of Tod Inlet,
was the blacksmith's helper. He also worked 10 hours a day for 23 days
in that same month. All of his time was dedicated to repairs in the
blacksmith shop itself.

Most other mill workers worked the same 10-hour days, but
J. Richardson, another blacksmith's helper, worked for 12 hours on
seven days (five days in the coal house), and for 28 hours straight while
he was working on a new elevator. A third of his time that month was
spent making special thread bolts, probably for the new wooden towers
of the aerial tram system. He also worked in the mill, on the kilns and
in the Butcharts' house.

Also among that treasure of old papers, I found old waybills that
listed the coal shipments brought from Nanaimo by steam tugs to
fuel the furnaces at the plant in March and April 1911. This was not
a find that would excite many, but it was one that made a confirming
connection to stories I would hear years later.

Several steam tugs from the Victoria Tug Company, including
Sadie, *Spray*, *Swell* and *Edna Grace*, brought the coal from the
Nanaimo Colliery of the Western Fuel Company on scows or barges
carrying about 300 tons. The Chinese workers and others unloaded the

(*left*) A sample of the paper treasure trove.

(*right*) Blacksmith Douglas Scafe's
time sheet for September 1911.
David R. Gray photograph.

(*left*) The coastal tug SS *Spray*.
BC Archives E-00651.

(*above*) Waybill from 1911 giving details of a coal shipment: "Nanaimo Colliery, Nanaimo, B.C. April 1911. Received from Western Fuel Company, on board S/S 'Sadie's' scow 'Progress,' One hundred & seventy six—tons # 2 Washed pea coal, One hundred & fifty three—74 tons Washed slack coal . . . Arrived. 1:30 P.M. 1st. Began 3. P.M. 1st. Finished 10. A.M. 2nd." Author's collection. David R. Gray photograph.

(*right*) The coastal tug SS *Edna Grace*.
Alex D. Gray photograph.

scows under a roofed section at the wharf, originally by hand, but later by a belt conveyor. The coal was probably loaded onto the scows by other Chinese workers employed at the Nanaimo Colliery farther north on Vancouver Island.

Unfortunately, most of the dates on the papers are illegible, but they do show that the tug *Edna Grace* made at least six trips in March and April, and the *Sadie* and the *Spray* made at least two each. Several of the shipping papers show that the coal barges from Nanaimo arrived at varying times of day, and often during the night, due to the timing of the required high tides for unloading.

> Received from Western Fuel Company, Nanaimo Colliery on board
>   SS Edna Grace's scow, 227 tons, Arrd. 1 A.M. March
> Received from Western Fuel Company, Nanaimo Colliery on board
>   SS Edna Grace's scow #3, 184 tons #2 washed coal, 112 tons
>   washed slack, Arrd. 1 A.M. March 30

When I met Dr. Wirk in Victoria, he shared stories he had heard from his patients about the nighttime unloading work at Tod Inlet: "When they had finished a full day's work, they finished at six o'clock in the evening. They were retired to bed . . . and if a barge happened to come in and had to be unloaded and reloaded, they were woken up. They had the option of saying no, but if a person said no, he was never called in for overtime. This fear of being blacklisted was enough for them to encouragingly get up and put in another full five hours' work."

Paul Singh Johal heard similar stories: "My grandfather Diwan Singh, he came in 1906, and with his other friends from the same village. I heard, I understand about 12 or 13 of them come on the same boat." If a ship arrived at the company wharf at night, the workers were summoned to unload by the ship's whistle. Some were happy to hear the sound of the whistle because it meant more work. Workers unloaded the scows at night even if they had already put in a 12-hour shift. Most people worked overtime. "If anyone refused to unload at night, they would not get additional shift work or overtime. Normally they carried 87-pound sacks of cement from the warehouse to the scow or ship. They carried two sacks, one under each arm. The Sikhs carried the sacks under their arms, the Chinese carried them on their backs."

Paul recalled for me an amusing story of one of those working nights: "They said one night, loading at night, one fellow had a sack on his shoulder and he put it down and just fell asleep, and everybody keep loading it [the ship]. Then they come back and they said, 'Where's so and so?' So they were looking for him, they had to come back and unload . . . and they found him, asleep" behind all the sacks!

Diwan Singh Johal, grandfather of Paul Singh Johal. Courtesy Paul Singh Johal.

THE CEMENT BOATS OF TOD INLET

The old shipping papers also gave me the names of the cement company ships that brought supplies and transported cement to construction projects along the Pacific coast, and these names sparked more research.

When Robert Butchart and the Vancouver Portland Cement Company decided to purchase their own ships to carry cement from Tod Inlet, they could not have known what a surprisingly important role these vessels would play in British Columbia's maritime history.

(*left*) Old shipping papers with the name *Marmion*. Author's collection. David R. Gray photograph.

(*right*) SS *Marmion* at Tod Inlet in 1915. BC Archives J-05137.

In March 1910, as production was increasing again, the company purchased the steamer *Marmion* from the Nobel's Explosives Company in Glasgow, Scotland. An iron and steel schooner-rigged steamer, 140 feet in length, she had been built in 1893 in Bowling, Scotland, by Scott & Sons. With a capacity for 300 tons of freight in holds sheathed with wood to protect the cargo, she was to carry cement from the Tod Inlet plant, bring the needed gypsum from Alaska and do general freighting for the company. She carried a master and a crew of 12: the mate, 5 able seamen, chief and second engineers, 2 firemen, a cook and a ship's boy. In 1914 their monthly wages ranged from $125 ($2,850 in 2020 dollars) for the chief engineer to $60 for the firemen and $22 ($500 in 2020 dollars) for the ship's boy. At that time, mate William Canterbury, able seaman Alex Croll and James Parsell, the chief engineer, all lived at Tod Inlet.

As a youth, Norman Parsell came to know the new steamer well: "Our father was on this vessel for many years as an engineer. It mainly carried cement to Vancouver and to a lesser degree to Victoria. But it hauled tons and tons to Ocean Falls as they were building the big dam there at that time and also the [pulp and paper] mill. . . . A highlight of my early years was when Dad would take me to Vancouver on the *Marmion*. I went with another boy, and while the longshoremen were unloading the cement we would be uptown taking in all the five and ten cent movies."[59]

(*top*) Cement boats—probably *Marmion* and *Leona*—at the Tod Inlet wharf, about 1912 or 1915. Author's collection, from BCCC photo album.

(*bottom*) The SS *Leona* at the Tod Inlet wharf, about 1915. Watercolour by David R. Gray.

It is interesting to wonder if any of the Sikhs who had left Tod Inlet for Ocean Falls ever connected with the crew of the *Marmion* when the ship delivered cement from their old workplace. James Parsell in particular must have been a familiar face.

Marmion made the newspapers in March 1911 by running aground at Vancouver's Second Narrows while outward bound in heavy fog. She tore out two water mains serving Vancouver's east.

The company bought another ship in 1912, the *Leona*, a 185-foot former collier built in 1905. As well as carrying cement, *Leona* transported bags of salt from San Francisco to Victoria and gypsum for the cement works at Tod Inlet. In March 1913 she arrived at San

The SS *Leona* at the company wharf between 1912 and 1915. The photo also shows the making of cement pontoons near the wharf.

Courtesy of the Butchart Gardens.

Francisco with 3,000 boxes of salt herring from Nanaimo. *Leona* was larger than *Marmion*, with a registered gross tonnage of 700, but with a similar crew: master, mate, four able seamen, chief and second engineers, two firemen, cook, messboy and donkeyman. The masters, Cochrane and Ludlow, and the chief engineer, Parsell, lived in Tod Inlet. These three and others served on both ships. Each of the cement company ships usually carried a Chinese cook as part of the crew. The cooks may not have been from the Chinese community at Tod Inlet, though, as at least some records give their place of residence as Vancouver.

As *Leona* joined the Tod Inlet fleet, the cement plant was reaching its maximum production of about 500,000 barrels a year, worth about $1 million at the time (about $22.8 million in 2020 dollars). The company had to charter other ships to keep up to the demand. One of them was the wooden coastal steamer *Matsqui*, 82 feet long and 113 tons, built in Vancouver in 1911. "With 1000 barrels of cement from Tod Inlet, the steamer Matsqui arrived at the Johnson dock Sunday," the *Vancouver Daily World* said on February 18, 1913.

The old soggy waybills and receipts from 1911 to 1912 provided details of the varied roles of the cement company's fleet, aside from the expected transporting of cement, and also of the company's dependence on merchants in Victoria and Vancouver. Some examples:

F. Jeune and Brother, Sail and Tent Makers, Victoria, British Columbia, May 30, 1912, Steamer Marmion, 6 curtains.

Vancouver Engineering works Ltd., February 26, 1913, S.S. Leona, 1 pc 3/8 plate as per template.

15 pounds of butter to the Vancouver Portland Cement Company by "W.S. BUTLER General Merchant Keating, B.C. Aug 19 1911."

Other firms mentioned on the waybills include the British American Paint Co. in Victoria (for an order of boiled linseed oil and white lead), the Canadian Puget Sound Lumber Company, Victoria Machinery Depot, Brackman-Ker Milling Co., Hinton Electric Company, E.G. Prior and Co., the Colbert Plumbing and Heating Co., Victoria Terminal Railway and Ferry Co., the Western Fuel Company, the Canadian Pacific Railway, and the Esquimalt and Nanaimo Railway.

With the increase in ship traffic and the additions to the Tod Inlet fleet of cement boats, the company required more docking space and so constructed a second wharf. It was built by driving wooden piles around a square perimeter and filling in the centre. The fill included debris from the dismantling of some of the original factory buildings, old machinery, discarded firebricks from the kilns, bags of cement that had been spoiled

Filling in the second wharf at Tod Inlet.
City of Victoria Archives PR134-5062.

by moisture, and clinker from the cement-making process. Two large cement and metal bollards for tying up ships were installed.

THE BUTCHART GARDENS: EXCURSIONS AND TOURISM

Tod Inlet's new and expanding cement industry continued to attract attention. It wasn't long before tours from Victoria and eventually visitors from far away came to visit the cement plant and learn about the process—and to enjoy beautiful Tod Inlet. In something of a foreshadowing of excursions to come, the Vancouver branch of the Canadian Society of Civil Engineers travelled by chartered ship to the Tod Inlet cement works in September 1911. As part of the excursion, Robert Butchart met them in his yacht and took them to his residence for a luncheon.

It wasn't long before the Butcharts' new house and gardens became a big part of Tod Inlet's attraction. Jennie Butchart's initial garden project was simply to make the area around their house more attractive. Once they completed the house gardens, they took to more ambitious projects. The Japanese Gardens were one of the first theme gardens to be developed away from the house, starting in 1906. The garden was developed with the help of Isaburo Kishida, a Japanese landscape artist. Having a cement plant close beside meant that the new gardens would have sculptures as well as flowers. In the Japanese garden, small pagodas made of cement were soon springing up.

As the cement company prospered, Jennie Butchart persuaded her husband to allow a few Chinese workers at the plant to garden for her part-time instead. Starting in about 1911 some of the Chinese workers from the cement plant were given a new full-time job. Jennie

Jennie Butchart's initial garden project was simply to make the area around their house more attractive. Once they completed the house gardens, they took to more ambitious projects.

The developing garden in the limestone quarry, with the cement plant in the background, about 1912. City of Victoria Archives PR134-5063.

had been distressed by the gaping hole of the abandoned limestone
quarry resulting from her husband's enterprise, and she purposed to
transform that unattractive space into something of beauty. The new
initiative likely started with a comment by a friend of hers about the
barren landscape: "Even you would be unable to get anything to grow in
there."[60] Perhaps that was the only prompting Mrs. Butchart needed.

The Butcharts hired local farmers to bring in and spread wagonloads
of soil from neighbouring farms onto the floor of the quarry. Gardeners
designated areas to be outlined with borders of poor-quality limestone
left over from the quarrying and filled them in with soil. The 1911
Canada census lists four Chinese "labourers—in gardens" in the
Butchart household: Joe Ling, Lim Dow, Joe Chong and Louie Ching.

The Butcharts had made a habit of travelling to a new European
country each winter for a holiday. While there, Mrs. Butchart would visit
gardens and learn about exotic flowers, shrubs and trees, bringing home

Butchart's new yacht *Nooya* in Tod Inlet, 1912. Courtesy of the Butchart Gardens.

new ideas and specimens. Though busy with his own cement business and involved with many other business interests about the country, Robert Butchart used the same trips to cultivate new markets for his cement. Soon, in 1915, he would turn his attention to the struggling Oregon Portland Cement Company in Portland, Oregon, and manage that business until it became a successful plant. When this plant and one built in eastern Oregon merged into a new company, he became its president.

He continued to have an interest in boating, too. In August 1912, his new yacht arrived in Victoria from New York. The 70-foot launch *Minnie W.* was carried on the deck of the freighter *Queen Amelia,* which had come around Cape Horn. The yacht had been built in New York in 1910 and was equipped with a new acetylene system of lighting, cooking and heating. The *Victoria Daily Times* reported, "The Minnie sits nicely in the water and has been built on lines giving her the best seagoing qualities." [61] Butchart renamed his new yacht *Nooya.*

In 1915 the local natural history society met at Tod Inlet, and Reverend Robert Connell, a well-known naturalist, spoke on the geology of the area. L.C. Newlands, chemist for the Vancouver Portland Cement Company, led the group on a tour of the cement works.

This was a sign of things to come. While Robert Butchart's cement plant still attracted visitors as a novel and exciting industrial excursion, Jennie Butchart's garden prospered and became the growing point of interest. With the addition of new plants, the old quarry began taking on a beauty that attracted both locals and visitors and became known as the Sunken Garden—the focal point of what was becoming formally known as "The Butchart Gardens." The gardens surrounding the Butcharts' house had already begun attracting visitors from all over the world, and the development of the Sunken Garden in the old quarry generated even more interest. By 1916, there had been an amazing 18,000 visitors.

As the limestone quarry was transformed into a spectacular garden, the cement boats of Tod Inlet were joined by coastal steamers that brought boatloads of visitors to the old factory wharf to see it. One of the many visitors arriving by boat in 1917 to view the gardens commented on the "small army of Chinese gardeners," under the direction of the head gardener Yorkshireman Hugh Lindsay. Mrs. Butchart had employed Lindsay to complete the transformation of the depleted quarry.

The Butcharts' care for their employees' families showed through annual Christmas parties with presents for each child, occasional group outings on the Butchart launch, and once, an invitation to the Butcharts' house to listen to a new pipe organ.

Stella Wright, of Tsartlip, recalled that when the gardens first started, people from the reserve were allowed to go there at "no charge."

The developing garden in the limestone quarry, with the cement plant in the background, after 1912. Coloured glass lantern slide in author's collection.

TRAGEDIES IN THE COMMUNITY

The Sikhs had left Tod Inlet because of the health conditions. The men who stayed on still faced dangers and death. As well as the dangers from exploding dynamite and the long-term perils of cement and coal dust, there were many other dangerous aspects of work at the cement plant operations.

In 1913 three fatalities at Tod Inlet were reported in the local newspapers. In February, Oscar Ross was accidently electrocuted. Thomas Greer was killed in a cave-in in the quarry in March. Harry Erskine went missing and probably drowned in the inlet in May.

Another blow to the company and the community was struck in 1915, when the company steamer *Leona* was lost in a severe storm off Active Pass in Georgia Strait. Although several of the crew survived, Captains Ludlow and Cochrane, as well as five others, were drowned. The ship was carrying ore concentrates from the Britannia Mine to Tacoma, Washington, and it was believed that shifting cargo in the rough seas caused her to capsize.

In a letter written in 1978, Norman Parsell shared a personal angle of the ship tragedy: "We knew both Capt. Cochrane and Capt. Ludlow very well as they were personal friends of my parents. The sad part of the sinking of the *Leona* and the loss of the two Captains, was Capt. Ludlow had only been married a week or so before, to one of the Butler girls, a pioneer family in Saanich."[62]

The two captains, Cochrane and Ludlow, were working together while the *Marmion* was out of service. They had been with the company for many years and were very well liked and trusted. They were experienced navigators in the open sea and along the coastline, and the company felt their loss deeply. They were very much an integral part of the company, not just employees. The *Daily Colonist* for November 2, 1915, covered the tragedy: "'This disaster has completely keeled us over,' said an official of the Vancouver Portland Cement Company, yesterday. 'The two captains were to be absolutely trusted, and we reposed every confidence in them. They were sterling fellows and knew their business.'"

The community suffered another loss in September 1916 with the death of long-time company master mechanic Thomas Haggart. While working on the roof of the electrical sub-station, he became entangled in an electric wire charged with 60,000 volts. He was badly burned and died three days later at St. Joseph's hospital.

THE INTERURBAN RAILWAY

In spite of these tragedies, life moved forward in the community. Before 1913, the only access to Tod Inlet by rail was via the Keating Station of the Victoria & Sidney Railway. When the BC Electric Company began surveying a rail line from Victoria to Deep Cove, the people of Tod Inlet were excited—the line would be only about 2.5 kilometres from the village. By December 1910 the route had been surveyed as far as the planned Tod Inlet station.

When the line was finally completed in 1913, a station with a covered shelter was built at the intersection with Lime Kiln Road. The station was on the north side of Lime Kiln Road, east of the railway tracks. The service provided the people of Tod Inlet with six round-trips a day to Victoria, now only 45 minutes one way. This meant young people could go to school in the city, and families could more easily get supplies and fresh food.

The BC Electric Tod Inlet Station.

Author's collection, from BCCC photo album.

To attend the closest high school in Victoria, Norman Parsell and his schoolmates had to catch the 6:30 train and disembark three-quarters of an hour later in Victoria, in plenty of time for a 9:15 start to classes. For a while the high school and elementary schoolchildren travelled to their schools easily. But the convenience was not to last: the service was discontinued after only a few years.

Although several sources mention a railway spur line down to the village of Tod Inlet,[63] and such a line is shown on published maps,[64] there is no mention of a spur in the BC Electric company papers listing all other spur lines. Also, there is no evidence on the ground of the existence of such a spur—the grade from the main rail line to the inlet is too steep—and aerial photographs from 1926 show no spur. The imagined BCER spur line probably arose from confusion with the small-gauge electric railway that the cement company built from the upper quarry down to the clay mill on Tod Creek.

COMPETITION: THE BAMBERTON CEMENT WORKS

A small limestone-burning operation, located five kilometres across Saanich Inlet from the Tod Inlet site, was known as the Elford deposits. Elford & Company originally quarried these limestone deposits and burned the limestone in a kiln as early as 1907. The Vancouver Island Directory of 1909 listed the Malahat Lime Company, with J.P. Elford as manager, under the entry for Tod Inlet, and Elford appears as a resident of the village. The operation was abandoned by 1911, but this small Saanich Inlet lime kiln, situated on the shore below the Malahat, foreshadowed a much larger operation that had a huge impact on life at Tod Inlet.

The Associated Cement Company of London, UK, had been a major exporter of cement from England to British Columbia before Robert Butchart formed the Vancouver Portland Cement Company. The British company's business in western North America had plummeted when Butchart started producing cement at Tod Inlet. To regain some of their North American market, the company acquired the Elford Malahat property. There they constructed a plant and began operating in 1913.

The Associated Cement Company of London, UK, had been a major exporter of cement from England to British Columbia before Butchart formed the Vancouver Portland Cement Company.

The new site was named Bamberton after Henry K.G. Bamber, who had come out from England on behalf of the Associated Cement Company. In consultation with the British Columbia Department of Mines, Bamber had learned that the veins of limestone, which had cropped out at Tod Inlet, reappeared on the hills directly across Saanich Inlet. Bamber investigated the site, had the overburden of vegetation and soil stripped off, and found enough limestone to warrant construction of a cement plant. The company purchased land at the foot of Mount Jeffrey as the plant site. Henry Anderson, an electrical engineer, came out from Scotland to supervise plant construction. There was no road access at that time, and the entire plant had to be shipped to the construction site by water.

By 1914 Bamberton's smokestacks were emitting the familiar whitish-grey gases and fumes from the kilns, and their sales department was equally active.

The Portland Cement Construction Company of London, which was hired to build the new plant, ordered a new ship to help in the transport of people and supplies: a 50-foot wooden freighter named *Bamberton*, to be built by the Hinton Electric Company in Victoria in 1913. Her ownership was transferred to the Associated Cement Company in 1915.

By 1914 Bamberton's smokestacks were emitting the familiar whitish-grey gases and fumes from the kilns, and their sales department was equally active. The 1914 report of the BC Minister of Mines compared the annual production of cement for the two rival companies: "The Vancouver Portland Cement company with works at Tod Inlet is said to have produced 360,000 barrels worth $560,000 [almost $13 million in 2020 dollars]. The Associated Cement Company with works at Bamberton made a production valued at about $300,000 [almost $7 million in 2020 dollars]." But unfortunately for Bamberton, for Tod Inlet, and for many others, World War I broke out.

WORLD WAR I AND ITS AFTERMATH, 1914-1921

World War I reached its fingers into the remote Tod Inlet community in many ways.

By 1915 the wartime recession in the building trades had already reduced the production of cement at Tod Inlet. Competition from two other new companies in the province, and the gradual exhaustion of the limestone deposits, further reduced cement production there.

There was a dramatic slowdown in cement sales, but there was also a human cost, as there was in every Canadian town and city. Day by day, newspapers documented the toll: "William Satterthwaite, of Tod Inlet, B.C., serving with the First Pioneers, was reported wounded in April 1916." [65] "Private Angus McIntyre was killed in action in 1917. He was employed by the cement company at Tod Inlet before enlisting with the 48th Battalion and serving with the 7th Battalion." [66] (I also came across a reference to a cement plant worker receiving a special war medal: "The Belgian Croix de Guerre was awarded to Sergeant J. H. Strudwick, of the 67th Western Scots of Victoria. Before going overseas he operated a rock drill at Tod Inlet.") [67]

None of the Sikh workers at Tod Inlet were among the 10 Sikhs who enlisted in the Canadian Army in WWI. Though there were some 300 Chinese men who joined the Canadian Army, we have no information on whether any of the Tod Inlet workers were among them.

Although the production of cement at Tod Inlet had slowed considerably, the cement boats were still active. In the "Marine Notes" section, the *Vancouver Daily World* reported on May 11, 1915, that the Grand Trunk Pacific freighter *Henrietta* would arrive from Alaska with a full cargo of some 800 tons of gypsum for the cement works at Tod Inlet.

There was a huge snowfall in February 1916. The inlet was isolated for several days until the snow was cleared and the interurban railway cars were able to run again. Mary Parsell remembered, "When one of the Cement boats came in, the Company officials sent it around to Sidney to pick up supplies for the residents. . . . When the interurban cars began to run again a young girl friend of ours came up to our place to attend a farewell party which was to be held in the West Road Hall. The party was to honour six of the local boys who had lately joined the Forces and were due to sail almost any day." [68] The men's bunkhouse at Tod Inlet, built shortly before the war broke out, became the centre for community Red Cross meetings.

At the Bamberton plant, many employees who had come out from England to work hurried back after the war broke out to fight for their homeland. The plant, only recently completed, was left with only a skeleton crew—an eerie, echoing place. Even Robert Butchart took up

Although the production of cement at Tod Inlet had slowed considerably, the cement boats were still active.

the cause: in 1917, he was appointed to mobilize British Columbia's wartime shipbuilding effort by the Imperial Munitions Board. As Director of Wooden Shipbuilding, Butchart oversaw the building of 135 vessels significant to the war effort in the last two years of the war.[69]

There was little local demand for cement during the war, and in 1916, after bitter competition for what business there was, Bamberton closed down for a time. This closing left the market for cement to be supplied exclusively from the Tod Inlet plant.

Wartime changes left vacant positions at the plant. They had to be refilled, and the newspapers recount efforts to find good men from as faraway as Vancouver: "BLACKSMITH WANTED—Good Practical all round man; steady work assured; for cement works Tod Inlet, B.C.," ran an advertisement in the Vancouver *Daily World*.[70]

By 1918 there were only 36 names listed under Tod Inlet in Wrigley's British Columbia Directory. (Of these men, only 27 worked for the Vancouver Portland Cement Company.) This was down from 41 names in 1915 in Henderson's Greater Victoria City Directory, and from 43 in 1910–1911, at the height of Tod Inlet's industrial success. Only a few of the men did not work for the cement plant. In 1915 there were four: the Butcharts' gardener, Hugh Lindsay; Captain MacKinnon of Butchart's yacht *Nooya*; and two farmers, Herbert Hemmings and Frederick Simpson. In 1918 there were also just two farmers listed: D. Woodward and C.S. Fox, both practising "mixed farming."

Farming was not a large part of life at Tod Inlet, even at the time of the first settlement. The closest farmer to the village was William Pitzer, who lived up Lime Kiln Road. In Henderson's Directory for 1904 he was listed as a farmer in the community of Sluggett—Tod Inlet had not yet been established. He and his wife, Fanny, raised 10 children on their farm. In 1909 John Beetlestone was the lone farmer at Tod Inlet. In 1913 and 1915 the only farmers listed were Herbert Hemmings and Frederick Simpson, and both lived farther up the road.

THE BRITISH COLUMBIA CEMENT COMPANY

In part because of the slowdown due to the war, it soon became evident to the plant officials at the Associated Cement Company at Bamberton

> There was little local demand for cement during the war, and in 1916, after bitter competition for what business there was, Bamberton closed down for a time.

that the market was too small for two plants operating under separate companies. They also recognized that Robert Butchart would give no ground in a fight for control. When overtures for an amalgamation were made to him, Butchart proved a ready participant and a tough bargainer. He knew that he held the best card in the game: the market for cement. He also knew, as his competitors did not, that the last active quarry at Tod Inlet had only limited accessible deposits, as the new interurban railroad line restricted access to the last significant limestone deposit.

As a result, in 1918 the Vancouver Portland Cement Company amalgamated with the Associated Cement Company, and the new company was to be called the British Columbia Cement Company, though the new name was not adopted until the following year. Butchart became the managing director of the new company. When he surveyed the prospective market for the next few years, however, he decided to not reopen the Bamberton plant and instead concentrate all activities at Tod Inlet. Bamberton remained closed from 1916 until 1921.

In the spring of 1918 Norman Parsell started working for the BC Cement Company. "I went to work in the rock quarry on Wallace Drive. . . . I was seventeen and was fireman and craneman on a Marion steam shovel and my father was engineer. The rock was crushed there and transported to the plant in buckets running on a cable supported on large wooden towers."[71] When Norman operated the steam shovel in the upper quarry in 1918, there were only about a dozen Chinese quarrymen in the gang, down from the 80 men who had shovelled rocks into the small railway cars by hand before the arrival of the big and efficient steam shovel.

In an article in the *Islander* in 1980, Norman described the complex operation and structures at the upper quarry. A heavy steel cable, five centimetres in diameter, was stretched between two large wooden towers at either end of the quarry. The hoist operator up in the control house manipulated two large cable drums that pulled a carriage, which was attached to the cable, back and forth. The quarrymen or the steam shovel operator filled a rock skip (a bucket-like container) with several tons of limestone. The operator would then hoist the skip up out of the

(*top*) Power shovel similar to one the Parsells worked on in the old Tod Inlet quarry, at Bamberton, 1966. Alex D. Gray photograph.

(*bottom*) Another view of a similar Marion power shovel. Still from *The Manufacture of "Elk" Portland Cement.* See p. 67.

(*top*) The system for transporting limestone out of the upper quarry. The quarry itself is to the right. The roadway running left to right below the structure became the BC Electric Railway line, now Wallace Drive. The Partridge Hills are in the background. Author's collection, from BCCC photo album.

(*left*) The concrete bases that supported the towers in the system for transporting limestone out of the upper quarry, 2014. David R. Gray photograph.

(*right*) The heavy bolts that attached the wooden beams to the cement bases of the limestone transport system at the upper quarry, 2014. David R. Gray photograph.

quarry and dump the limestone into a large holding bin. The limestone then passed through a crusher below the bin, and onto a heavy conveyor belt that carried it over the roadway (now Wallace Drive). From there it was loaded into one of the large buckets that transported the excavated limestone on the telpherage cable system down to the cement plant.

Norman also related a frightening experience in the quarry that occurred when the turnbuckle holding the main cable broke. The broken cable tore through the cross braces of the tower, and the carriage and the skip, loaded with eight tons of rock, crashed down alongside Norman's steam shovel. "It smashed into my boom engine and fractured a large gear. . . . There was considerable damage and it took a month to get things fixed. Luckily no one was injured."[72]

With the Tod Inlet plant operating at full capacity, shipping was critical. Having sold the *Marmion* the previous year, in 1919 the company decided to purchase the small freighter *Matsqui*, which had already been carrying cement from Tod Inlet on a charter basis. Other ships, including the CPR's *Princess Ena*, also continued to pick up cement at Tod Inlet. The company purchased another ship in 1920, the 117-foot motor vessel *Teco*, to transport cement from Bamberton and cement tile products from the Tod Inlet plant. *Teco*, a wooden semi-diesel coastal freighter, was built in 1918 by the Taylor Engineering Company of Vancouver.

A beautiful five-masted wooden schooner also found its way to Tod Inlet in December 1920, after a tragic voyage early in her career. *Laurel Whalen* was built in Victoria in 1917 by the Cameron-Genoa Mills Shipbuilders as a lumber carrier for the Canadian West Coast Navigation Company. She was wrecked in Tahiti on a Pacific voyage and brought back to BC, where a survey of her hull showed extensive damage. The BC Cement Company bought the schooner, had her engines and three of the five masts removed, and towed her to Tod Inlet where she began her

(*top*) *Teco* at Tod Inlet in 1935. *Teco* was a regular visitor to the inlet even into the late 1930s. Alex D. Gray photograph.

(*bottom*) The schooner *Laurel Whalen* at launch in 1917. This view of the ship shows her great capacity for cargo. BC Archives E-00675.

The schooner *Laurel Whalen* as a floating cannery in 1928. BC Archives D-09060.

new career as a barge and depot supply ship for the storage of bags of cement, as there was no large storage building on site.

By 1920, Bamberton was preparing to reopen. BC Cement Company began advertising for "an experienced foreman for Limerock Quarry at Bamberton" in September. An article about how Vancouver Island's cement industry had "suddenly struck a vein of prosperity" appeared in the *Financial Post* of Toronto in the fall of that year. Among other things, the BC Cement Company had gained a distinct advantage over other Pacific districts producing cement because of its tidewater location and easy access to sea transportation. In the past year, the cement company had shipped 7,000 barrels of cement to Australia and another 3,000 to South American ports.

At the same time, smaller freighting vessels such as the *Trader* and *Grainer* were busily carrying cement from Tod Inlet to Victoria's outer wharf for loading onto transoceanic ships, including the *Iris* bound for Cuba and *Talthybius* bound for China. Cement was also being shipped to Bellingham, Washington, where the local cement company was partially shut down for repairs.[73]

The CPR liner *Princess Mary*—later the famous Princess Mary Restaurant in Victoria—sailed from Victoria to Tod Inlet in May 1921 to take on a consignment of cement bound for Vancouver. The entire passenger accommodation on the ship was booked for the trip, which continued north to Alaska after dropping its cargo in Vancouver.[74]

When Bamberton reopened in 1921, Tod Inlet was indeed running out of limestone. This was seen as an opportune time to reduce the older plant's capacity, with a view to closing down and making Bamberton the only production facility. As the limestone deposits at Tod Inlet were used up, the cement production was transferred to Bamberton, and in June 1921, the Tod Inlet plant and quarries would close.

4

The Community Adapts (1921–1940)

THE CRAZY '20s

The closure of the Tod Inlet cement plant was accomplished with little fanfare. The *Vancouver Daily World* announced the news in the back pages on June 18 under "Mining Notes": "The British Columbia Cement Company has closed its plant at Tod Inlet, near Victoria. The plant employed principally Chinese labor."

There seems to have been little notice of the closure in the Victoria newspapers, nor any reaction. Four days after the official closure, the Victoria *Daily Times* reported on the presentation of a gift to plant superintendent Harvey Knappenberger by his employees: "On the occasion of the closing down of the Tod Inlet plant of the B.C. Cement Company on Saturday last, H.L. Knappenberger . . . was presented with a pair of military hair brushes, suitably initialed and engraved."[75]

As the closing of the plant in 1921 coincided with the taking of the Canada census, we have a good record of the men who were impacted. When the census of Tod Inlet was taken on June 16, 1921, there were 66 men recorded as working at the Tod Inlet cement works.

There were 24 white workers, many of them immigrants from Europe, and 42 men in the "Chinese Quarters" of Tod Inlet. The census gives an interesting picture of the men from China. Five of the men were 50 or older; the oldest was 60. The youngest was 25 and four others were 30 or younger. Only two of them were not married. Twenty of the men had arrived in Canada in 1911 and 1912. The others had arrived as early as 1881 and as late as 1918.

All were recorded as "labourers" except two: Chow Fung On and Goody On were each listed as "Chemist Assistant." They would have worked in the company lab helping run the constant testing of the cement. Both were listed as speaking English.

With the closing of the plant some of the Chinese workers at Tod Inlet probably went to work and live at Bamberton, while others began to work at the Butchart Gardens or sought other work in Victoria. Some may have gone back to China. The Chinese workers played an important role in the Bamberton story as well. There were 39 men from China already working at Bamberton in 1921, one as a foreman, the others as labourers at the cement works. At Bamberton, they had their own bunkhouse and cookhouse. They were diligent workers in the kilns, mills, quarry, yard and laboratory.

The engineers and other plant workers who stayed on with the company and continued to live at Tod Inlet had to make the daily commute to Bamberton by boat. At first the men were taken to Bamberton by Oscar Scarf of Tod Inlet in his 32-foot double-ender *Mary S.*, a former fur-sealing boat from the Pribilof Islands, named after his daughter Mary. Scarf also had a contract to carry mail from Tod Inlet to Bamberton. He lived at Tod Inlet on his boat until 1946.

With most of the company activities now centred on Bamberton, mail delivery at Tod Inlet became more complicated. Edwin Tomlin, president and managing director of the BC Cement Company, was appointed postmaster for Tod Inlet on February 2, 1921, and held

Men at the tile plant. See p. 134.

As the closing of the plant in 1921 coincided with the taking of the Canada census, we have a good record of the men who were impacted.

The active cement plant at Bamberton
in 1966 with the kilns in the foreground.
Alex D. Gray photograph.

that position until his death in 1944. The post office was moved from
the plant's office building to the former cookhouse when the cement
plant buildings were abandoned. James R. Carrier was an assistant
postmaster under Tomlin from about 1921.

Norman Parsell, one of the Tod Inlet men who followed the industry
to Bamberton, began work in the quarry there, first as a driller's helper,
and then as a driller in 1922: "Those big old burly machines with the
tripods and weights were heavy hauling around that quarry!"[76]

In 1919, the BC Cement Company had taken over ownership of
the *Bamberton*, the 50-foot ship built in 1913 by the Hinton Electric
Company of Victoria, and in about 1923 this ship took on the daily role
of carrying men from Tod Inlet to Bamberton and back.

The population of Tod Inlet rose and fell with the highs and lows of the
cement plant. The number of men listed in Wrigley's BC Directory for Tod
Inlet went from 36 in 1918 to a low of 19 in 1924. For the next two years the
list reached a new high of 55 names, most employees of BC Cement.

Adapting to change seemed to be standard procedure for the
cement business as it adjusted to the times, the demands and the
competition. Even the name of the product changed. Their cement was
no longer sold as Vancouver Brand Portland cement, probably to avoid
confusion between Vancouver Island and the city of Vancouver. It was
now Elk Portland cement, perhaps inspired by the elk that were once
common in the hills around Saanich Inlet. When advertising their
high-grade Portland cement in 1920, the British Columbia Cement
Company still listed their "Works" at Tod Inlet as well as Bamberton.

One of the big dryers from the Tod Inlet plant was sold to the
Canadian Kelp Company of Sidney, BC, in about 1917. It was then
purchased by the Portland Cement Company of Oswego, Oregon,
in 1922. A long-time employee of the BC Cement Company at Tod
Inlet, James Haggart, was now in charge of the work of moving the
dryer to Oregon by ship and rail. H.L. Knappenberger, who had been
superintendent of the Tod Inlet plant, also moved to Oregon at the
same time to work for a different cement company.

After the war, the demand for cement finally increased, as cities
replaced older wooden buildings with new, more permanent and

fire-safe structures. By 1923 more capacity was needed. The company took the largest of the kilns at Tod Inlet out of the old plant building and moved it to Bamberton. The weight and size of the kiln must have made for a tricky set of manoeuvres to say the least. The installation of the "new" old kiln increased production from 2,000 to 3,000 barrels each day.

Robert Butchart retired as managing director of the BC Cement Company in 1926 at the age of 70 and turned the directorship over to Edwin Tomlin, who had been treasurer of the company for many years. Butchart was made Freeman of the City of Victoria in 1928.

While things were slowing down at Tod Inlet in the 1920s, to the west, on the other side of the Partridge Hills, a new community was just beginning. The land between Saanich Arm and Tod Inlet, which includes the Partridge Hills, is sometimes referred to as Willis Point, though the name really applies to the point of land at the northern corner. This whole area was an important place for the Tsartlip people. Traditional hunting and fishing camps were situated along the coast. The local W̱SÁNEĆ name for this whole area is SX̱OX̱ÍEM, meaning still or rising waters. The area was first surveyed in 1894, and two sections at the northwest end were granted by the Crown to Sewell Moody in 1905. The land began to be settled in the 1920s.[77]

According to Elder Dave Elliott Sr., white men were not allowed there, but Tsartlip chief David Latasse sent Sam Whittaker and his First Nations wife there as land markers.[78] The Whittakers lived in a cabin at Smokehouse Bay, south of Willis Point, in the 1920s. They picked berries and fished, selling their catches in Tod Inlet and at what is now Brentwood.[79] Whittaker was a taxidermist who worked for the BC Provincial Museum (now the Royal BC Museum) from 1911 into the 1920s. He also offered boats for rental, and his name appears under Tod Inlet in the 1930 BC Directory as "Whittaker S boats for hire." Josiah Bull, who built a wooden shack near Smokehouse Bay, was the only other resident at the time. Within 20 years, this would change.

With the increased use of cars and buses came improved roads, and the BC Electric interurban railway suffered substantial losses. The service finally came to an end in 1924. No more would the freight

(*top*) The *Bamberton* at Tod Inlet in the ice and snow. Alex D. Gray photograph.

(*bottom*) The new Elk brand shipping sack used by the BC Cement Company. Author's collection. David R. Gray photograph.

The Bamberton cement works, 1930.
National Air Photo Library.

service haul freight and logs, nor would mail and milk from local farms be carried to Victoria.[80] The rails were removed in 1925, and the route once again became a local roadway, eventually becoming part of Wallace Drive from Brentwood south to Tod Creek Flats, and Interurban Road on towards Victoria.

INTO THE HUNGRY '30s

Even though production increased throughout the 1920s, in about 1930, at the beginning of the Great Depression, the Bamberton plant was closed and most of the employees were laid off, including all of the Chinese men. Only a skeleton crew was kept on to watch over the plant. The Chinese workers did not return when the plant reopened.

During the years of the Depression, Tomlin, the managing director, made a number of improvements to the Bamberton plant. One was the retrieval from the old cement plant at Tod Inlet of another tube mill for grinding limestone and its installation at Bamberton.

The BC Cement Company planned annual events for the families of its employees, including those who lived at Tod Inlet. There were picnics every year, among other summer excursions. Mary Parsell recalled an excursion to Maple Bay on the company boat. "Oh! what an enjoyable time we had. They provided all the food and gave tickets to all the children for ice cream and pop."[81] Another time—sometime after 1929—they were taken to Deep Cove on the *Island King* (purchased by the company in 1929), and in later years they went to the federal government's Experimental Farm in Saanichton for their annual outing.

THE TOD INLET TILE PLANT

After closing the main plant at Tod Inlet in 1921, the company continued to operate a tile plant at the site, making cement drainage tiles and flower pots on a small scale. The plant was situated at the shore, between the large wharf and coal shed and the power station, just east of the coal unloading dock. The foreman of the plant was James Carrier, who had

arrived at Tod Inlet with his wife, Evelyn, and family just after the World War I. The family appears in the 1921 census as living at Tod Inlet; Wrigley's Directory of 1921 lists Carrier as postmaster for the village.

The tile plant was a simple building with corrugated tin for the roof and siding. Inside was a 1.5-metre mixer machine. Sand and cement were poured into a chute that led to the machine. The tile machine made straight, tube-shaped tiles of solid wet cement, which the plant workers had to bore out to make them hollow before the cement had completely set. They also made special tile fittings in hollow T, Y and C shapes by hand.

The flower-pot- and tile-making process was complicated. The men had to let the tiles partially set overnight after they were hollowed out, 50 tiles to a tray, then stack them the next day and spray them with water for two or three days until they set completely. Specially made nozzles created a fine, fan-shaped spray. The cement flower pots, which came in at least six sizes, the smallest 4 inches across and the largest 12, also had to set under a water spray.

The big ships were still seen occasionally in the inlet in the 1930s. Cement to make the flower pots and tiles came from Bamberton on the company ships or by tug and barge, usually five hundred 87.5-pound bags at a time. The sand for the tile plant came from Victoria or Metchosin on a barge, and the men unloaded it using wheelbarrows.

(*above left*)
James Carrier,
postmaster
and foreman of
the tile plant.
Carrier family
collection.

(*right, top to bottom*) The tile
plant, with the peaked roof,
at Tod Inlet in 1973.
David R. Gray photograph.

Cement drain tile on the
beach at Tod Inlet, 2018.
David R. Gray photograph.

Flower pots from the
Tod Inlet tile plant.
David R. Gray photograph.

A spray nozzle from the
Tod Inlet tile plant.
David R. Gray photograph.

134

Men who worked at the tile plant.
Carrier family collection.

At age 23, Sluggett's wage was 30 cents (about five dollars in 2020) an hour; he lived in the Tod Inlet bunkhouse, where the cost of each meal was 35 cents.

From 1921 to 1936 the company freighter *Teco* carried cement from Bamberton to Canadian west coast ports, but was also seen in Tod Inlet on occasion. In 1928 *Teco*'s master, R. Hunter (age 41); the mate, James Smith (age 28); the second engineer, James Parsell (age 63); and the winchman, Peter Hunter (age 29), all lived at Tod Inlet.

The company steamer *Matsqui*, purchased in 1919, also visited Tod Inlet. In May 1923 *Matsqui* ran aground on a rock at D'Arcy Island, where in the late 1800s the Canadian government had quarantined Chinese people who had leprosy, without medical care, leading to its reputation in the Chinese community as the "Island of Death." *Matsqui* was pulled free and sent to Yarrows Ltd. in Victoria for repairs.

Mike Rice, who lived at Tod Inlet, recalled that initially it was Chinese men who worked at the tile plant in the 1920s. When Claude Sluggett began working at the plant in 1932, he took over from three Chinese men who worked there. He thought they might have gone on to the Butchart Gardens. At age 23, Sluggett's wage was 30 cents (about five dollars in 2020) an hour; he lived in the Tod Inlet bunkhouse, where the cost of each meal was 35 cents. Sluggett worked at the tile plant until war broke out, and he went back to Bamberton in 1939.

Dem Carrier, son of the plant foreman, was born at Tod Inlet in 1925. When he began working at the tile plant as a teenager in 1940, sand was brought in on a barge nudged in by a tug. Workers had to unload the sand across large planks over four and a half metres of water to the shore. They also had to unload bags of cement that the *Island King* brought from Bamberton, for local sale and for making the flower pots and cement tiles.

LIFE IN THE COMMUNITY

When I interviewed Lorna Pugh (née Thomson) about her memories of the Chinese and Sikh workers of Tod Inlet, she gave me a little book of memories of the 1930s, *Brentwood Bay and Me: 1930-1940*. I had no idea at the time that her book would turn out to be such a gold mine of stories about Tod Inlet. Her memories provide a glimpse into the social life of the community, consisting of about 150 people in the 1930s, from the perspective of a teenager.

> Sunday afternoons were often spent walking to the Carriers' home in Tod Inlet, having tea and listening to the 5 P.M. news and Big Ben on the radio before walking home, a distance of approximately two miles. The Carrier household was a friendly place and I have spent many enjoyable hours in their company. My mother and Mrs. Carrier were very close friends… Their friendship led to Joyce Carrier and myself sharing many outings together. We did much exploring in the Partridge Hills and named one of the creeks flowing into Tod Inlet "Joylorn." We loved to hike or row across the inlet to explore this creek and thought it mysterious because it went underground for a way and then reappeared.[82]

> Spring was my favourite season. Everything seemed to come alive. The Indian drums and

The Cement Song

This song comes from the BC Cement Company's *Community Song Book*, a book that was created "for Use at Community Functions at Bamberton." But the lyrics obviously would have had a lingering connection to Tod Inlet.

NOTHING BUT CONCRETE

(To the tune of "My Bonnie Lies over the Ocean")

The children of Israel in Egypt
Made brick in four thousand B.C.,
But we have escaped out of bondage,
It's nothing but concrete for me.

Chorus:
Concrete, concrete, nothing but concrete for me,
    for me,
Concrete, concrete, nothing but concrete for me.

Don't build a cottage of lumber,
I want something modern, you see
And building of lumber's a blunder,
It's nothing but concrete for me.
(Chorus)
Don't spoil any roads with macadam,
For that is as frail as can be;
As long as I'm paying the taxes
It's nothing but concrete for me.
(Chorus)
In picking the dates for our lifetime
The fates worked with kindly intent
In placing us here on this planet
To live in the age of cement.
(Chorus)

The tennis court at the Carrier home. The net posts are still in place, and one of the walking trails passes right over the court.
Carrier family collection.

their chanting at [ceremonies] on the Tsartlip Reserve competed with the frog chorus in the swamp. Both could be heard from our house and seemed to usher in spring.[83]

I still roamed the hills [as a teen] but usually in the company of others instead of alone. Good Friday hikes to Durance Lake with a group of local school friends, Girl Guide hikes and compass tests in the Sooke Hills and up Mt. Work under the capable hands of our Guide Leader, Ethne Gale, are happy memories.[84]

The old West Road Hall was a meeting place for the social and recreational needs of Brentwood and Tod Inlet for many years. The hall was built at the corner of Lime Kiln Road (now Benvenuto Avenue) and West Saanich Road on land owned by Jack Sluggett. When the local Women's Institute built its own hall in 1924, the old hall began to be used for basketball, and the Tod Inlet cement company men formed their own team.

When a few of us showed interest, Miss Jean Bagley, the primary teacher at West Saanich School used to take us to the West Road Hall and taught us the rudiments of badminton. This game became very popular in the early thirties and a court was built in an unused building in the B.C. Cement plant in Tod Inlet.[85]

When the Mount Newton High School was built nearby in 1931, students from the area no longer had to take the bus into Victoria to attend high school. Lorna first went to Mount Newton in 1934 after grade 6.[86]

Lorna and her school friends enjoyed occasional wiener roasts on Fernie Beach at night and swimming or playing tennis at the Carriers' on days off. Sometimes they fished for perch off a wharf below the village or from the Butcharts' boathouse.

In the latter part of the 1930s, the young people of the area were delighted on cold winter nights when the Carriers would flood their tennis court and visitors were allowed to put on their skates in the warmth of the Carriers' kitchen. The Carriers used to scrape and

reflood the court after skating was finished so that it would be in top condition the next day. They also served coffee and delicious refreshments to top off the wonderful evenings.

> One very cold year Tod Inlet froze sufficiently that skating was possible out to the buoy off Fernie Beach. It was said Jack Stewart's team of horses was taken across the inlet to test the ice. Mrs. Carrier, who was not a strong skater, in her stately manner pushed a chair in front of her for support.[87]

(left) Bamberton *in ice.*
Carrier family collection.

(right) Rescuing a boat sunk by the ice at Tod Inlet in 1935. Note the laundry house in the background to the right and the foreman's house behind the men. Alex D. Gray photograph.

Photos from the Carrier family photo album show James Carrier, the postmaster, pulling a bag of mail across the inlet to the edge of the ice, where the tug *Bamberton* waited to take the mail across Saanich Inlet to the plant at Bamberton.

QUARRY LAKE

The Reverend Robert Connell, an Anglican minister who was later the first leader of the BC Co-operative Commonwealth Federation party (a predecessor of the New Democratic Party), wrote articles about local natural history and geology for the *Daily Times* and *Daily Colonist* newspapers in the 1920s and 1930s. He visited Tod Inlet often, and in his articles, a series entitled "Rambles Round Victoria," he described in observant detail the plants and geology of the area.

Connell described what it was like to follow the road down to the inlet from the old interurban line in 1924:

Kangaroo at the Inlet in winter, with
Tod's Cabin in the background.
Alex D. Gray photograph.

The road descends into the valley which, extending from Prospect
Lake, passes into the head of the inlet by way of a little stream whose
waters go tumbling seaward under a simple bridge of timbers.
Here the maidenhair [fern] luxuriates in the damp interstices of the
rocks shaded by the overhanging trees and shrubs.... The road, in
its lower part, at present the scene of woodcutting operations with
their accompaniment of fresh surfaces and resinous odor, winds up
the hillside and eventually brings the traveler to a little cottage in an
open clearing starred with flowers.[88]

He was probably referring to the cabin at the head of the inlet,
just south of the mouth of Tod Creek on the small terrace above the
shoreline. This old log cabin was known as "Tod's Cabin" (though it had
no connection to the inlet's namesake). It had become pretty dilapidated
by the 1930s. Joyce Jacobson (neé Carrier) recalled the building, known
to them as "the Hut," as a shack papered with newspapers—in particular,
a 1905 edition of the *Calgary Herald* with a headline reading "Reform of
the Senate Required." Some things never change!

Connell's writings give an interesting perspective on the old limestone
quarry just east of Wallace Drive, now called Quarry Lake. Water began
to seep into the quarry sometime around 1921 after drillers checking
the depth of the limestone deposit drilled through to the water table.

Connell described the quarry both before the flooding, in 1924,
and after, in 1931. In the earlier account, he wrote, "At the crossing
of the derelict electric railway we looked down into the quarry of the
cement company, very bleak and cold, with its bare walls of dark grey
limestone. Vegetation has scarcely as yet succeeded in establishing
itself in the inhospitable crevices, and the contrast is great with the
lawns and flowerbeds of the other quarry, once as naked as this but
now the celebrated 'Sunken Gardens.'"[89]

Seven years later and ten years after the aerial tramway and quarry
were abandoned, Connell wrote about what was still to be seen at the
now water-filled quarry:

Then come the appendages of the quarry, the overhead railway, engine-house, pumps, loaders, and what not. What a sight the quarry presents! It is filled from end to end with water, which over the pale rock below has a blue-green color, and in its motionless surface the walls of marble with their abrupt changes of tint, their crevices and cracks, and all the irregularities due to Nature or to the operations of the quarryman's art, perfectly reflected.[90]

In those days the quarry was not fenced off as it is today, and people went there to swim. Quarry Lake was also a bathtub for some of the berry pickers who worked on neighbouring farms. Many would often head there after work with their towel and a bar of soap.

People also swam in the flooded lower quarry—the first quarry, abandoned before the cement plant was built. In the summer of 1931, 20-year-old Patrick Hogan, a soldier from Heal's Camp, was swimming with friends in the lower quarry, then climbed up onto the roof of the vacant plant. In an unfortunate accident, he was electrocuted when he touched a live high-power wire leading to the crusher machine in the building. The secretary of the BC Cement Company told the inquest into Hogan's death that although the plant was not in operation, the live wiring had been retained for occasional use. Signs had been posted stating that the land was private property and that swimming was prohibited, but they had been torn down. Sometime after this incident, the quarry and plant were fenced off, though they remained accessible from the beach at low tide.

When the film studio Central Films of Hollywood was shooting a series of films in Victoria in the mid-1930s, the inhabitants of Tod Inlet had a front-row seat for one of the movies. Dem Carrier and other youngsters were asked to help with the filming of a scene in the 1936 movie *Stampede* where outlaws spooked a herd of horses in an attempt to kill the hero, played by Charles Starrett.

The "Black Canyon," the scene of the stampede, was actually the Tod Inlet gulch, the cement company's electric railway cutting, where clay from the upper pit and rock spoil from the upper quarry had been carried west towards the plant by the electric railway trolley. Dem Carrier helped in the action shot by throwing clods of dirt at the horses, all from the Thomson and Sluggett Farms, to keep them moving.

Quarry Lake in the 1960s (*top*) and in 2019 (*bottom*).
David R. Gray photographs.

(clockwise from top left) Newspaper advertisement: "Victoria's Own Motion Picture Production! Peter B. Kyne's Roaring Yarn of Thundering Hoofs! 'Stampede' Filmed Entirely in Victoria and Vicinity under the Title 'Gunsmoke' with Charles Starrett, Finis Barton." Author's collection.

A section of a poster for *Stampede* showing the star, Charles Starrett, wrestling with an antagonist in the Tod Inlet gulch. Central Films, 1936. Author's collection.

The "Black Canyon," just west of the entrance to the main trail through Gowlland Tod Provincial Park at Wallace Drive, 2018. David R. Gray photograph.

WILLIS POINT PASTURE

The making of the movie *Stampede* was not the first roundup of horses at Tod Inlet.

On the northwest side of Tod Inlet, along the coast and inland towards Willis Point, is an area where the Tsartlip people took their horses to graze in a grassy opening.[91] A fence marking the Tsartlip territory ran across the land, from Tod Inlet to Saanich Inlet, approximately in line with the high smokestack at the old power plant at Brentwood Bay. Tsartlip Elder Dave Elliott Sr. remembered often hunting along that fence. The whole peninsula south of the Willis Point itself had beautiful springs year-round and plenty of forage. Elliott's people used to leave their livestock there while they went to the Gulf Islands to fish. They drove their horses and cattle up to the mouth of Tod Inlet and swam the animals across so they would be inside the fence. The animals could look after themselves there.[92]

Beatrice Elliott (née Bartleman) was 82 years old when I spoke to her in 2001. She described how the Tsartlip people used the land at Tod Inlet across from the ferry dock in Brentwood as hunting grounds, probably in the 1930s. There were grouse in the wooded areas. The Tsartlip also had land there as a place to take livestock when they left to go to the US or to the mainland to do seasonal work or to fish in the Fraser River—there was a good grazing area for horses. People lived on clams, hunted deer and shot pheasants and grouse. Beatrice remembers a group of people going up into Tod Inlet digging clams: "Everything was clean, the water was so clear."

Manny Cooper and Marshall Harry also took their horses across Tod Inlet to the area opposite Butchart Cove. There was good pasture and lots of free water in the summer there. Harry took geese along with his horses.

In the early 1940s, the people from the Tsartlip Reserve still made their traditional trips in summer to Yakima, in Washington State, for the hop harvest. Everyone from Tsartlip to Duncan went to Yakima for the harvest. They picked blackberries first, then hops. There were five or six different camps: the Yakima people had their own camp, as did the Blackfoot. The Tsartlip people were part of what were known as the "BC Camps." While Manny Cooper was away, "Old Man Chubb" (Fred Chubb, Robert Butchart's chauffeur, who lived at Tod Inlet) kept an eye on the horses to make sure they didn't swim back across. In September the Tsartlip people would come back to retrieve the horses.

The Thomson family of Brentwood also swam their cattle across Tod Inlet in the years around 1935 to let them graze on the south side of the inlet. If they drove the cattle in along Durrance Road, the cattle would simply walk out again, but if they were swum across, they would stay, grazing opposite Fernie Beach. Lorna Pugh recalled her dad, Lorne Thomson, leading the young stock not being milked, about 10 to 12 head, across by rowboat. On Sundays, the Thomson children rowed across to check on the cattle and have a picnic. Manny Cooper remembered working on Lorne Thomson's farm for a dollar a day, cutting and baling hay for the livestock.

> The Thomson family of Brentwood also swam their cattle across Tod Inlet in the years around 1935 to let them graze on the south side of the inlet.

THE CHINESE VILLAGE

When the Tod Inlet plant shut down, many of the married men continued to live at Tod Inlet, working in the tile plant or at Bamberton. The population of Chinese workers, however, must have fallen rapidly. A few men continued to work at the inlet, in the tile plant or the gardens, but most of the 200 or so probably left by the 1930s. Unlike the white workers, the Chinese did not commute by boat to Bamberton. For the few that remained, a truck from the cement factory went to Victoria to pick up groceries in Chinatown in the 1930s. The store that supplied the provisions was Hang Ley's, at the corner of

(*top*) Aerial photograph of Tod Inlet in 1926. National Air Photo Library.

(*bottom*) The old laundry house in 1966. Alex D. Gray photograph.

Government Street and Herald Street. Lorna Pugh remembers selling perch to the few Chinese workers still living at Tod Inlet.

The first aerial photographs of Tod Inlet, taken in 1926, show at least four buildings still standing in the Chinese-Sikh village area. The field in the centre of the photo at left is where the company horses grazed. North of this is the row of white family housing and the entrance to the Butchart Gardens. South of the field is the Sikh and Chinese workers' village. At the southwest corner of the field, near the mouth of Tod Creek, is the laundry house. To the southeast is the larger two-storey Chinese bunkhouse.

When Dem Carrier went up to the village to sell fish in the 1930s, there were still three houses on the north side of the road east of the stable, but only one on the south side. The large house visible in the 1926 air photo was no longer there.

The longest-standing building used by members of the Chinese community was the former laundry building at the edge of the hayfield. The Butcharts' big house at the gardens had no place to do laundry; the basement was low and was heated with radiators, and so unsuitable for drying laundry inside. As former gardener Pat van Adrichem recalled, "There is no way Mrs. Butchart was going to hang out sheets." The laundry building at the Chinese village was built by the Butcharts, probably in the early 1900s, and all their laundry was sent down there to be done. The laundry workers, almost certainly Chinese, used a big water boiler to "cook" the sheets. As there was no electricity, irons were heated on the stove. The working area included a smaller room at the back of the house with two larger chimneys.

At some point a two-inch pipe was put in for a waterline to the laundry house from the fire hydrant at the intersection of the two paths in what was the Chinese village. This pipe can still be traced from the fire hydrant at the main road junction to where the house stood. The position of the fire hydrants is marked on the 1916 map of the cement company structures.

Yat Tong, who came to Tod Inlet in 1912, lived in the old laundry house with another man in the 1940s—the only residents in what was once a bustling village of hundreds of immigrants from China. At first Tong lived in a bunkhouse with 30 other Chinese labourers. Later, he moved to the former laundry house with another gardener, Bing Choy, who joined the gardens in 1941.

Former gardener Pat van Adrichem worked with Tong and got to know him well, learning at least a part of his story. When Tong was delegated by Robert Butchart to work in the gardens on one or two days a week, his work apparently impressed Mrs. Butchart. From an interview in the *Islander* in 1961, we can almost hear the only words directly from Tong that have survived. In his own description of how he came to work at the Butchart Gardens full-time:

> Missy say to me, "Tong, you like work here allatime?"
> I say, "yes."
> Missy say, "I see Missiter."
> Next day, Missy say, "Al'ight, Tong. You work here allatime."[93]

The transcription may seem like an uncomfortable stereotype, but the piece reflects the way the speech of Chinese labourers was perceived at the time. Tong's English was clearly sufficient to communicate with his employers.

Allan Ferguson was a shift worker at Bamberton from 1947 to 1954. The Ferguson family lived in the house at the top of the row of company dwellings at Tod Inlet. The house was freezing cold, with no basement. His wife remembers the three Chinese men who worked at the gardens: Tong, Choy and Wing. She recalls that they "got on great" and were good to the kids of the village. Although Tong and Choy lived in the same house—the laundry house, in the field—she never saw them talking to each other and always saw them walking one behind the other. One was from Guangzhou, then called Canton by westerners; the other from Beijing (Peking). Wing lived in the bunkhouse. He was older and had been there longer. He left before Tong and Choy, retiring in 1949 or 1950. Mrs. Ferguson remembers

The fire hydrant and the shut-off valve in the Chinese village area, 2019.
David R. Gray photograph.

Glazed ginger pots found at Tod Inlet.

David R. Gray photograph.

Tong as more outgoing and generous. The kids loved them. The two men always brought treats for the kids after a Saturday's bus trip to Victoria's Chinatown.

Joyce Jacobson (neé Carrier), who was born at Tod Inlet in 1921, remembers that the Chinese men lived in about four houses, arranged in a semicircle, of which she never saw the interiors. Choy and Tong worked with her dad at the cement tile plant. When they finished work, they walked up the road past the village. Jacobson would watch for them and run up from the beach and sell them perch or cod at 5 cents (75 cents in 2020) each, or even 15 cents ($2.25) for large perch. She recalls that they "were nice guys to us." At Chinese New Year, the men who worked with James Carrier at the tile plant would bring the family a gunny sack of dried lychee nuts and green-glazed jars of sugar-syrup ginger, and a silk handkerchief for Mrs. Carrier.

THE BUTCHART GARDENS

With more and more visitors now coming to the gardens by car, the Butcharts decided to improve the old Lime Kiln Road to Tod Inlet. The route was smoothed out by eliminating a few corners east of Wallace Drive and rounding off the major curve just north of the present entrance to the gardens. The remnants of the former roadbed can still be seen on both sides of the road east of Wallace Drive and on the inner (east) side of the curve near the gardens. The roadbed was newly constructed, and the road was surfaced with cement in 1929. In the same year, it was renamed Benvenuto ("welcome" in Italian) Avenue, reflecting the name of the Butcharts' residence, and their famous welcome.

It is interesting that this project was an early demonstration of the use of cement for road surfacing. In a company ad in the *Nanaimo Free Press*, the BC Cement Company declared, "Concrete Roads surpass all others. They save public time and public money. They are always safe to drive on, and are permanent investments. It pays to have the Best." [94]

The Canadian Pacific Railway Company ran excursions from Vancouver to Butchart Gardens in the early 1930s. The CPR SS *Princess Patricia* left Vancouver at 10 a.m. and started the return journey from the Tod Inlet wharf at 4 p.m. "One of the most enchanting beauty

spots on this continent, Butchart's Gardens are visited by tourists from all parts of the world. You'll enjoy every minute of this scenic cruise to Tod Inlet, with a delightful visit to the Gardens," ran an ad in the *Vancouver Sun* on July 20, 1932. The return fare was $2 ($30 in 2020 dollars), "children half fare."

Mrs. Butchart received the City of Victoria's medal for Best Citizen in 1931 because she opened her gardens to visitors each day of the year. By then tens of thousands of people had visited Butchart Gardens. *Maclean's* magazine described it that year as "more than 20 acres in which every flower and shrub of the temperate zone grow at their best: where anyone at their leisure could wander without encountering a 'Keep off the grass' or a 'Do not pick the Flowers' sign."

(*left*) Excursion ship arriving in Tod Inlet for a tour of the Butchart Gardens.
BC Archives F-04193.

(*right*) Stern view of the cement ship *Shean* leaving the Tod Inlet dock.
Carrier family collection.

THE CEMENT BOATS IN THE INLET

With the increased production of cement at Bamberton, the company ships *Teco* and *Matsqui* could no longer handle the growing transport requirements up and down the coast. Consequently the company managers once again looked to Great Britain to augment the cement fleet. In 1924 they purchased the coaster *Fullagar*. She was built by the

The new cement ship *Shean* in Tod Inlet. Author's collection, from BCCC photo album.

But again the output of Bamberton cement surpassed the capacity of the ships in use, and in 1928, the BC Cement Company sent word to their United Kingdom representative to look for another ship.

Cammell Laird shipyard in Birkenhead, the first shipyard in Great Britain to use electric arc welding. When *Fullagar* was launched in February 1920, she was the world's first all-welded cargo ship. She was 150 feet long, with a gross tonnage of 398. Renamed *Shean*, the new company ship crossed the Atlantic, traversed the Panama Canal, and arrived in Victoria in good condition. She replaced *Matsqui* to join *Teco* in the cement trade, mainly carrying cement to Vancouver. *Matsqui* was sold to the Coast Steamship Company of Vancouver in November 1924. She ended her career as a barge for a fishing company in the early 1960s.

But again the output of Bamberton cement surpassed the capacity of the ships in use, and again, in 1928, the directors of the BC Cement Company sent word to their United Kingdom representative to look for another ship. A year later the company purchased the *Granit*, built in Norway in 1920. She was 166 feet long and carried one ton in her hold. Renamed the *Island King,* she began her eventful career on the west coast with an adventurous voyage across the Atlantic and into the Pacific—a trip that lasted an incredible nine months! The journey included a minor mishap on leaving port, a three-day stranding off

the coast of Kent, continuous engine trouble, months of delay in the Azores, where an engineer and some of the crew quit, the death and burial at sea of the second engineer, a 25-day drift without engines, adjustments to the engine in the Virgin Islands, and another change in crew. She finally made it safely into the Pacific Ocean and up the coast to Victoria. *Shean* was summoned to tow *Island King* to Bamberton, where her cargo of gypsum from Rouen, France, was off-loaded. *Shean* then towed *Island King* back to Victoria, where a new Union engine was installed at Yarrows Shipyards.

In 1930 *Shean* hit a rock off Victoria at full speed and shattered her forepeak bulkhead. The welded plates of her hull held, though severely buckled. Only 400 bags of her cargo of 10,000 bags of cement were damaged, and *Shean* made port under her own power.

At various times during the Depression, one or another of the cement boats—*Shean*, *Teco* and *Island King*—were taken out of service due to lack of work. When not in use, they were tied up at the wharf in Tod Inlet. Bob and Alice Guisbourne lived aboard as caretakers. Joyce Andrews, who lived at Tod Inlet, used to go down to visit the Guisbournes, make fudge and dance to the radio.

Teco and *Shean* were seen periodically in Tod Inlet until the mid-1930s, and *Island King* probably up until 1944, as the ships were

Aerial views of Tod Inlet showing the plant, office buildings, bunkhouse and company housing, 1930. In the two photos on the right, you can see the Butchart Gardens in the background. In the top two photos, you can see the *Island King* at the wharf. In the left photo, the road to the Chinese village and the trail to the laundry house can be seen on the right. For a detailed map, see pages 218–19. National Air Photo Library.

(*left*) Dem Carrier near the mouth of Tod Creek with a company scow in the background. Carrier family collection.

(*right*) Remnants of the large cement tiles used to form the grids on the mud flats near the mouth of Tod Creek.

David R. Gray photograph.

occasionally called to deliver cement to the tile plant. In later years of operations, *Teco* also picked up cement tiles and flower pots from Tod Inlet. Her captain, mate and crew of six (the chief and second engineers, a winchman, two deckhands and a cook) remained the same during this period, but their monthly wages dropped dramatically as a sign of the hard times. The mate's wage dropped from $142.50 to $80, and the chief engineer's from $205 to $100. *Teco*'s cook, Quon Don, earned $75 a month in 1926 (equal to $1,115 in 2020 dollars), but nine years later his wages had dropped to only $45 (equal to $855 in 2020 dollars). By 1936, the last known year of ownership by the BC Cement Company, only the master, Captain Hunter, lived at Tod Inlet.

After the other ships were sold—*Matsqui* in 1924, *Shean* in 1935 and *Teco* in 1936—*Island King* continued loading cement at Bamberton. By 1944, when the *Island King* was sold, cement was already being shipped by tugboats pulling scows (barges), or by larger ocean-going freighters not owned by the company.

To make the cleaning and painting of the BC Cement Company scows easier, a system of "grids" was placed on the tidal flats at the east end of Tod Inlet between 1930 and 1940. A series of 14-inch-long cement tiles, two stacked upright and filled with concrete, were placed in a grid pattern to support the scows, which were manoeuvred into place at high tide, then allowed to settle onto these short pillars as the tide went out.

The tiles were placed about one metre apart, allowing the men and boys hired by the company to crawl underneath and scrape barnacles,

HMCS
Armentieres.
BC Archives A-00213.

mussels and algal growth from the undersides of the company barges, a job described by Dem Carrier as "simply terrible." In later years he found the grids were a good place to collect pile worms for fishing bait. The grids show up on aerial photos of the time, and some broken tiles can still be seen there at low tide.

MILITARY USE OF TOD INLET

The story of Tod Inlet saw yet another twist when the inlet was the site of an extensive military practice manoeuvre involving the Royal Canadian Air Force, navy and army. On the night of June 30, 1932, the 600 "attacking" troops from Vancouver were embarked on the warships HMCS *Skeena*, HMCS *Vancouver* and HMCS *Armentieres*, and landed in the early morning at Tod Inlet. The 800 "defending" troops were local military units camped at the Heal's Range, just south of Tod Inlet.[95]

As the two forces engaged in mock battle, two aircraft from the Vancouver air station arrived to take part in the training: a Fairchild on floats and a Vickers Vedette, a small wooden flying boat. These aircraft were likely the first aircraft to land in Tod Inlet, and among the few ever to do so.

Vedette wooden flying boat, 1930. This is the type of aircraft from which the 1930 aerial photographs of Tod Inlet were taken. The pilots flew on training missions from the Royal Canadian Air Force station at Jericho Beach near Vancouver. Author's collection.

In the Vedette was Flying Officer Costello, on the defenders' side. He located the landing party in Tod Inlet and dropped information to the headquarters of the defending troops using the World War I–style message bags. Noting the three naval ships steaming north after landing the troops, Costello landed the Vedette in Tod Inlet twice to discuss the operation with the military observer. After patrolling the area of the operations, he noted it was "difficult to distinguish attacking troops from defending troops. Practically all movements were along roads." [96]

In support of the attacking force, Squadron Leader Shearer flew the Fairchild to Tod Inlet with a signaller and an observer. They located the attacking battalion's headquarters, sent messages with an Aldis signalling lamp, dropped message bags, made an attack on an "enemy aircraft" and patrolled the area until the "battle" was over and all the troops were marching to their training camp at Heal's Range. After returning to their temporary base at Esquimalt, both pilots made additional flights to Tod Inlet carrying militia officers who wanted to view the battleground.

At some point in the late 1930s, just before World War II, the remaining kilns and all other large iron fittings were stripped out of the Tod Inlet cement plant as scrap iron and put on barges bound for Japan. Clarence Sluggett (Claude's brother), who probably watched the proceedings from the tile plant, commented at the time, "It will all be coming back to us as bullets pretty soon."

Japan had been a major buyer of scrap metal in the US and in Canada in the years leading up to the start of World War II. Japanese freighters loaded cargoes of scrap metal in Victoria in 1935 and 1937. When Japan invaded China in 1937, Canadians expressed their dismay that Canada would continue to allow Japan to buy scrap iron, copper and other metals that were obviously important to Japan's military needs. In Victoria, Chinese Canadians protested the shipping of metal to Japan. The Saanich council sent a resolution to Prime Minister King calling for an embargo on exports of scrap metal to aggressor nations in July 1939.

White and Chinese Victorians picketed truck operators trying to move scrap metal aboard a scow intended for Japan in August 1939, just a month before Canada declared war on Germany.

At some point in the late 1930s, just before World War II, the remaining kilns and all other large iron fittings were stripped out of the Tod Inlet cement plant as scrap iron and put on barges bound for Japan.

5

Another War, Another Ending (1941–1970)

THE INLET AND THE WAR

World War II had a relatively minor impact on Tod Inlet. The men working at Bamberton were kept on, as the military needed cement for coastal defences and other installations. Though they had some trouble finding staff during the war, the company was able to keep the plant in production.

At the Butchart Gardens, though, the impacts were more deeply felt. In 1939, the Butcharts presented ownership of the gardens to their grandson, Ian Ross, on the occasion of his 21st birthday. Ross enlisted in the Royal Canadian Navy at the beginning of the war, and the gardens did not flourish during his absence. At the end of the war he resigned his commission and decided to make the running of the gardens his full-time job.[97]

At Tod Inlet, part of the old system of taking clay from the clay pit by the upper quarry to the cement plant was brought back into service in order to meet increased demand. The clay deposit up at Wallace Drive was reactivated, and clay was once more sent down to what is now called the Old Mill. An old metal skip still at the site was probably used for scraping and loading the clay. At the mill, the clay was mixed with water, then piped down to the old plant through a wood and wire pipe system. At the plant, they pumped the clay mixture into a barge at the wharf for shipment to Bamberton.

The Butchart family, left to right: Robert Butchart, daughter Jennie Ross, Jennie's son Ian Ross, and Mrs. Jennie Butchart.
Courtesy of the Butchart Gardens.

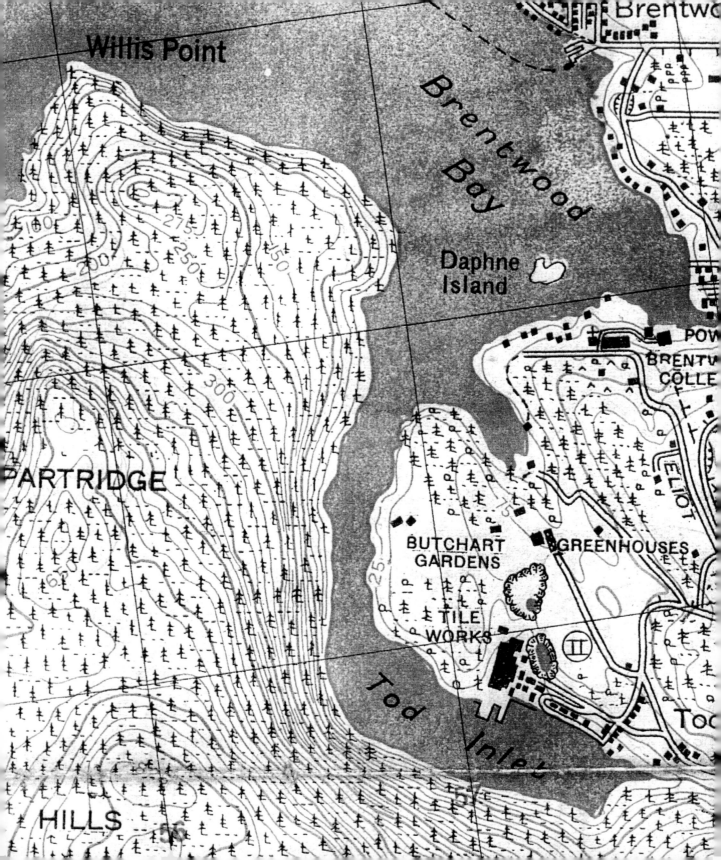

Map of Tod Inlet in 1935 showing the quarries (in blue) at the Butchart Gardens and the clay works and upper quarry at Wallace Drive. Department of National Defence, Geographical Section, No. 415. Author's collection.

The trial run for this new endeavour didn't pan out as expected. Because of the vibration of the tug's engines, transmitted through the taut tow line to the barge, the clay settled out, and by the time it reached Bamberton, they couldn't pump it out as planned. The men had to drill and dig it out, it had settled so hard.

When Bamberton started running out of limestone on the main mill site, they opened a new quarry at Cobble Hill, and later, in the mid-1940s, brought limestone in from the Blubber Bay quarry on Texada Island, north of Nanaimo. The BC Cement Company was one of three companies then quarrying limestone on Texada.

On June 16, 1944, the Vancouver *Province* reported that there was a large increase in demand for lime, for both war-related industries and agricultural needs. However, with the wartime shortages of manpower, lime plants were unable to operate at maximum capacity. Anticipating the future expansion of the British Columbia lime industry, the Roche Harbor Lime Company, based on San Juan Island in Washington State, established a new company and bought the lime works at Eagle Bay on Texada Island. The new company was called the McMillin Lime and Mining Company, and it had its headquarters in Vancouver. It was headed by Paul McMillin of Roche Harbor, son of Robert Butchart's old acquaintance and competitor, John McMillin.

The remnants of the old clay mill, 2019. David R. Gray photograph.

(*top*) Barnard's yacht *Quenca* at
the Point Hope shipyards, Victoria.
Alex D. Gray photograph.

(*bottom*) *Kangaroo* at Tod Inlet.
Alex D. Gray photograph.

PLEASURE BOATS IN WAR AND PEACE

As far back as the 1930s, cement company workers and others had kept their private pleasure boats moored in the inlet. Sir Frank S. Barnard, lieutenant-governor of BC from 1914 to 1919 and a friend of Robert Butchart's, kept his 67-foot yacht *Quenca* in Tod Inlet at least until 1935. The big yacht was housed in a large boathouse that was kept in place by piles driven into the sea bottom. At least part of the flotation system supporting *Quenca*'s boathouse was large cement pontoons made at Tod Inlet around 1915. One of the pontoons is still lying on the beach below the village site, partially filled with mud. (Incidentally, my family's connection to Tod Inlet started when my dad, Alex Gray, a Victoria resident and shipwright, became an occasional deckhand on *Quenca*.)

The 40-foot *Kangaroo*, built in Nanaimo in 1914 and owned by dentist Dr. Sam Youlden ("Doc Youlden"), first came to Tod Inlet in 1930. A small white wooden boathouse with red trim was towed to Tod Inlet from Victoria by the *Kangaroo* in July 1936. The boathouse was a centre of activity in summer for picnics, fishing and swimming, as well as a storehouse for rowboats and boating equipment.

Our family boat, *Squakquoi*, a 25-foot cabin cruiser launched at Portage Inlet in 1939, joined the group in 1941 after a few short stays in 1940. Squakquoi is probably derived from the word SҠOҠI,—meaning "dead" in SENĆOŦEN, the Saanich language. The name comes from my dad's friends joking about how long it was taking him to build the boat. They said that the original wood in her hull would have dry rot before he finished building the rest. Dad wanted a First Nations name for his boat, and "Squakquoi" was the closest translation he could find for the term "dry rot."

By March 1942, all of the Canadian Navy's corvettes and armed merchant cruisers stationed on the Pacific coast had been diverted either to Alaska, because of the threat of Japanese invasion there, or to the Atlantic for convoy duty. To replace them, the navy organized the civilian Power Boat Squadrons (PBS) to fulfill a need for surveillance and protection of the British Columbia coast. More than 200 civilian

boats, based in marinas from Victoria to Courtenay, began training with the navy, army and air force. British Columbians were concerned about a possible Japanese invasion, and the PBS had to be trained to respond. Simulated air attacks and beach landings in the dark of night prepared the squadron members for possible action.[98]

At least four of the private boats moored at Tod Inlet became active members of the local Power Boat Squadron: *Dennis*, *Kangaroo*, *Squakquoi* and *Tum Tum*. Along with the other 223 boats in the volunteer squadrons, the Tod Inlet boats were painted dark grey, with their individual PBS numbers in large white digits on the bow. In September 1942 the squadron practised with the Royal Canadian Air Force, which made mock attacks and dropped smoke bombs. In November, the squadron practised various manoeuvres outside the Victoria Harbour breakwater. *Squakquoi* was moored at Tod Inlet and Shoal Harbour during the war, depending on where the Power Boat Squadrons were sent for exercises.

One of the squadron's most challenging exercises was the nighttime transport of troops during a simulated invasion of Vancouver Island. In July 1943, the PBS, including the four Tod Inlet members of the fleet, the Royal Canadian Navy, the Royal Canadian Air Force, and the Home Defence Forces, prepared for a possible invasion. In the evening darkness, the boats left Deep Cove, in North Saanich, loaded the infantry troops of

(*above*) PBS137 *Squakquoi* in her war colours, 1942. Alex D. Gray photographs.

(*below*) Alex Gray's Power Boat Squadron's badges and membership cards. Author's collection.

Victoria Daily Times

VICTORIA, B.C., SATURDAY, JULY 24, 1943—30 PAGES

n Hails 'Complete Liq
azi Offensive; Lists B

Commandos Strike at Dawn

When the sun peeked into Saanich Arm this morning landing barges, operated by Vancouver Island powerboat squadrons, stuck their blunt noses on beaches there and men of Canada's Reserve Army leaped ashore to carry out manoeuvres designed to outwit the defending forces. Men wading ashore in above picture are from 3rd Reserve Battalion, Canadian Scottish Regiment. (See story of combined operations on Page 2.)

The landing of troops during a PBS manoeuvre in 1943. *Victoria Daily Times,* July 24, 1943. Author's collection.

the attacking landing parties and proceeded to Brentwood and Tod Inlet. There the troops leapt ashore at dawn to engage the defending forces.

> It was the most realistic operational maneuver, simulating real warfare, ever engaged in by these units, whose men are preparing themselves to defend these shores…. A fleet of grey-painted, numbered boats made a rendezvous overnight at a well-known cove. At 3 a.m. today, blacked out, they slipped quietly away and crossed to the point where the invading troops… were embarked…. At 5 a.m. the boats ran for the beach and just as dawn was breaking the first landings were made…. Waist high into cold waters the men jumped… rifles held aloft, full kit on their backs. Dripping wet they crouched along the beaches awaiting the order to attack…
>
> Along the barnacled rocks and over clam shells the men crept cautiously beneath protecting trees and up the banks, where they took up firing positions to engage the enemy, entrenched behind barns and fences…. By sun up the battle was in full swing…. On stretchers the "wounded" were packed through heavy underbrush and down sloping banks to dressing stations. Before the battle ended the troops were subjected to gas attack.
>
> Following the maneuver the powerboats returned to their regular anchorages and the soldiers marched to their Heal's camp.[99]

Four of the powerboats were already home.

With the passing of the immediate threat, the pressure on the PBS decreased, and by the end of the war, the squadrons had been disbanded. The nucleus of one squadron, however, the North Saanich Squadron at Deep Cove, was preserved. This became the starting point for a civilian yacht club promoting training in good seamanship. In 1947, the squadron became the Capital City Yacht Club. Today, the Canadian Power and Sail Squadrons, an organization of recreational boaters with over 20,000 active members, continues the legacy of the PBS throughout Canada.[100]

PEACETIME ON THE WATER

In 1946 the Tod Inlet Power Boat Owners' Association was formed by the small group of boaters who still moored their pleasure craft at Tod Inlet. The objectives of the association were to improve the conditions for boat owners mooring in the inlet and to provide proper landing facilities. At the start there were 29 active members. In later years the number of regular members was kept at 34 to avoid overcrowding. Fred Chubb, who lived at Tod Inlet and had worked at the cement plant in the early days, before becoming Butchart's chauffeur and later the engineer of the *Bamberton*, was appointed honorary port warden.

The objectives of the association were simple: "to install, operate, maintain and repair docks, wharves, floats, gangways, marine ways, mooring buoys, and similar facilities for the mooring, docking, repairing, maintaining, and servicing of boats owned and operated by members."[101]

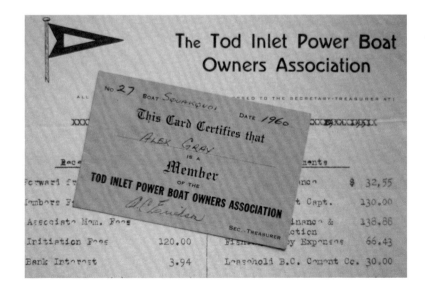

Alex Gray's membership card for the Tod Inlet Power Boat Owners' Association.

Author's collection. David R. Gray photograph.

My own early involvement with Tod Inlet also began
in 1946. At seven months old, I experienced my first trip
on our family boat, *Squakquoi*. My mother recorded
my reaction in a baby book: apparently I "just loved the
water, couldn't keep [my] eyes off it."

That year the association also began building a
wharf and small marine railway, known as "the ways,"
for hauling out boats. Tom Ward, owner of *Tarpon* and
vice-president of the association, talked directly to Nigel
Tomlin, president of the BC Cement Company, who
agreed to supply the cement for the construction of the
ways, though many of the club members thought it was a
bad idea to be indebted to the company.

Often working at night using floodlights to take
advantage of low tides, the members expended
about 2,000 man-hours under Tom Ward, the acting
construction engineer. The ways were probably finished
in early 1947, as the date "Feb 16 1947" is inscribed in
the cement foundation. The ways used a unique system
of chains and plates to support a boat and adjust its
position as it was hauled up out of the water on the rails
and held in a wooden cradle. The lower part of each
chain was sheathed in rubber tubing to protect the boat's
hull. The supporting chains on each side fitted into the
holed and grooved plates at the top of the wooden side
posts of the cradle. They could be adjusted as the boat
on the cradle was winched up out of the water. The ways

could take boats up to 65 feet long and weighing up to 35 tons. They were still in use in the 1970s.

The annual Tod Inlet fishing derby, started in 1948, was popular with the community of Tod Inlet as well as with the members of the association. There were prizes for the largest and smallest fish, and plentiful cake and green fish candy as treats for the children. The winning fish were described as "small" in the second annual derby in 1949: the first-prize fish weighed only 10 pounds.

The black can buoy moored close to a rock on the eastern side of Tod Inlet was a popular spot to fish for lingcod in the 1950s. As a family, one of our favourite weekend outings was to go with Doc Youlden on the *Kangaroo* to tie up to the buoy and fish for cod. We would lower our lines, baited with small live pile perch that we had caught back at the wharf, and watch them sink. It was thrilling to see the lingcod moving below through the clear green water—though I don't remember much success at catching them.

I well remember the exciting summer activity of fishing for the big striped sea perch that lived under the boat dock. The only way we could catch them was by dropping a hook, baited with small mussels, through a knothole in the planks of the wharf. When a perch got hooked, you dropped your line that was attached to a dowel of wood through the knothole, then dove under the wharf, swam up to the surface under the dock, retrieved the dowel and the line, then swam back out from under the wharf to emerge triumphantly with the fish.

My personal memories of this unique time at Tod Inlet are powerful. There was a great sense of camaraderie amongst the boat owners—and an inappropriate sense of ownership of the inlet, at least among the children. But it was a playground unimagined by most: the water perfect for swimming and fishing, the fun of meals aboard the boat, the other families, and of heading out for summer adventures in Saanich Arm and the Gulf Islands. There was also the excitement when a big racing canoe from Tsartlip came into the inlet.

(*top to bottom*) *Squakquoi* on the ways at Tod Inlet, 1948. Note in the left background the clear-cut logging on the hill south of Tod Creek and the log dump, and the logging road running up towards the Partridge Hills. Alex D. Gray photograph.

The Tod Inlet anchorage in 1947.
Author's collection.

Members of the Tod Inlet Power Boat Owners' Association who worked on building the ship ways in 1947.
Author's collection.

The fishing derby at Tod Inlet with the *Kangaroo* at the dock. Alex D. Gray photograph.

Children with dogfish shark, with the tile plant and ship ways behind, 1954. Alex D. Gray photograph.

The dock decorated for the annual fishing derby, early 1950s. Alex D. Gray photograph.

Boys on *Squakquoi*, about 1960.

David R. Gray photograph.

CANOE RACING

The long tradition of people from Tsartlip using Tod Inlet to train for canoe races continued into the 1940s. Ivan Morris recalled that the most common training course was from Tsartlip Reserve to Tod Inlet and back. Ivan was part of the crew of the well-known racing canoe *Saanich #8*. When he started going to Tod Inlet, the cement plant was already abandoned and falling apart. They saw the buildings, and the boats tied up there, but never saw the plant in operation.

People at Tsartlip who made dugout canoes included Marshal Harry, Philip Tom and Tommy Paul. Harry worked on both racing and other canoes. He made one of the best, and best-known, racing canoes: *Saanich #5*. Beatrice Elliott's dad, Joe Bartleman, paddled in that canoe. "They won so many races in that canoe," Beatrice recalls. "I remember as a girl the practices before the races, when everyone went to the beach. Afterwards, the paddlers were served lime cordial or lemonade from a big bucket. The canoes were taken by gas boats to races on the coast or by truck to the races at the gorge."

LAND USED AND LAND LOST

On the opposite side of Tod Inlet from the cement plant and village, there was little or no industrial activity into the 1940s. The forested hills leading up into the Partridge Hills maintained their quiet stillness in spite of the commercial activity facing them. The people from the Tsartlip First Nation at Brentwood, just around the corner, were the primary users of this forested land. They continued using the land for traditional hunting, fishing and trapping, as well as for the grazing of livestock, well into the 1950s.

After the war, all the timber rights to the forested land around Tod Inlet were sold by BC Cement to logging companies. As Dave Elliott Sr. recalled in 1983, "We knew it was our land, we never had any other thought but that it was our land." But "we lost the land somehow. One after the other—land, fishing rights, hunting rights were legislated away. . . . The treaty with James Douglas said we could hunt and fish as formerly. We can't."

(*top*) Canoe race at the Tsartlip Reserve, Brentwood, May 1965.
Alex D. Gray photograph.

(*bottom*) After the canoe races at the Tsartlip Reserve, May 1965.
Alex D. Gray photograph.

Although the Douglas Treaties had stated the Indigenous people could keep their "village sites and enclosed fields," as well as the right to fish and hunt in traditional territories, in reality they were denied these rights by the practice of the government selling all lands outside of the reserves, which the government itself had designated.

Hunting

The Tsartlip people continued to hunt on the Partridge Hills, the high land above Tod Inlet, throughout the 20th century, as their ancestors had for hundreds, perhaps thousands, of years.

When Ivan Morris was born, his family lived in a longhouse on the Tsartlip Reserve with fire and no electricity. At the age of 13, Ivan would go hunting about three times a week up in the Partridge Hills above Tod Inlet to get food for the table. They would take three deer a day, sometimes, to feed the community.

In an interview in 2001, Ivan explained to me that "at that time, the law at Tsartlip was that whenever the head of the family went out hunting, no one was to play around. Just sit still, not even wash the dishes. The law of the Elders was to do nothing until the hunters returned home." When Ivan and his older brother went hunting, his younger brother had to keep still in the home. "We always went by canoe to the mountain, pulling up on a patch of gravel at the end of Tod Inlet walking up into the hills, though we never got many deer there. There was always a great feeling when we got home. The family was always happy that there was food on the table."

John Sampson (1945–2014), a respected Tsartlip Elder, also shared his memories of Tod Inlet with me in 2001. John and his family used to dig clams up at the end of the inlet. He would row to "the red house" on the west side of the inlet narrows and go hunting all day long up as far as Durrance Lake. That was in about 1958, after the logging. "As kids we used to go through the old cement plant, play around the area and swim in the inlet. Sometimes we saw smoke from the plant. White people used to scare us off the property, but later we made friends with other boys from Tod Inlet, and then we didn't worry about being chased off." Tod Inlet was the only place they could go to hunt because they had no car—

Tsartlip Elder John Sampson during an interview in 2001. David R. Gray photograph.

or they could go to the Goldstream Reserve by canoe. People often hunted along the shore from the canoe.

John also remembered when the white families who moved into houses up there (near Willis Point) kicked his dad and others off of the mountain. Even though they protested that they knew how much to take and how much to leave, they still were not allowed to use the area—this was not an issue of conservation but an issue of perceived ownership and possession.

Even after their rights to use the traditional lands were denied, Manny Cooper hunted all through the hills around Tod Inlet, starting when he was 12 years old (about 1940; he was born in 1928). He hunted from the mouth of the inlet over the hills to McKenzie Bight on Saanich Arm. There the salal was thick and grew as tall as your head.

Deer eat the leaves and berries of the salal, and Manny also believes the leaves are medicinal for deer. Once, at Sheppard Point, on the west side of Saanich Arm, Manny shot and wounded a deer, pulled his canoe up on the beach, then followed the deer as it took off. He watched the deer eat salal leaves, chew them and put the chewed leaves into the wound. There was no more blood, and Manny was not able to catch up to the deer.

Manny was active in trying to get some compensation for the loss of traditional hunting territory around Tod Inlet. The change in hunting patterns has been drastic: in the days before logging they used to get a deer after walking only about 250 metres from the beach; and then they had to travel down to McKenzie Bight; and now they cannot hunt at all in the area.

Blue Grouse

The Tsartlip name for Tod Inlet, which translates as "Place of the Blue Grouse," indicates the importance of these birds. Tsartlip Elder John Elliott (STOLȻEȽ) talks about the historic relationship between the Tsartlip and the blue grouse on the FirstVoices' SENĆOŦEN website, which is dedicated to the teaching and learning of the SENĆOŦEN language. "Our Saanich ancestors could go out to gather the Blue Grouse just with a basket and a stick; because there was so many that they had become tame and wouldn't even fly away. Plentiful amount of Blue Grouse is a sign of a healthy environment."[102] At the time of the Bullhead Moon, SX̱ÁNEȽ (April–May), the almost full-grown grouse could be snared in the woods. A review of the history of this species in the area helps in understanding how that

Continued on page 164

Male blue grouse, in courtship display. SD MacDonald photograph. Canadian Museum of Nature Archives S95-22599 TG C55.

(Cont'd from the previous page)
importance has changed over the years. Hunting of blue grouse was an important fall activity for many hunters in the early 1900s. The *Victoria Daily Times* reported on September 10, 1903, that special trains were run on Labour Day by the Esquimalt and Nanaimo Railway to pick up hunters at the various stations south of Shawnigan. The reporter noted that there were many hunters with grouse in their bags, from two or three up to thirty.

The Vancouver Island Fish and Game Club was active in 1904 and 1905 in getting amendments to the Game Act to help protect the blue grouse. By 1905 the sale of game shot on Vancouver Island was prohibited, but the club was still urging the appointment of a special constable to patrol the districts near Victoria where blue grouse were being "sold in numbers" out of season.[103]

In another twist to the blue grouse story, Hungarian partridges (also called grey partridge) were released near the cement works at Tod Inlet in the spring of 1908. (They may have had an impact on the decline of the blue grouse.) By November, partridges had been seen near the cement plant, on Keating Cross Road, and in the Highlands on the west side of Tod Inlet.[104] This and other introductions in southern BC were not successful, and the grey partridge populations died out between the 1930s and early 1970s.

The suggested open season for blue grouse in the 1920s extended from early October to mid-November, and the bag limit was still 6 birds per day and 50 birds per season. By 1925, the open season for the area including Tod Inlet area had been reduced to the last two weeks of September.[105] The blue grouse hunting season for Vancouver Island currently extends from September 1 to December 31 with a daily bag limit of 5 birds (15 for the season).

Since 1970 blue grouse populations have declined, probably because of urban development. The current status of the blue grouse around Tod Inlet is unknown. I have never seen a grouse at Tod Inlet, even when exploring the Partridge Hills.

Ornithologists decided in 2004 that what we have called the blue grouse is actually two closely related species, now named the dusky grouse and the sooty grouse. It is the sooty grouse that lives on Vancouver Island and in the Tod Inlet area.

Tod Inlet was also known for lots of blue grouse. Cooper used to hunt them with a .22-calibre rifle. He loved fried grouse, and still hunted them into the 2000s.

Trapping

John Sampson's grandmother Christine Pelkey and her husband, Philip Pelkey, used to trap mink and otter around Tod Inlet, up to the Goldstream Reserve in the 1920s and '30s. They trapped whatever people would buy and took the pelts to Vancouver to sell. They had a 20- or 25-foot dugout canoe that carried all their trapping and camping gear, including canvas for a tent and a pole to hold up a sail. John remembered his whole family going clam digging with them. When he was young and travelling by canoe, he was told, "Sit and don't move."

Fishing

In the late 1930s or early 1940s, the Tsartlip people still followed their tradition of cutting cedar boughs during the herring run in March and placing them in the water. When the boughs were covered with herring spawn, they would strip the spawn from them to eat.

Around the same time, people from the Tsartlip Reserve would also come into the inlet during the herring run in one-man canoes and troll for spring salmon using 50-foot linen lines. Manny Cooper remembered going in with canoes and fishing for big spring salmon with a two-fathom line tied to his leg, using #4 or #5 Canadian Wonder spoons. They used abalone spoons for grilse and also speared lots of cod from the rocks.

Dem Carrier, as a young white fisherman in the 1940s, was intrigued by the almost magical success of the Tsartlip people. Was it due to some special local lure or bait? He was surprised to learn some years later that they used the standard Martin white-red gill plug, available from any fishing outlet!

In 2001 Beatrice Elliott told me about her husband's (Tsartlip Elder Dave Elliott Sr.) love for fishing: "David used to go fishing in Tod Inlet, where there was always good fishing. He used to go up there during the war. He netted small pilchards to use as bait for other fish. He caught dogfish in Brentwood Bay and took the livers to Ogden Point, where someone bought them for the oil. While fishing, he would line up different points to locate his fishing area for dogfish. He also caught lingcod and rock cod, and always gave fish away to people. He was a fisherman all of his life, until he couldn't fish because of his health."

Beatrice also remembered going to Tod Inlet in a canoe with Elder Genevieve Latasse, who took her up to the Butchart Gardens. Her eldest brother also took her out in a canoe and speared cod with a long spear.

John Sampson's great-grandmother Lucy Sampson, who died at the age of 106 in 1980, told him of seeing killer whales in the inlet. There was a pod of orcas known as the Seven Sisters who used to come into

(*top*) Fishing spoons made of abalone shell. David R. Gray photograph.

(*bottom*) Dem Carrier with a salmon in front of the Carrier house. Carrier family collection.

Saanich Inlet in the late 1950s, when John was about 13. The whales never bothered anyone, but when they were around, the younger guys were not allowed to go out fishing. As great-grandmother Lucy said emphatically, "There were *others* out there fishing!" She said the whales followed one at a time in and around at the mouth of Tod Inlet, along Willis Point and down to Mackenzie Bight.

In the late 1950s and early 1960s, John used to catch trout in Tod Creek and big grey perch at the ferry wharf. He would take a sackful of perch (about 20 fish) up along Wallace Drive to a Chinese man who lived on Durrance Road, who would buy the sack for two dollars. During this time John and his brother Chuck also speared cod behind Daphne Islet. John paddled while Chuck spotted the lingcod. He speared them with an eight-foot three-pointed spear made by his dad. John's brother Ken used to make fancy spear points like arrowheads, but they were hard to get out of the cod. They used to leave their spears where they fished in case they ran into fisheries people. While fishing at night in Goldstream River, they sometimes had to leave their spears behind on the bank. They rowed the dugout, rather than paddling, when fishing for salmon so that one could easily handle the canoe while the other fished. The five-foot oars overlapped while rowing because the dugouts were only about three feet wide. They tied the fishing lines to their feet so they knew when a fish was on the line.

Map of areas of clear-cut logging around Tod Inlet, 1940s–1950s. Philip Wilson and David R. Gray.

THE LOGGING ERA (1941–1956)

A few large old stumps in the valley of Tod Creek provide evidence of the selective logging carried out in the late 1800s and early 1900s. Large notches in these stumps indicate that the trees were cut by two men standing on springboards and sawing with a two-man crosscut saw.

Several areas around Tod Inlet were logged by clear-cutting between the late 1930s and 1950s. In the mid-1940s, the Copley Brothers of Victoria logged the area south of Willis Point and on either side of the locally named Joylorn Creek, running down into the south corner of Tod Inlet.

Aerial photo of the Butchart Gardens and
the cement plant at Tod Inlet in 1956.

Courtesy of the Butchart Gardens.

By 1946, three large areas on the west side of Tod Inlet had been logged,
from the mouth of the inlet opposite Daphne Islet, southward to opposite
Fernie Beach. Bob Copley recalled that they used a 24-foot boom boat,
Logger Lady, for the log-booming operations in the early 1950s.

By 1950 the logged areas covered most of the west side of Tod Inlet
from its mouth to its southwest corner, extending up over the Partridge
Hills halfway to Saanich Arm. From the head of the inlet, the logging
at Joylorn Creek had extended to the east, west and south, with logging
roads leading to Durrance Lake.

While logging around Joylorn Creek, the company established a
booming ground at the southeast corner of the inlet. They built a log
dump on the inlet's east shore, just south of the mouth of Tod Creek,
placing large cedar logs at a near-vertical angle on the slope above the
beach. I remember seeing the logging trucks dumping their logs into
the inlet in the contained booming area in the mid-1950s.

Squakquoi at the boathouse, about 1960.
Note the vertical logs of the log dump
in the background, to the left.

David R. Gray photograph.

Some of the Tod Inlet archaeological sites were damaged during
the logging. The midden along the shore south of the creek was
extensively damaged by the construction of logging roads, the log
dump and the booming ground. As earth was bulldozed towards
the sea, much of the central shell midden material was removed or
redistributed towards its southern end.

Areas on the south side of Tod Inlet were also selectively logged.
A logging road descended to the south shore of Tod Inlet opposite
the cement plant's wharf. Both fully loaded logging trucks and single
bulldozers pulling log arches came down the rough road to dump their
cargo into the water. The logs were held in a boom that extended west
along the south shore. Logging at Tod Inlet must have been completed
by the mid-1950s, because no booming grounds are visible in the 1955
or 1959 air photos.

 The logging rights to the BC Cement Company lands on the east
side of Tod Inlet up past Wallace Drive to West Saanich Road were held
by the Selective Logging Company of Victoria, owned by Stan Neff and
his brothers. They logged these areas between about 1945 and about
1956. Much of the operation was horse logging; trees were cut by hand,
rolled down banks, and loaded by hand onto horse-drawn trailers. On

steep hills they loaded the logs onto the trailer using skids on the side of the road. When coming down a steep hill, the driver stopped the horse when necessary by running the log it was pulling behind a stump. Selective Logging also operated two trucks, a tandem rig built out of a 1940-or-so Diamond T and an army truck, and a 1939 International single-axle truck with a trailer, formerly owned by Island Freight.

The company built a small sawmill on the west side of Wallace Drive, near its intersection with Benvenuto. They dumped logs into a small pond—Butchart's flooded clay quarry. A jack ladder, a V-shaped trough with a spiked conveyor belt, pulled the logs up from the pond to the mill. Rough lumber was trucked from the mill into Victoria for planing at the company's lumberyard on Douglas Street. Some was sawed for export and some for railway ties. The mill ran two shifts in summer, but shut down sometimes during fire season.

Workers at the sawmill in the 1950s included Rene Henderson, Woolly Smith and Tommy Paul from Tsartlip. John Sampson's dad, Francis, and John's oldest brother, Tom, also from Tsartlip, worked at this mill. The sawmill probably closed in about 1954.[106]

Settler Land Use in the Logging Era

As the Tsartlip First Nation lost access to, and "ownership" of, Tod Inlet, the use of the area by settlers and other newcomers increased.

At Willis Point and south along the shores of Saanich Inlet, a whole new community was forming, at first of cottagers and summer residents, and later of permanent residents. Glen Twamley had purchased two sections of land in 1946, just before they were logged by the Copley Brothers. He later subdivided one into waterfront lots.[107] This was the beginning of a permanent residency at Willis Point. The Rickinson family bought three properties in Smokehouse Bay and became the first permanent residents. The old Whittaker cabin still stood, until it was finally demolished in 1978.

At Tod Inlet, there were still a few people who could be described as farmers in the mid-20th century. One of them was Albert Cecil, the truck driver for the tile plant. Cecil kept horses for riding and pastured them in Yat Tong's field, near the Tod Inlet Chinese village. He also

At Willis Point and south along the shores of Saanich Inlet, a whole new community was forming.

The three-room "larder" storehouse, still with its wooden roof, in 1979.

David R. Gray photograph.

kept cows in a pasture on the east side of Wallace Drive and ploughed two acres of land parallel to Benvenuto Avenue on the flats. He had a barn near the road (now a walking trail) up to the third quarry.

In about 1931 a huge fire burned over much of the area south of the intersection of Wallace Drive and Benvenuto Avenue, reaching almost to Cecil's barn above Tod Creek. Dem Carrier remembers watching the treetops exploding during the fire. After the fire, Cecil grew potatoes on the burned-over land.

At one point in the 1940s, when housing in the village was scarce, Cecil lived in the tiny three-room larder or storehouse between the cement plant cookhouse and bunkhouse. With no connecting doorways, he had to go outside to move between rooms. This concrete storehouse is the only one of the cement plant buildings still standing.

During World War II, when sugar was rationed, James Carrier, who was foreman at the tile plant, tapped the local bigleaf maple trees and made maple syrup. The process required lots of sap and lots of boiling, as the sap was not as productive as the eastern sugar maples.

In the 1930s, settlers at Tod Inlet hunted deer and grouse in the land extending from the company barn through the burned-off area north to Wallace Drive. The construction of logging roads in the 1940s brought greater access to the backcountry, and there was more hunting in the hills around Tod Inlet. I remember in the 1950s the excitement of walking from the inlet up into the hills on the logging roads with adults who were "hunting." We never left the roads, we never saw a deer and I suspect the guns were never loaded. For us hunting was just an excuse for an adventure, not an effort to put food on the table.

Bernard Woodhouse, who lived near Tod Inlet, held a trapping licence for the area in the 1930s. After him, Dem Carrier trapped mink all around the inlet and along Tod Creek. He also trapped muskrats on the upper part of Tod Creek, where it leads up to Durrance Lake.

He remembers picking up salmon in Tod Creek and carrying them upstream, to help them reach their spawning area.

When the staff of the Butchart Gardens opened the dam on Tod Creek, cutthroat trout and bass from Prospect Lake would come out with the rush of water into Tod Creek below the dam. To catch the trout in the pool below the dam, Carrier and other young fishermen would splash water over the dam into the pool. The trout would only bite after there were waves in the pool from the splashed water. The children of Tod Inlet also regularly fished for large perch (probably striped sea perch) from the company or village wharf to sell to the Chinese workers. With their long working shifts, they probably appreciated the opportunity to buy fresh fish.

Claude Sluggett, born in 1909, grew up near Brentwood and saw the changes in abundance of Tod Inlet sea life. He remembered a run of pilchard into Tod Inlet one year when he was a kid, a run so large the fish piled up on the beach. Claude remembered when there were herring galore in Tod Inlet, and when people from Tsartlip came in dugout canoes to fish. But that came to an end.

Jim Gilbert of Brentwood Bay also witnessed great changes in the productivity of Saanich Inlet. Jim became a fishing guide in 1948 at the age of 13, working for his father, Harry, who had owned Gilbert's Boathouse since 1927. As a guide and fisherman, he came to know Tod Inlet well. In his early days, Jim witnessed tremendous populations of herring coming in to spawn with the afternoon tides every April, followed by chinook salmon. The chinooks would move into the inlet at dusk and come back out in the early morning. When Jim was in high school, he and many others would go out in rowboats and dugout canoes to catch the salmon as they fed. He remembers how the Tsartlip Elders watched the diving ducks and noted the time they spent submerged to tell how deep the herring were, and thus how deep the salmon were.

And there were more than just fish in the inlet. Families in the cement company houses were woken in the night by the sounds of orcas splashing and blowing. On the smaller side, there were also littleneck and butter clams. The boys speared octopus, flounder and

> And there were more than just fish in the inlet. Families in the cement company houses were woken in the night by the sounds of orcas splashing and blowing.

skate, and they fished for pile perch and lingcod off the old cement plant wharf, sometimes catching lingcod of 15 or 20 pounds.

Jim Gilbert's dad, Harry, caught a 53-pound lingcod in the inlet when Jim was very young. In the 1930s, '40s and '50s, there was a tremendous population of cod and pile perch, and cutthroat trout of three or four pounds spawning up Tod Creek. Tod Inlet was a safe place for Jim and his friends growing up—Jim learned to swim there. As kids, they had seven-foot cedar rowboats that they could easily haul up on shore, and they hand-trolled Tod Inlet from the rowboats. In 1941, Jim and his sister, six and eight years old, caught eight- and ten-inch cutthroat trout with hook and worm.

In 1951, local fishermen notified Jim and his parents that there was a large shark in Tod Inlet. Wrongly assuming the shark was competing with them for salmon, they asked the Gilberts to catch it. The Gilberts went after it in an 18-foot boat, harpooned it, fired several rounds into it and looped the rope around a tree before they finally killed the shark. It was a five-metre-long basking shark, the largest ever caught in Saanich Inlet. There must have been substantial numbers of plankton in Tod Inlet for such a shark to feed.

Ivan Morris from the Tsartlip Nation also "used to see basking sharks, close to the beach here, huge things. . . . When kids started hitting them with rocks when close to shore, I stopped them."

Basking sharks were common in British Columbia waters until the federal Fisheries Department began to actively encourage and participate in killing them. A fisheries patrol vessel chased and killed basking sharks by ramming them with a specially outfitted and sharpened bow. This eradication program killed at least hundreds, if not thousands, of basking sharks between 1945 and 1970, and the population has never recovered.

THE END OF THE TOD INLET COMMUNITY

City directories for the years 1930–1945 list the "white" and mostly only the male population of Tod Inlet, with a maximum of 256 in 1940. This listing must have included men living at Bamberton—the directories had not yet caught up to the growth of the new community at the time.

The BC Directory (Victoria City and Vancouver Island) for 1950/51 shows a reduction of the population of Tod Inlet to 171 and lists 156 names, almost all men. Of the names listed, 123 worked for the BC Cement Company. Another 20 had jobs likely related to the plant (for example, "lab"), and five were gardeners. Three women were also listed: Phyllis Hamilton, A. Trowsse ("wid") and Irma Trowsse, the latter a schoolteacher at Bamberton. Although women were listed in the census records, they were not usually listed in the directories.

The single men's bunkhouse in 1965.
David R. Gray photograph.

When the Bamberton plant manager, Edwin Tomlin, died in 1944, the British Columbia Cement Company applied to become a corporate postmaster in his stead. James Carrier, manager of the tile plant, was the company-appointed postmaster in charge. He held that position from June 1944 until the post office closed in October 1952. Claude Sluggett was the postmaster's assistant from 1939 to 1952.

The Vancouver Island Coach Lines bus service to Tod Inlet began with the Victoria–West Saanich route in the early 1930s. The buses also delivered the mail to Tod Inlet in the 1940s and 1950s. For the kids who came out to the inlet on weekends, there was always a bit of excitement when the Coach Lines bus came roaring down the road, around the sharp corner at the plant, and pulled up in front of the post office near the bunkhouse. The 1930s Coach Lines advertising colourfully described what we remembered of the 1950s buses: "A Streak of Orange . . . The Staccato Hum of the Exhaust, and It's Gone!" For the villagers the bus meant mail or visitors; for us weekend kids, it was just a big, colourful, noisy attraction, as we didn't see these big buses at home in Victoria.

When the post office was closed on October 8, 1952, the Tod Inlet & Victoria Mail Service became the Brentwood Bay & Victoria Mail Service, and the 1.1-kilometre route into Tod Inlet was deleted from the contract held by Vancouver Island Coach Lines. An extension to the mail courier's "Route of Travel" from Brentwood Bay Post Office was requested to serve the 18 families who still lived within less than a kilometre of the former Tod Inlet Post Office. The heads of four of these families were employed at Butchart Gardens, and the remainder were employees of the BC Cement Company. Ron Tomlinson was living in the old company cookhouse, and Joe Hiquebran, carpenter for the company, was in the big house east of the vacant men's bunkhouse.

After being rebuilt at Victoria's Point Hope shipyards in 1923, the *Bamberton* continued in the cement company's service until 1952, when she was sold to a logging company. After that, workmen were transported from Tod Inlet to Bamberton in smaller boats hired by the company. Claude Sluggett operated such a boat between 1940 and 1950, carrying 15 people back and forth across Saanich Inlet, "a routine

Hunter at the wharf in Tod Inlet in 1979.
David R. Gray photograph.

job with no problems." In about 1950, the company bought the 25-foot *Hunter*, to transport some 20 employees from Tod Inlet to Bamberton. *Hunter* was built in about 1940 for Canadian Industries for the run to James Island. Claude operated *Hunter* between 1955 and 1965, then the company took it over. *Hunter* may have been named for the captain Hunter who captained the *Teco* for the cement company for many years.

The last city directory entry for Tod Inlet appeared in 1952. After that, people living in the village were listed under the heading of Brentwood Bay. The directory for 1959 listed 14 households on Benvenuto Avenue below Wallace Drive. Among the names were still some familiar to people who grew up at Tod Inlet: van Adrichem and Shiner, who worked at the Butchart Gardens, and Tomlinson, Hiquebran, Rice and Ferguson, who all worked for BC Cement. Hiquebran was harbour master for the Tod Inlet boaters' association between 1957 and 1963, though he was no longer living at Tod Inlet by 1961.

The company houses along the Tod Inlet road were all in good repair and occupied at least until 1958. After that, they were gradually abandoned. The last inhabitant was probably Evelyn Carrier. Her family negotiated with the BC Cement Company to allow her to stay in her house until she was unable to live alone, probably in the early 1960s. By then, even the Butcharts had moved to Victoria, when their declining health made living at Benvenuto more difficult. Robert Butchart died in Victoria 1943 and Jennie in 1950. Their ashes were scattered on the waters of Tod Inlet.

(*top and middle left*) The lower row of houses in the village at Tod Inlet in 1967. Alex D. Gray photographs.

(*bottom left*) *Squakquoi* at the boat owners' wharf in 1965. David R. Gray photograph.

(*centre top*) The Gray family on their last trip to *Squakquoi*, 1965. Alex D. Gray photograph.

(*centre bottom*) The boathouse beginning its last journey in 1965. Alex D. Gray photograph.

(*top right*) Treasures from the boathouse: an old ship's lantern from the days of oil lamps, and a wine bottle full of varnish. David R. Gray photograph.

The village itself was finally abandoned, and the pleasure boats became the sole occupants of the port. The little wooden boathouse lasted until about 1965 when, more-than-somewhat waterlogged, it slowly sank into the inlet. One day just before it completely sank, my dad and I clambered gingerly in through the attic window as the water level reached that height and retrieved a ship's lantern and an old wine bottle full of varnish. These were the only treasures we could reach to remind us of the structure's 30 years of service to the boating families.

The last houses at Tod Inlet were destroyed by the local fire department during a training session in the 1970s.

Remnants of the Chinese community
in 1968. Alex D. Gray photograph.

THE CHINESE VILLAGE SITE

We don't know when or how the Chinese village was destroyed. The
dwellings of the Chinese workers who left Tod Inlet in 1921 or so would
have likely deteriorated fairly quickly, as they were not solid structures.
Materials from the abandoned buildings may have been used by the few
remaining Chinese residents to improve their own houses. When the
Butchart Gardens began dumping compost, grass clippings and other
materials over the banks of Tod Creek in the 1950s, most of the Chinese
village was already gone.

However, a few crumbling remnants of the Chinese community at
Tod Inlet still exist. The old "Chinese midden" keeps a silent record of
who lived there and provides hints of what their lives might have been
like. When my brother and I first discovered the numerous pig skulls

(*top to bottom*) A pig's jaw in the Chinese midden.
David R. Gray photograph.

Pigs' teeth: the start of the whole story.
David R. Gray photograph.

Chinese pottery and mineral water/gin container from Tod Inlet.
David R. Gray photograph.

there in the mid-1950s, it was the large curving tusks in their weathered and earth-stained jawbones that were our treasure. We passed by the shards of broken pottery, cooking utensils and chopsticks.

Later we came to realize that there was a beauty too in the old food and drink containers. Although many were broken, there were some intact Chinese pots: beautifully glazed "Tiger Whisky" or rice wine jugs, delicate blue-patterned rice bowls, squat soy sauce and ginger pots, and many tiny opium bottles. We soon discovered that the best-preserved and intact vessels were often found in the soil and maple leaves banked up against the upslope side of larger trees.

The community's international flavour was evident to us in the hundreds of bottles with embossed writing. Some came from local sources, like Victoria's Silver Spring Brewery, but many others were from around the world. Some were imported Chinese beer bottles, with names like "Wingleewai"; others came from unexpected places such as the "San Miguel Brewery, Manila, P.I." and "Steinike & Weinlig Schutz Selters" in Germany.

Many of the square-holed Chinese coins found were too corroded to read, but some indicated a source in Annam, now part of Vietnam. The hundreds of ebony wood "dominoes" and round glass gambling pieces that we found on the site are typical of the Chinese communities that sprang up in many parts of British Columbia around the turn of the century. The wooden dominoes are playing pieces for the Chinese game called *gwat pai* in Cantonese, which is likely the forerunner of the European game of dominoes.

On one outing in the early 1960s, David Neilson (my frequent partner in exploring Tod Inlet) and I explored a new area upstream on the bench above Tod Creek and found the broken bases of several

(*above left*) Sealing wax container found by Pat van Adrichem at the Chinese village. David R. Gray photograph.

(*above right*) Chinese toothbrushes and ivory razor handle from Tod Inlet. David R. Gray photograph.

(*below*) Corrugated tin roofing material at the Chinese village site. Alex D. Gray photograph.

of the large Chinese containers still popular among gardeners today. Beyond on the flats, where the main part of the village was, we found more solid remnants. Bricks, foundation platforms, and sheets of corrugated tin roofing indicated the location of some buildings. Bottles and pottery, cooking pots and two-man saw blades were scattered throughout the trees and clearings between the creek and the road to the cement plant.

When we first explored the site in the late 1950s, the only building still standing in the area was the old laundry house at the far end of the pasture, above the mouth of Tod Creek and overlooking the inlet. We used to avoid this house, as it was evident that it was still lived in. As kids we were a little afraid of meeting the people who lived there in fear they would forbid our further explorations. Evidently they took the bus into Victoria for the weekends, which is when we would leave Victoria for Tod Inlet. Much later on I came to realize that the men who lived there were probably Chinese, and that they could help me understand the artifacts we were finding nearby. So I tried to contact them by writing a message and my phone number on a cedar shingle and placing it on the front door of the old house.

The response to my wooden letter came from Alf Shiner, head gardener at the Butchart Gardens. He told me about Yat Tong and explained that he shared the former laundry house with Yem ("Bing") Choy, a gardener who joined the Butcharts in 1941. Shiner suggested that I go to the Loy Sing Meat Market on Fisgard Street in Victoria's Chinatown and ask for Tong there. I did, but I guess my request seemed suspicious—a young white guy asking after an elderly Chinese man—and although Tong was well known in Chinatown, I got no help in finding him. Without a personal introduction, there was a wall between his culture and mine.

My next attempts to contact Yat Tong in the late 1960s included phoning and then writing to all of the Tongs in the Victoria phone book. This too proved fruitless, though I did talk with some very kind people. So I never met Yat Tong. I did learn more about him, eventually, through gardener Pat van Adrichem. Yat Tong and Bing Choy lived in the house until sometime in the mid-1960s. In the later years, Tong and Choy lived in each end of the building. A third man had once lived with them; when he died, the room he'd lived in was never used by the other two. Tong told van Adrichem that they would not open the room because the man had died.

Roy Carver, who began working at Butchart Gardens in the fall of 1949, also remembers Tong and Choy well: "One of my duties in later years was to drive Tong and Choy to Chinatown in Victoria where they purchased their sacks of rice and other items, delivering them and their purchases to their house in Tod Inlet." Only three houses remained in the Chinese village at that time. Roy also remembered Choy with a box of cigars, handing them out when his wife in China had a baby.[108]

(*top*) Yat Tong and Mary Todd (née Butchart) at the Butchart Gardens. Courtesy of the Butchart Gardens.

(*bottom*) The Loy Sing Meat Market in Victoria, 2019. David R. Gray photograph.

Unknown youths digging for artifacts in the Chinese village area, 1979.

David R. Gray photograph.

The house, the last remnant of the workers' village, stood until the late 1960s, when it too was burned in a training exercise by the local fire department.

The site of the Chinese village was thoroughly scoured by bottle and artifact collectors in the years after our discoveries, and looks pretty empty today. There are stories of antique dealers and "pickers" coming into the area and breaking any ceramic pots they could find, in order to maintain the price of these Chinese antiques. However, there is still more than enough evidence of the community remaining to provide a valuable window into the past for park visitors.

THE END OF THE CEMENT PLANT (1941–1960)

The cement plant buildings at Tod Inlet remained relatively intact into the 1950s and 1960s.

In 1949, 15-year-old Roy Carver rode his bicycle from Prospect Lake to work at the Butchart Gardens: "I helped in the early years to unload barges of coal at the wharf in Tod Inlet for the furnace that heated the greenhouses, later changing over to oil. . . . I wandered through the cement plant ruins a few times, picking up a large bolt cutter and a few other tools." Roy used a tractor with a bucket to unload the coal, at the same place where the Chinese workers had unloaded coal by hand almost 50 years before. It took him a week to unload a barge load of coal. The bolt cutters that Roy had salvaged from the abandoned plant are now destined for a place in the Royal BC Museum collections.

When Pat van Adrichem was working at Logana Farms, a loganberry farm in Saanich, at the end of 1951, the farm brought a truckload of cement tiles from the tile plant at Tod Inlet. At that time the tile plant was "going full bore."

He started work at Bamberton soon after, in March 1952, and worked there full-time for 19 months as they were supplying cement to Kitimat for the construction of the hydroelectric dam and other facilities for the new Alcan aluminum smelter. Laid off on a Friday

at the end of 1952 or early in 1953, he met with
Ballantyne, the head gardener at Butchart Gardens,
and was hired to start work at the gardens on
Monday. When Bamberton received a big order for
cement for a road in Calgary, the company asked Pat
to come back to Bamberton, but he elected to stay
with the gardens.

Pat recalled that customers were still getting
flower pots from Tod Inlet in 1952, and the tile plant
was still operating in 1953, but the increasing use
of clay and plastic tiles was changing things. The
cement tiles were cheaper but didn't last as long.
They collapsed when used in septic tank disposal
pipes because of the constant wetness and corrosion.

When the tile plant finally closed in about 1953, Heaney's, a
moving company, dismantled it and took the equipment out by truck.
Afterward, a company called Evans, Coleman & Evans bought all the
works from the plant, including the machinery for making flower pots.

Ian Ross, then the owner and manager of the Butchart Gardens,
was in the United States for the winter when he received a letter
saying that the equipment for making tiles and flower pots had
been taken out. He was upset, as he had neither been informed nor
given his approval. He returned to Victoria and drove down in his
old Ford to Evans, Coleman & Evans and brought the pot-making
equipment back to the Butchart Gardens.

When the old flower-pot moulds arrived at the gardens, Yat
Tong was the only one who knew how to use them. The mould was
bell-shaped, made of heavy metal and set upside down. The mix of
sand and cement had to be just right because there was no internal
reinforcement. Tong taught the others how to use sticks to tamp the
cement down into the mould before the outer mould was lifted off.

When an early batch failed to set, Tong understood the problem—
the pots had to set underwater. The gardens staff went back to town
for the metal trays and tanks from Evans, Coleman & Evans, and Tong
showed how to use them. Making flower pots became a usual winter

Bolt cutters from the abandoned
plant, 2019. David R. Gray photograph.

chore at the gardens in the 1950s. The several different sizes of flower-pot moulds are still at Butchart Gardens and were put on display during the garden's centennial year in 2004.

For years after the closing of the tile plant, hundreds of the cement flower pots—possibly rejects—were stored under the old cement plant office building. Some are still in use in various gardens in Saanich, and the Royal BC Museum now has some in their collection.

Sometime between 1953 and 1960, a Vancouver scrap dealer spent most of a winter cutting up the metal still left at the old plant. The workers cut large pieces up into chunks and welded eyes onto each so that their rickety crane could lift them onto their two old trucks and take them to Victoria. On one occasion, one of the men had a large piece of metal drop onto his finger. He shook off his heavy gloves and was quickly taken to hospital. Pat van Adrichem, who had witnessed the accident, collected the man's gloves and placed them on top of the machine. When the injured man returned several days later, Pat pointed out the gloves to him. The man recoiled in horror from the gloves—part of his finger was still in there! Pat asked why he hadn't taken the glove with him so that the finger could be reattached, but it seems he hadn't even thought of that possibility. He certainly didn't want to use the gloves again. Pat simply shook out the offending fingertip and put the gloves to good use for many years.

One piece of machinery that remained in the plant area near the kilns was a small rock-crusher, with jaws about 75 centimetres long and 15 centimetres wide. Pat and Roy Carver used to get it going and toss in small rocks to demonstrate its effectiveness. Eventually it was all removed, as people would often come from Bamberton to get "stuff" they needed from the abandoned plant.

The BC Cement Company merged with the Victoria firm Evans, Coleman & Gilley Bros. in 1957 and continued to do business under a new holding company, Ocean Cement and Supplies.

In December 1957, an appraiser from the firm Ker & Stephenson inspected and investigated the BC Cement Company property at Tod Inlet and prepared an appraisal: "I am of the opinion that a developer would be prepared to pay $30,000.00 for this site after the buildings

For years after the closing of the tile plant, hundreds of the cement flower pots—possibly rejects—were stored under the old cement plant office building.

have been demolished and removed, and that he would pay this sum in the expectation of putting in a subdivision and selling lots for the price mentioned above, namely $63,000.00. If the buildings were not demolished, then I am of the opinion that the property would not be as attractive to a developer and that it is unlikely that it could be sold as is for more than $20,000.00." [109]

BC Cement became a wholly-owned subsidiary of Ocean Cement in January 1964. When Genstar, a large diversified company based in Montreal, purchased Ocean Cement in 1971, the BC Cement Company became part of a subsidiary, Inland Cement Industries of Edmonton. The cement company land around Tod Inlet land became an asset of a different nature.

ENVIRONMENTAL DECLINE

An account that describes the early 1900s, written by columnist Gus Sivertz in 1958, sets the scene that would endure for the whole life of the Tod Inlet cement plant and beyond: "And here was the little cement mill with everything in a shroud of light grey dust: the workers' gardens bravely battling the relentless encroaching pall of infinitely fine particles that rained down on the earth endlessly." [110]

The most obvious pollution from the plant was airborne: a fine dust spewing from the chimney stacks, the product of grinding and burning coal, limestone, clay and gypsum.

On the forest floor to the west of the cement plant site, near the sole remaining chimney, the accumulation of cement dust from the plant, mixing with rainwater, has left a thin coating of concrete over large areas of ground. As the moss

The Fate of Bamberton

In 1959, the BC Cement Company donated land near the Bamberton cement plant to the Province of British Columbia for the creation of a new park. Bamberton Provincial Park includes a Douglas fir and arbutus forest, a salmon creek, coastal eelgrass beds and a 225-metre-long beach.

Between 1960 and 1980 production at Bamberton declined as costs increased and workers engaged in a prolonged strike. As with the Tod Inlet cement plant, ownership changed from the BC Cement Company to Genstar, who decided to sell the property in 1982.

After several failed development proposals and millions of dollars spent in environmental cleanup, the Malahat First Nation bought the Bamberton property in 2015, a purchase that tripled the size of their land holdings.

(*above*) The active cement plant at Bamberton in 1966. Alex D. Gray photograph.

(*above*) Old drainpipes on the shore leading from the plant to the wharf area, 1994. David R. Gray photograph.

(*left*) Dr. Sam Youlden ("Doc Youlden") on the *Kangaroo* in 1973.
David R. Gray photograph.

has grown over the cement covering, it is not immediately obvious that the ground is in fact covered in concrete.

Tsartlip Elder Manny Cooper told me of a time many years ago when he shot a big buck up on the side of the hill near the cement plant, where on the whole hillside the ground was grey with cement dust. The deer had been eating salal leaves. When he cut the deer's throat, he heard a strange rasping sound. He checked his knife, but there was nothing wrong there; he cut again and saw that there was cement at the bottom of the deer's windpipe.

The pollution of the waters of Tod Inlet began in 1905 with the installation of septic tanks at the first 10, then 14 houses in the village, as well as the cement plant buildings. The overflow from the septic tanks in the village was carried by a single pipe into Tod Inlet. We have little knowledge of what other sorts of water-borne pollution came from the cement plant itself.

In the early 1950s my family harvested clams at the mouth of Tod Creek. A special treat was digging clams with Doc Youlden, taking them back to the *Kangaroo*, steaming the clams and eating them from the shell with vinegar, with a mug of hot sweet tea. The water must have been polluted then, but who knew?

Ivan Morris's father, William, used to paddle from Tsartlip to Tod Inlet by canoe to harvest clams, as he and his family had always done. Ivan shared with me the story of the last time they harvested clams at Tod Inlet in the late 1950s: "When Father was an old man, digging clams, he had a sack about half full of clams. A fisheries guy went down and told him he shouldn't be digging clams. He grabbed the sack and spilled them all over the beach. This was unheard of. You can't treat an Elder that way. It hurt the family quite a bit. They gave no warning."

Eventually the Department of Fisheries posted a sign on the boat dock reading, "Shellfish Contaminated—Harvesting Prohibited." The sign was still there in 1980.

Durrance Lake, which drains into Tod Creek, was a man-made lake, dammed up to provide a constant water source for the Tod Inlet cement plant. In the area known as Tod Creek Flats, the course of Tod Creek was rerouted in about 1915 to make a flat, dry area for Heal's Range, the practice range for the Canadian Armed Forces. On many maps, Tod Creek's upper reaches are labelled "Government Ditch."

The most serious changes in the quality and structure of Tod Inlet water probably began with the Hartland Road dump, located about three kilometres due south of Tod Inlet. Starting as an unregulated dump site in the mid-1950s, for 30 years uncontrolled dumping created a dangerously toxic source of water-borne pollution.

The effluent discharge and runoff from the dump ran into Heal Creek, the outflow from tiny Heal Lake, and a tributary of Durrance Creek. Durrance Creek in turn flows into Tod Creek. An example of the kind of contamination the dump created comes from the removal of the contents of a paint works in Victoria to the dump, which resulted in a flow of lead and lethal metal components into the water system. The polluted material introduced into Tod Creek and Tod Inlet was a major blow to the life and vibrancy of the inlet. It began to kill much of the life in the inlet, including the eelgrass beds on the mud flats.

Tod Creek water became so polluted that the Butchart Gardens couldn't pump it onto the lawns

Alex Gray at the Tod Inlet Power Boat Owners' Association wharf. Note the sign prohibiting the gathering of shellfish.
David R. Gray photograph.

because of the smell, and the pollution of the stream due to leachate from the Hartland Road dump and agricultural waste resulted in the loss of the salmon run.

Populations also suffered because the Department of Fisheries allowed uncontrolled herring fishing. Jim Gilbert, the former fishing guide, thought that herring might have ceased to spawn in Tod Inlet because of changes in water oxygen content or temperature or the loss of vegetation, or maybe that larval forms of the herring couldn't survive. Lingcod and chinook salmon populations disappeared; even dogfish didn't frequent the area. By the late 1950s the creek and inlet were dying. By the 1960s, only the shells of mussels and the skeletons of barnacles remained. Deposits of grey-blue muck sludge covered the creek mouth and estuary of Tod Creek.

Among the last positive reports of salmon at Tod Inlet were published in Stewart Lang's fishing column in the *Victoria Daily Times*: "Right in the mouth of Tod Inlet and near Willis Point and Indian Bay might be a weekend hot spot for those fishing Saanich Inlet. Salmon weighing up to 20 pounds are following an influx of big herring into the Inlet," he wrote in 1968,[111] and in 1970: "Main spring returns are coming from Indian and Coles Bays, to a lesser degree near the entrance to Tod Inlet."[112]

6

Protection, Parkland and Recovery (1971–2019)

(left) Aerial view of Tod Inlet in 1982.
BC Archives I-03141.

(overleaf) Fountain in the old first quarry.
See p. 214.

For many years, the future of Tod Inlet was in doubt, both from the perspective of pollution of the inlet and from the perspective of the use of the land, which was dependent on development decisions made by local governments.

On the environmental side Beatrice Elliott recalled that in the mid-1960s, her husband, Tsartlip Elder Dave Elliott Sr., had given a big speech at the BC parliament buildings about the terrible state of Tod Inlet: the sewage on the beaches, how disgusted he was at what was happening, and how he wanted to claim back some of the old ways. Not much had changed in the next decade.

Beginning in about 1975, Genstar submitted several plans to the local municipal council to turn the lands surrounding Tod Inlet into a huge hotel-resort complex or an extensive housing development.

Finally, following a meeting called in June 1970 between Hugh Curtis, Capital Regional District (CRD) chairman; officials from the Butchart Gardens; and representatives of the health, fish and game, and pollution-control agencies, action was taken to stop the pollution of Tod Creek and Tod Inlet. The owner of the Hartland Road dump was required to divert three small streams from entering the dump and to build a permanent dam to prevent dump seepage from reaching Tod Creek. In addition, the dump stopped accepting oil and paint, and posted signs directing garbage trucks to specific dumping sites. Eventually the CRD moved ahead and constructed facilities at the site to collect waste, which was then taken back to Victoria and sent out into the Strait of Juan de Fuca to be dumped.

There were also changes on the development front. Beginning in about 1975, Genstar, the newest owners of the old BC Cement properties, submitted several plans to the local municipal council to turn the lands surrounding Tod Inlet into a huge hotel-resort complex or an extensive housing development. There were various plans, but all of them included levelling the remnants of the old cement plant and building a marina, hotel, golf course and restaurant. Housing developments were proposed for the site of the workers' homes, the old farm, the Chinese village and even the majestic forested hills that form the south shores of Tod Inlet.

On behalf of Genstar, BACM Development Corporation, a Winnipeg development company, proposed a 3,000-person community. This was just the beginning of the plan to develop the entire 1,200-acre site around Tod Inlet. They had further plans that would provide for recreation, commercial and other needs of the development. It included five to ten acres for a 150-berth marina with shore buildings and a parking lot, and a commercial zone of shops to serve the future neighbourhoods, which would eventually cover the entire acreage.

The first phase plan was to build the 900 units that would house up to 3,000 people. Seven acres of land were deemed suitable for apartment complexes, and two such complexes were proposed, with as many as 250 rental units. In total the development would include about 70 detached homes, 170 "terrace and cluster buildings" and up to 500 multiple-dwelling units. The 1,000-acre Partridge Hill area to the west of Tod Inlet and extending across to Saanich Inlet would wait for future development.

Part of the plan was to build a dike across the inlet, with a road on the dike to provide access to the marina and commercial area. The proposed dike location was at the Tod Creek estuary, perhaps one of the most fragile ecosystems of the whole inlet. The dike also would have destroyed two of the archaeological sites.

Citizens began urging local governments to pursue the idea of a park at Tod Inlet as a more suitable land use than the aggressive development proposed by the owners. My own letters to various politicians and government departments and the newspaper in 1978 were typical of what so many of us wanted to see: "I would like to suggest that the whole area at the head of Tod Inlet be purchased by the provincial government and developed, in moderation, as a historical-natural marine park. Tod Inlet is worth saving, not only as one of the most delightfully scenic areas on the Saanich Peninsula, but also as an interesting example of the growth and disappearance of a community and an interesting natural area in the process of growing back from a period of intense industrial development. The development of a marine park would beautifully complement Butchart Gardens, would ensure a certain increase in tourism, and would preserve the area for the education and enjoyment of future generations."

Ian Ross, owner of the Butchart Gardens, was one of many people who spoke out at public meetings urging the local council to pursue the idea of a park. The developers recognized the cultural value of the property and, hoping for approval, offered to donate the area of the cement plant and up to 20 acres on Tod Creek, including the site of the Chinese village, to the local government for park use if their proposals were accepted. In the meantime, Genstar had three of the towering chimneys toppled as a safety precaution in 1978.

Tod Inlet marine park development perfect complement to Butchart Gardens

Colonist June 3, 1978

I have just recently learned of the controversy over the Genstar Development Company's proposal to develop the Tod Inlet area, and the battle to save this area around Butchart Gardens from such development.

I feel very strongly about the future of Tod Inlet as I spent many happy hours there as a youngster. It would be a tragedy for that beautiful spot to be lost to development in the way that so many other wonderful places on southern Vancouver Island have been lost.

I fully agree with Ian Ross's assessment of the situation with regard to the preservation of the surroundings and atmosphere of Butchart Gardens, but there is an important aspect of the atmosphere of Tod Inlet that has been neglected, namely the historical value.

Though most Victorians know the story of Mrs. Butchart's transformation of an unsightly limestone quarry into a world-famous garden, few know that in 1909 the settlement of Tod Inlet boasted a population of nearly 200 oriental workers plus 30 white workers and their families. There is little trace now of the orientals' village and collectors have removed all of the portable evidence of their community. But the ruins of the B.C. Cement plant and the associated structures are a valuable visible link with the past. These buildings are more than just "a mess of unsafe, derelict buildings" on an abandoned industrial site as suggested by Genstar's Bothwell in the April 28 *Colonist*.

The early 1900s was an important time in the industrial development of the province and any surviving relics of that time should not be dismissed so off-handedly or destroyed without careful and qualified assessment by industrial historians. With the judicious dismantling of some buildings and restoration or preservation of others, the old cement plant could become an attraction in its own right.

I would like to suggest that the whole area at the head of Tod Inlet be purchased by the provincial government and developed, in moderation, as a historical-natural marine park. Tod Inlet is worth saving, not only as one of the most delightfully scenic areas on the Saanich Peninsula, but also as an interesting example of the growth and disappearance of a community and an interesting natural area in the process of growing back from a period of intense industrial development. The development of a marine park would beautifully complement Butchart Gardens, would ensure a certain increase in tourism, and would preserve the area for the education and enjoyment of future generations.

DAVID GRAY, 1701 Kilborn Ave., Ottawa.

Letter about Tod Inlet marine park in the newspaper, June 3, 1978. Author's collection.

(*left*) Three of the old chimneys in the cement plant, in 1967. One is an original brick chimney from about 1904, and the other two were built in 1911–1913.

David R. Gray photograph.

In the early 1980s, Genstar had most of the outbuildings demolished—the powerhouse, office building, machine shop and blacksmith shop—seeing them only as a "mess of derelict buildings" without historical significance.

When BC Cement and Ocean Cement, under their parent company Genstar, sold their Tod Inlet holdings to a local developer, Sam Bawlf, in March 1981, a new battle was engaged. One ramification of the change was that the members of the Tod Inlet Power Boat Owners' Association were informed that all of their boats would have to be relocated.

RESTORING TOD CREEK

While the new development proposals were being considered, environmentalists continued to do what they could to enhance the ravaged environment of Tod Inlet and Tod Creek.

In 1983 the Tod Creek Water Enhancement Society released 4,700 coho salmon fry into Tod Creek. A year and a half later there was a

(*centre and right*) The toppled chimneys
in the cement plant, 1978.

David R. Gray photographs.

small but healthy run of returning salmon. Unfortunately, they were all eaten by the resident seals of Tod Inlet before they could enter the safety of Tod Creek.

During the stream enhancement the volunteers removed part of a rocky ledge across the creek by blasting and improved several pools by minor damming with small rocks. They also removed large fallen logs that were partially damming the creek. An area just above the creek mouth had been used as a local dumping ground as late as the 1960s, and large amounts of garbage and debris had been dumped down the banks into the creek. The society volunteers cleared out most of the larger debris, including old car bodies, as part of the stream enhancement program. As the restoration of the Tod Creek aquatic environment was under way, another project, under the federal government's Katimavik program, had a team of students building streamside trails. These new trails gave better access to the creek and a more natural feeling for visitors than the wider, well-used former road above the creek.[113]

As the restoration of the Tod Creek aquatic environment was under way, another project had a team of students building streamside trails.

(clockwise from left) The CASE march and rally at Tod Inlet in 1990 in support of a proposed park. CASE photograph. Author's collection.

Tsartlip councillor John Elliott addressing the rally at Tod Inlet, 1990. CASE photograph. Author's collection.

Derrick Mallard, of CASE, addressing the crowd at the rally at Tod Inlet, 1990. CASE photograph. Author's collection.

By 1990 the leachate from the Hartland dump was finally blocked from the drainage area of Tod Creek, and agricultural runoff problems had been partially mitigated. The quality and flow of water in the creek improved through volunteer programs carried out under the guidance of the Peninsula Streams Society of North Saanich.

A PARK IS BORN

Though the pollution in the inlet was beginning to lessen, people remained dismayed at the prospect of Tod Inlet being "developed" from a unique, beautiful, ecologically and historically significant area into another golf course, another marina and another collection of stores and houses. The Citizens Association to Save the Environment (CASE), under the charismatic leadership of Derrick Mallard, conducted research, gathered information and presented proposals for protection. Derrick and his team organized many events, including a march of 500 people, with the active participation of the Tsartlip Nation, to Tod Inlet in September of 1990.

Action erupted from the groundswell. Various submissions were put forth to the Saanich councils expressing a desire for the inlet to be preserved in some way, and a public meeting vote gave a black-and-white statement of that desire when 90 per cent of 120 attendees said yes to a park. One year after the march, we produced a thorough report of Tod Inlet's character, history and resources under the direction of CASE president Derrick.

In the face of the strong and determined opposition to the development of Tod Inlet, Bawlf and his partner Murray Pezim sold their Tod Inlet holdings to a Vancouver company, FAMA Holdings, owned by Saudi Arabia's King Faisal, for $7.2 million.

In 1992, some 15 years after Genstar's first development proposal, development was still very much an active plan. FAMA Holdings planned to start development with a resort, golf course and housing on 1,200 acres stretching from the highlands of the Partridge Hills to the southeastern shore of the inlet.

However, CASE's persistent work with politicians, in cooperation with the Tsartlip people and the Provincial Parks Branch, finally brought Tod Inlet to a long-hoped for and long-awaited new status.

GOWLLAND TOD PROVINCIAL PARK

In 1994, Moe Sihota, minister of the environment for BC, announced that under the Commonwealth Nature Legacy—a unique partnership between the provincial and local governments, organizations and companies—a new park would be established along the east side of Saanich Inlet and would encompass much of Tod Inlet. The Legacy, established to commemorate the spirit of the XV Commonwealth Games held in Victoria in 1994, preserves the important heritage of green space on southern Vancouver Island for present and future generations.

The land at Tod Inlet was designated a part of the Commonwealth Nature Legacy Park after the last owner, FAMA Holdings, donated $1 million worth of property after their development plans stalled at Saanich council.

The Legacy, established to commemorate the spirit of the XV Commonwealth Games held in Victoria in 1994, preserves the important heritage of green space on southern Vancouver Island.

Crane after removing the last of the cement plant buildings, 1995. David R. Gray photograph.

The old three-room larder or storehouse, the only remaining cement company building.

David R. Gray photograph.

In 1995, the area of the Legacy lands, including Tod Inlet, became part of the new Gowlland Tod Provincial Park. The name reflects the park's dual natures: it includes both the Gowlland Range, a rare dry coastal Douglas fir habitat in the south, and the natural shoreline and uplands of Tod Inlet to the north. John Thomas Gowlland, for whom the range of hills was named, was a second master on Captain George Richards's survey crew aboard HMS *Plumper* during the Vancouver Island survey of 1857–1862.[114]

But this legacy for the majority meant a change for the few remaining members of the Tod Inlet Power Boat Owners' Association. "I'm glad it's not a development," said Daryll Youlden, president of the association. "I'd much rather see it as a park, but we hate to give up something we've had."[115] The association members had enjoyed the privilege of mooring in the quiet inlet since 1946, but they would not be allowed to moor their boats long-term in the park.

The newest and tallest of the cement plant buildings, the mill and aerial tram terminal, were among the few structures to survive the long years of private ownership. Both bordered the Butchart Gardens and dated to about 1911. In the summer of 1994, following an accident in one

The trail above Tod Creek, formerly the road to Victoria. David R. Gray photograph.

of the buildings, the Parks Branch decided that they too would have to be demolished. The old concrete horse stable remained standing, but by 1998 it too was gone. This left the larder, a small three-room concrete building situated near the foundation of the bunkhouse, as the only cement company building still standing.

Shortly after Gowlland Tod Provincial Park was established, BC Parks drafted a management plan for it. The key objectives of the park as presented in the 1996 management plan include a reasonable level of access for visitors to experience the park; a minimal impact on the environment, wildlife and cultural features; and educating park visitors about the natural and cultural value of the park and the importance of the area to local Indigenous peoples. The park plan aims to ensure that visitors gain a better appreciation and understanding of the park's natural and historical significance and the principles of conservation and park stewardship.

The main way of accessing the park at Tod Inlet is the walking trails. Some of these trails follow the routes of roads established at the time the Vancouver Portland Cement Company began operations at Tod Inlet. Others follow logging roads constructed in the 1940s and 1950s and the newer trails made in the 1980s.

A number of projects relating to the objectives of the management plan have been completed since the park was created. Millennia Research completed further archaeological inventory studies of the Tod Inlet area for the First Nations of Saanich and BC Parks in 1996. The team located a few additional sites and assessed the impact of recent history on all of them.[116]

TSARTLIP FIRST NATION AND THE PARK

Tod Inlet is an important part of the ongoing Tsartlip First Nation's land claims. When Derrick Mallard and I met with the chief and council of the Tsartlip First Nation in 1994 to discuss the successful campaign to protect Tod Inlet from development, we were encouraged and thanked for what was happening. When I asked about interviewing Tsartlip Elders about their memories and knowledge of Tod Inlet and its current and historical importance, the chief suggested that in view of the ongoing land claim, it would be better to hold off on the interviews. Seven years later, with no apparent progress on the land claim, John Elliott, a member of the Tsartlip council, suggested that it would now be a suitable time to begin interviewing the Elders. Their stories, as related in this book, are an important part of the Tod Inlet story. Many of those I interviewed have since passed on, and so their words and stories are now of even greater significance.

As Gowlland Tod Provincial Park is within the area covered by the North Saanich Douglas Treaty of 1852, the Tsartlip First Nation

Tod Inlet is an important part of the ongoing Tsartlip First Nation's land claims.

Culturally modified western red cedar trees in the park, 2019. A thin strip of bark is harvested by cutting at the base and pulling up. David R. Gray photograph.

people have the treaty right to "hunt on unoccupied lands and fish as formerly." The *Gowlland Tod Provincial Park Management Plan* states that "the creation of this park does not restrict these First Nations from continuing to use the park area for traditional medicinal, ceremonial and spiritual purposes." The parklands are to be "administrated recognizing that the rights identified in this [the Douglas] treaty must be considered when developing strategies to manage the park's fish and wildlife." The management plan also states that "there will be no archaeological research conducted without prior consent of the Saanich and Malahat First Nations." The plan commits the park to consult with the First Nations on an ongoing basis on appropriate archaeological and cultural research and appropriate information to share with the public.

The Interim Reconciliation Agreement

The population of the five Saanich First Nations, including the Tsartlip First Nation, declined significantly between the late 1700s and the mid-1800s due to the introduction of new diseases, particularly smallpox and tuberculosis.

After the "signing" of the Douglas Treaties of 1852 and the supposed "selling" of their land to the Colony of Vancouver Island, the Tsartlip First Nation lost control of much of their territory through the McKenna-McBride Commission of 1913, which established the location of the current reserves. Lands outside the reserves became government-owned and were eventually sold to private landowners.

When Bawlf and two companies proposed the huge development at Tod Inlet in 1982, Tsartlip Elder Dave Elliott Sr. spoke out: "All of the [Saanich] peninsula belongs to our people and always will. We have to speak out and oppose this development because it will hurt the environment."

Tsartlip chief Tom Sampson noted that Tod Inlet "has profound significance as a spiritual site." He was alarmed that the proposal to develop "traditional Indian Territory" was made with no consultation of or consent from the Tsartlip.[117]

After Tod Inlet was included in the new provincial park in 1994, John Elliott, a Tsartlip band councillor, stated that the sale of lots near Tod Inlet but outside the park should be halted until the Tsartlip site-specific land claim was dealt with. The claim covering all of Tod Inlet was filed in January 1995.[118]

The Tsartlip First Nation and the Province of British Columbia reached an interim reconciliation agreement in 2017 as a first step in holding comprehensive reconciliation negotiations.

Regarding Tsartlip history and culture, the Province agreed to provide funding for consultations with Elders, to explore changes or additions to official place names and to develop a community cultural recognition strategy. In terms of heritage protection, BC will provide the First Nation with support to complete an inventory of heritage sites and objects of spiritual, ceremonial or cultural value.

With regard to the park management plans for Gowlland Tod Provincial Park, the Province and the Tsartlip agreed to discuss the First Nation's interests, culture and history as they relate to the park. The BC government and the Tsartlip First Nation will also discuss the nation's interests in acquiring a park-use permit for a portion of Gowlland Tod Provincial Park.

Representatives of the federal government and other interested parties will also be invited to discuss strategies to protect the environment, the waters and the wildlife of Saanich Inlet.[119]

As well as being owners of the reserve on the eastern shore of the Saanich Inlet in Brentwood Bay, the Tsartlip First Nation also own Goldstream Indian Reserve #13. The nation weighed in on a proposed LNG project for the Saanich Inlet in 2017, pouring cold water on an announcement by the proponent, Steelhead LNG, which claimed the support of the neighbouring Malahat First Nation. Tsartlip chief Don Tom warned both groups that they were jumping the gun. Tsartlip's Goldstream Indian Reserve is located directly south of the proposed LNG terminal location. That project is thankfully no longer on the table.

SEARCHING FOR THE SIKHS

In 1998, I began working on a documentary film that told the story of the Sikh workers of Tod Inlet. Dr. Manmohan Wirk and I took the Pallan brothers, Mukund (Max) and Nad Lal, to Tod Inlet to see where their father had lived and worked in 1906. This was the first time that descendants of the original cement plant workers from Asia had visited the site of the Tod Inlet village. Together we investigated the old brick structures that I had been convinced were the remnants of the cooking ovens, still showing their Sikh origins after 100 years. The brothers' consensus was that these structures were the same pattern as the ovens common in cookhouses in India. Max recalled his father telling how one man used to look after the ovens, and that there was always a big pot of water boiling, and anybody could come and have tea or make his own coffee.

One of the highlights of the protection of Tod Inlet within Gowlland Tod Provincial Park for me was the guaranteed possibility of people being able to visit the place where their fathers or grandfathers had lived and worked 100 or more years before.

Max and I visited Tod Inlet and the Butchart Gardens again together in 2006. We were delighted to find what looked like one of the old cement sacks eroding out of the banks of Tod Inlet near the old plant site. Looking closer, it was clear that the cement had set, and that the sack had rotted away, leaving only the impression of the burlap. Finding and touching that old "fossilized" cement bag—still full, but of solid cement rather than powder—gave us a moving glimpse into the

One of the highlights of the protection of Tod Inlet for me was the guaranteed possibility of people being able to visit the place where their fathers or grandfathers had lived and worked 100 or more years before.

past. There on the beach at Tod Inlet we could see and touch one of the cement bags that was carried from the plant to the ships by the Sikh workers. We can better imagine their toils and hardships through these voiceless reminders.

TOD INLET TODAY

More than a hundred years of industrial activity has had a powerful impact on the wildlife, vegetation and ecological processes of Tod Inlet.

From the present point of view, the remnants of the two cement company wharfs at Tod Inlet provide an interesting contrast. The largest wharf, with its skeleton of vertical concrete pilings, has been there since about 1907, though it was not the first wharf at Tod Inlet. It replaced the original wooden wharf built by John Greig or Joseph Wriglesworth for the Saanich Lime Company around the turn of the century. It is now the location of a colony of purple martins, nesting in a series of nesting boxes attached to the cement pilings.

The second cement company wharf, built by infilling with various materials sometime before 1916, is now eroding around the edges.

(*left*) Max Pallan and the author inspecting a "fossil" cement bag on the beach, 2006. David R. Gray photograph.

(*right*) Close-up view of the fabric imprint on a solid piece of cement.
David R. Gray photograph.

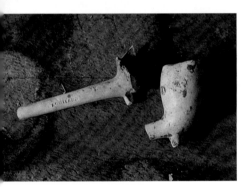

(*clockwise from top left*) The cement piles of the first wharf, 2012. David R. Gray photograph.

The bollard for tying up ships at the second wharf, 2019. David R. Gray photograph.

Clay pipes found on the shoreline near the plant. David R. Gray photograph.

Debris from the original factory buildings, discarded firebricks from the kilns, fragments of bags of cement, and clinker from the cement-making process are now eroding out onto the shore, revealing odd pieces of history. The former wharf now supports a picnic area, and two large cement-and-metal bollards once used for tying up ships accompany the picnic tables as a playground for children.

A wide range of natural habitats at Tod Inlet support a diversity of wildlife species. Unfortunately, the only major biological studies that have been carried out in the area to date are those on plant communities.[120] The major plant habitats are those associated with the Douglas fir, western red cedar and arbutus.

There have been few specific surveys or studies of other forms of life. The waters, the shorelines and the uplands of Tod Inlet are known to support many mammals, including cougars, black bears, black-tailed deer, raccoon, red squirrel, river otter, mink and harbour seal. Among

the more common species of forest birds recorded are bald eagle, raven, turkey vulture, pileated woodpecker, hairy woodpecker, winter wren, towhee, robin and flicker. Along the shores of Tod Inlet many water birds are seen, including great blue heron, belted kingfisher, Canada goose, American merganser, bufflehead, goldeneye, American widgeon and glaucous-winged gull.

In the marine waters of Tod Inlet, coho and chinook salmon, Pacific herring, lingcod and rock cod, striped sea perch, three-spine stickleback and tidepool sculpins all abounded into the 1960s. Current numbers and distribution of these fish species are unknown. Up until the 1950s, basking sharks and orcas also occasionally appeared in the inlet. Today the fish species confirmed to exist in the waters of Tod Inlet are limited: three-spine stickleback, coho salmon, cutthroat trout and Pacific herring for sure, and probably lingcod, rock cod, minnows, dusky sea perch, yellow shiner and bullhead sculpin.

Many marine invertebrates are still found in the inlet, among them moon jellyfish, octopus, clams, oysters, mussels, crabs, acorn barnacles and nudibranchs, but there have been few surveys to show their diversity or their current numbers. No intensive studies have investigated the long-term impact of industrial activities and settlement on these organisms.

A white-line dirona (a nudibranch) at Tod Inlet. David R. Gray photographs.

Making cement
pontoons at the wharf
about 1913. The caption
reads, "Raising cement
pontoon with blocks
to insert skids for
launching."
Courtesy of the
Butchart Gardens.

THE RECOVERY OF THE MARINE ENVIRONMENT

When I interviewed Jim Gilbert in the spring of 2000 about his
recent observations in Tod Inlet, his comments were encouraging.
There were live Pacific oysters and other shellfish in the area, though
the Department of the Environment has continued to flag the inlet
as having high levels of coliform bacteria, so no shellfish harvesting
is permitted. In 1999–2000 the return of herring to Saanich Inlet
showed hope for the possibility of recovery. When Jim was a kid,
Elders from the Tsartlip band told him that what he saw in the
1940s and 1950s would one day fade away and again return, on a
50- or 60-year cycle.

The old cement pontoon, made at the company wharf in about 1913
and now resting in the mud below the old village, shows one small
aspect of the recovery of life in the inlet. Photographs taken in 2011 and
2013 show more-or-less bare cement on the pontoon's surface. Six years
later the pontoon was covered in oysters and barnacles.

(*left, top to bottom*) The
old cement pontoon on
the shore in winter 2011.
David R. Gray photograph.

The same cement
pontoon in 2013
with no oysters.
David R. Gray photograph.

The same cement
pontoon on the shore
in 2019, encrusted with
oysters and barnacles.
David R. Gray photograph.

In April 2000 a group of students from Camosun College surveyed Tod Inlet from a 23-foot survey vessel, the *Aluminator*, utilizing a towfish with a video camera and an altimeter. The survey used the Seabed Imaging and Mapping System (SIMS), which provides images of the sea floor and records the depth at which fish and other species are detected. The students developed a classification system to identify and quantify both biological and geological objects on the bottom of the inlet.

The encrusted ring for lifting the cement pontoon, 2019. David R. Gray photograph.

The 2001 Marine Survey

Purple sea star at Tod Inlet. David R. Gray photograph.

The 2001 report on the Camosun College study found that the distribution of plants and animals is directly related to the type of material on the sea floor (the "substrate") of Tod Inlet. There was a higher percentage of gravel near the shoreline and more mud and sand sediment in the deep central part of the inlet. Over half of the sediment in Tod Inlet is composed of mud, sand and slightly gravelly mud and sand. The shoreline areas with more gravel showed more biological diversity. The substrate suitable for the important marine plant eelgrass (*Zostera marina*)

is abundant in the inlet, but only a few eelgrass "meadows" were present. Other important plant groups identified were brown algae, kelp, green algae, red algae and coralline red algae. None of these groups had a wide distribution, and were most dense along the west shoreline and southernmost tip of the inlet. The most widely distributed bottom-dwelling animals were sea stars, especially the ochre and spiny pink sea stars. Sea stars were most abundant in the northern half of the inlet and least abundant in the area near the former cement plant. Piddock and horse clams were present, but not abundant, in the mud/sand areas along the east and west shorelines. Other animals noted were tubeworms and sea anemones, and in relatively sparse numbers, crabs, sea cucumbers, moon snails and nudibranchs.

Small fish species were recorded in limited numbers at the mouth of Tod Inlet, along the west side of the narrows and west of the village area, but they were not identified.

Man-made objects noted were mostly bottles and miscellaneous metal objects, as well as pipes, garbage and sunken logs.[121]

(*above*) Tsartlip First Nation sign near the beach. David R. Gray photograph.

The Friends of Tod Creek Watershed, established in 2001, took on some of the objectives of the former Tod Creek Water Enhancement Society. The Friends' stated mission is to protect and enhance the integrity and biodiversity of the Tod Creek watershed.

The SeaChange Marine Conservation Society, with a 100-year vision and a largely volunteer crew, has raised money and worked successfully to begin restoring the original marine habitat of Tod Inlet. They identified Tod Inlet as a promising locale in which to restore the natural aquatic environment because it is now a provincial park and because the cement industry and other sources of pollutants have moved out or been controlled.

To aid the recovery of habitat for marine life, SeaChange began transplanting shoots of eelgrass in 2000. That first year, volunteers planted almost 2,000 shoots. Eelgrass, a flowering intertidal marine plant, is a vital species that had disappeared from Tod Inlet. Its thick root mats had been badly disrupted by activities including log booming, the dragging of anchors, and pollutants. Eelgrass is vital to a rich marine environment because of the habitat it creates for marine life. It is also a direct source of food for the Tsartlip people.

Another part of SeaChange's 100-year vision includes the planting of native plant species, especially traditional W̱SÁNEĆ (Saanich) food and medicinal plants. Up beyond the shoreline, in areas where native vegetation has been replaced over the years by introduced and invasive species, volunteers, including schoolchildren, are removing invasive plant species like Himalayan blackberries and instead planting native cottonwoods, rose plants and redcurrant bushes.

The Friends of Tod Creek Watershed recently achieved a goal that was first suggested back in 1905: a fishway to help coho salmon and cutthroat trout make their way up Tod Creek and over the dam near Wallace Drive. Starting with planning visits and monitoring of water

flow in 2002, they worked for 13 years to achieve the goal. In 2015 the
Peninsula Streams Society worked with BC Parks, the Department of
Fisheries and Oceans, local First Nations and the Butchart Gardens
(owner of the dam) to complete a 30-metre fishway to help the fish get
past the dam to spawn upstream. Fittingly, the fishway was financed
by the Butchart Gardens and thus named Butchart's Fishway—110
years later! Today, the fish passing through are monitored by camera.
They include both resident and sea-run cutthroat trout, three-spine
stickleback and coho salmon. Some fish have been tagged, but so far,
as of 2020, no tagged salmon have returned as adults.

The Butchart Gardens also purchased a pump-out boat in 2015 to
collect sewage from boats in Brentwood Bay and Tod Inlet to decrease
the amount of sewage dumped into the sea.

SeaChange began another recovery project in 2017: the location and
removal of underwater debris on the inlet bed to reduce contaminants
and allow space for the natural habitat to recover. Society volunteers
removed bags of old concrete, boats, tires, metal pieces, bottles and tins
from the seabed and took them away for safe disposal.

In the same year, with the assistance of BC Parks, SeaChange led
the creation of a new beach near the old wharf. This involved clearing
the cement footings and backfill—including industrial waste from the
cement factory, polluted topsoil, and metal debris from the tile plant—
of the old man-made shoreline from about 1904, and replacing it with
gravel and sand.

(*left*) SeaChange sign at the land
restoration site near the wharf.
David R. Gray photograph.

(*right*) Clearing of invasive plant
species in the white village site.
David R. Gray photograph.

(*top*) The new fishway on Tod Creek below the old dam, 2019.

David R. Gray photograph.

(*bottom*) The sign at the new fishway on Tod Creek, showing the two fish species that are using the fishway, 2019.

David R. Gray photograph.

The newly restored beach is a perfect place for recreation and teaching. Earl Claxton Jr., an Elder of the Tsawout First Nation, teaches traditional knowledge here with storytelling, salmon bakes and the use of native plants. On my recent visit to Tod Inlet in 2019, I had the pleasure of meeting Earl on the beach at the tail end of a program he was giving to students from the University of Victoria.

A HERITAGE PLACE

In 2004, the hundredth anniversary of its humble beginning, the Butchart Gardens were designated a National Historic Site of Canada. In announcing the designation in 2004, the Historic Sites and Monuments Board of Canada stated the reasons for the designation of the gardens: "It represents the remarkable combination of three aspects of Canadian gardening history. First, the gardens represent the traits of an early 20th-century estate garden through its different types of gardens such as the Japanese Garden, the Rose Garden, the Italian Garden, the Star Pond and Jennie Butchart's Private Garden. Second, the gardens evoke the early twentieth century beautification movement as expressed through the Sunken Garden. And third, the gardens rely upon the Victorian bedding out system to achieve their outstanding floral displays. These three aspects of the Butchart Gardens have been conveyed through the successive visions of Butchart family members."[122]

The National Historic Site nomination had nothing to do with the cement industry, the immigrant community, preserving a piece of the

(*below left*) The totem pole at the Butchart Gardens, carved by Charles Elliott in 2004. David R. Gray photograph.

(*right*) Detail of the totem pole showing the blue grouse, carved by Charles Elliott. David R. Gray photograph.

traditional Tsartlip land or the ecological recovery of the inlet—just the gardens.

As part of the garden's centennial celebrations, Tsartlip master carver Charles Elliott was commissioned to carve a classic Coast Salish totem pole. The pole features Raven, Beaver and Grouse, Otter with pups and a clam, and at the base, Frog— beings of great importance to the Tsartlip people and of great significance to the ecology of Tod Inlet. The pole was dedicated on September 9, 2004.

BEAUTY AND THE BEAST

An article by "Ivanhoe," in the *Winnipeg Tribune* of September 14, 1922, entitled "The Sunken Garden or Beauty and the Beast," contrasts the remnants of the cement factory to the increasingly popular Sunken Garden: "In the foreground . . . stand the tall cement chimneys and the ungraceful bulk of a cement factory. You wonder why Mr. Butchart located beauty so near this beast until you are told that without the beast there would have been no beauty. The sunken garden with its multifarious charms is really a child of the ugly cement plant. . . . And out of that happy thought of reparation has come the far-famed garden of today."

One of the wonderful characteristics of the Tod Inlet story are the number of such unexpected developments—the occurrences no one could reasonably have predicted. Perhaps the most

(*above*) The last chimney as it begins to crumble in 2019. David R. Gray photograph.

(*below left*) The last surviving cement plant chimney from its base, 1980s. David R. Gray photograph.

(*below right*) Piles of unused piles in the winter snow. David R. Gray photograph.

significant of them is the story of Jennie Butchart's garden. As her husband immersed himself in producing cement, Jennie was busy encouraging gardens and beautiful flowers. Early on her house garden attracted visitors, and when her garden grew to include the spent quarry, her visitors started coming by boatloads and busloads. In the end, Jennie's gardens brought far more acclaim and fame to the family than did Robert's cement plant.

The garden was to grow to become a huge tourist attraction that benefited the whole province. Who could have imagined in 1910 that the cement plant would one day be overshadowed by the flower garden? Today, the Butchart Gardens is still a family business and is open every day of the year. A booming tourist destination, it attracts a million visitors a year from around the world. On the other hand, the cement plant has been reduced to the remnants of two wharfs, a last crumbling chimney, and a few stacks of cement wharf pilings made more than a hundred years ago and never used.

There is another Beauty and the Beast story at Tod Inlet, on a much smaller scale. The rare, threatened and beautiful phantom

orchid, known from only a few sites in BC, grows at Tod Inlet in an area that was once one of the most disturbed patches of ground in a vast industrial landscape. And why is this beauty now here? Phantom orchids prefer limestone soils, and there is plenty of exposed limestone left over at Tod Inlet, from the days of the beast.

Phantom orchid, the limestone lover.
David R. Gray photograph.

The cultivated gardens preserve two of the quarries where the Chinese labourers toiled by hand to remove limestone for the cement plant. The first quarry became the Ross Fountain; the second, the famous Sunken Garden. The third, Quarry Lake, is also owned by the gardens, and now serves as a water reservoir.

A HISTORIC DESIGNATION

When Heritage BC called for nominations for places in British Columbia of heritage importance to the Chinese Canadian and South Asian Canadian communities under the BC Heritage Conservation Act, I submitted nominations of Tod Inlet as a place of historical

significance to both. Along with several other nominations, the Tod Inlet nominations were accepted in 2016. Tod Inlet is now officially recognized as a Historic Place of Canada.

Tod Inlet is the place where an important part of BC's unique industrial history began. Though the individual stories of the Chinese workers of Tod Inlet are largely lost to us now, we can assume that among the more than 200 men who laboured here, there were those who made contributions of great significance. Certainly their experience as a whole, of hard work for low pay far from the place of their birth, is a familiar theme in the BC story. The story of the Sikh contributions began with a relatively few men from Punjab providing labour for BC's first major cement plant. Over time, it expands to involve people and communities across BC. When the Sikh labourers left Tod Inlet in about 1911, many of them travelled to Vancouver, Golden and Ocean Falls to work in the sawmills there. Their descendants became sawmill owners and operators, entrepreneurs and developers, company owners, politicians and businessmen. Their legacy, along with the long-standing legacy of the Tsartlip and other First Nations and the immigrant settlers, is an essential part of BC's story.

(*above top*) The first quarry today: the Ross Fountain in winter. David R. Gray photograph.

(*above bottom*) The Ross Fountain in the fall, 2019. David R. Gray photograph.

(*right*) The second quarry became the Sunken Garden at the Butchart Gardens. David R. Gray photograph.

Epilogue

In 2017, when Canada celebrated its 150th year since Confederation, one of the celebratory programs was the Canada C3 (Coast to Coast to Coast) Expedition. This voyage began in Toronto, travelled east down the St. Lawrence and around the Maritimes, north to Baffin Island and west through the Northwest Passage, then south along the west coast before arriving in Tod Inlet on October 28, 2015.

It was the last stop before C3's arrival at Victoria, its final destination, on the 150th day. There could not have been a more suitable place to gather and reflect together on Canada's history, in all its richness and challenges. The deep and sheltered waters of Tod Inlet hosted not only the 30 participants on that leg of the C3 journey, but also First Nations representatives, descendants of the workers at the cement factory—including one Sikh family—local schoolchildren learning hands-on about their nation, Butchart Gardens staff, provincial member of the legislative assembly and Tsartlip First Nation member Adam Olsen, federal member of Parliament Elizabeth May, and Catherine McKenna, minister of the environment.

As a member of the C3 Expedition planning team, I had proposed a stop at Tod Inlet right from the very beginning. On that remarkable October day when the ship arrived, I could not have been more

The Canada C3 team arrives at Tod Inlet by Zodiac, escorted by the Sidney Royal Canadian Marine Search and Rescue team from the C3 ship, *Polar Prince*, anchored at Brentwood, October 2017. Beverley Hall photograph.

pleased with, or proud of, our community. The First Nations participants who gave their thoughts on reconciliation; the teachers and students who came to

Students from Royal Oak Middle School at the site of the Chinese and Sikh village at Tod Inlet, October 2017.
Beverley Hall photograph.

Nicholas Singh Johal and his grandfather Paul Singh Johal, with Canada C3 participants at Tod Inlet, October 2017.
Beverley Hall photograph.

learn together; the SeaChange Society members who have showed such dedication to helping the recovery of the environment; the descendants of the cement company's immigrant workers who shared their heartfelt memories—all contributed to the great success of the event.

Perhaps C3 artist Karen Tamminga-Paton best expresses the magic of that afternoon on Tod Inlet's shores:

"I had no idea, when our small C3 crew landed on the sandy shores of Tod Inlet, of the rich and troubled human history hidden amongst the thick cedar and maple canopy."

I had no idea, when our small C3 crew landed on the sandy shores of Tod Inlet, of the rich and troubled human history hidden amongst the thick cedar and maple canopy. David Gray was our guide. We walked the trails, heard the stories, saw remnants of the immigrant workers who once lived here and worked long shifts at the Portland Cement Company. Our trail then led us to the famous nearby Butchart Gardens. I was especially inspired by the account of Jennie Butchart, wife of the cement plant owner, who hated the sight of the excavated limestone quarry and did everything in her power to bring beauty to that ravaged landscape. She planted flowers. She accessed steep banks with ladders and ropes to carefully place vines and shrubbery. She planted trees, and she ceaselessly tended them all. Eventually, this gaping and wounded landscape became the famously beautiful destination that it is today.

In some ways, David Gray's insights are like the work of Jennie Butchart who lived a century before us. Like Jennie gathering her plants, David gathered stories and fanned them into life. The landscape is quiet there at Tod Inlet, protected from offshore winds and urban noise, yet as David talked, one couldn't help but be more attentive. It was so much more than just a lovely walk through a gorgeous forest. And it wasn't much of a stretch to imagine the old cedars leaning in as though to say, "did you catch that"? We listened, imagined, witnessed, and shared responses together, all of us deeply impacted. David's humble curiosity, sharp eye and ear and suspension of judgement modelled for us how to be in that space. As Canadians, we all need to understand these stories that give any given piece of geography within our borders its particular tenor and character. We will occupy it very differently when we do.

(*above*) Canada c3 group on the new beach. David R. Gray photograph.

(*below*) Ahmed Saffar, a Canada c3 participant from Calgary, takes his first trip in an Inuit-style kayak from the beach at Tod Inlet out to the c3 ship in Brentwood Bay, October 28, 2017. David R. Gray photograph.

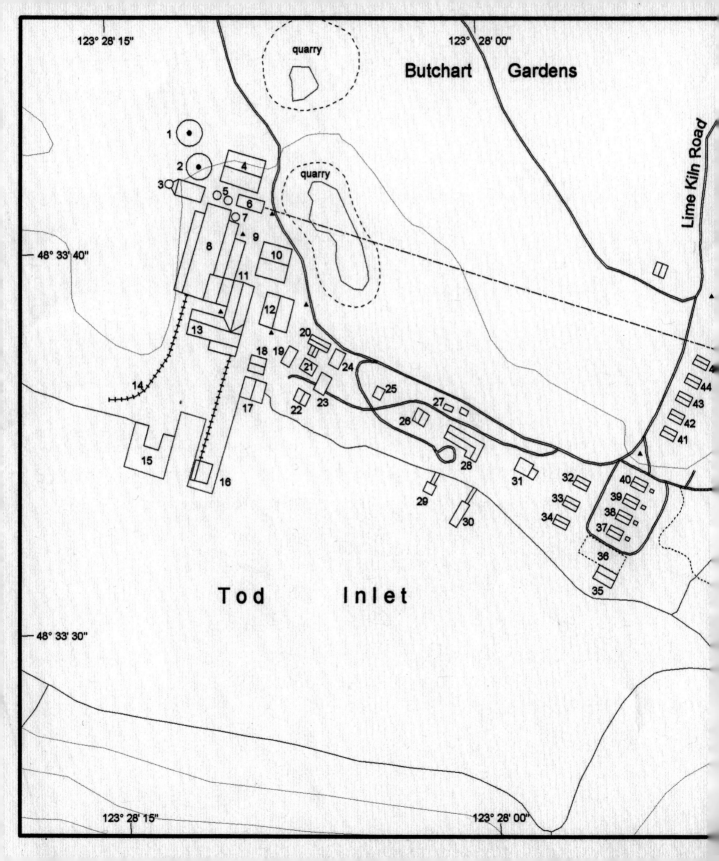

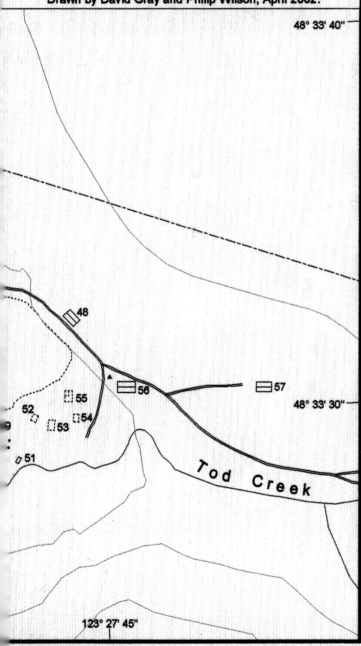

Historical Map of Western Part of Tod Inlet Area in 1926.

50   0   50   100   150 Meters

Based on 1:20,000 TRIM Map Sheet 92B.053

20 m contour interval

Drawn by David Gray and Philip Wilson, April 2002.

48° 33' 40"

48

56

57

55

52

54

53

51

48° 33' 30"

Tod Creek

123° 27' 45"

1   Slurry mixer (concrete)
2   Slurry mixer (concrete)
3   Concrete chimney stack
4   New mill
5   Two concrete chimney stacks
6   Aerial tram terminal
7   Brick chimney stack
8   Kilns (steel and concrete posts)
9   Open area (formerly grinding mills)
10 Machinery storage
11 Stock house no. 1 (concrete)
12 Coal house
13 Stock house no. 2 (concrete)
14 Rail line carrying rock for dumping
15 Secondary wharf
16 Main wharf with loading warehouse
17 Coal unloading (roof only)
18 Bag warehouse, pump house and sack cleaner
19 Dynamo (concrete)
20 Blacksmith shop (concrete), with warehouse
21 Office building, oil room and post office
22 Tile plant
23 Transformers and substation (concrete)
24 Machine shop (concrete)
25 Laboratory (wood frame)
26 Mess house
27 Larder (concrete, with wooden roof)
28 Bunkhouse (two storeys, concrete)
29 Small boat wharf
30 Small boat wharf
31-34 Wood-frame houses (two storeys)
35 Foreman's house (wood-frame)
36 Tennis court
37-45 Wood-frame houses
46 Ireland's store/house
47 Pasture
48 Stable (concrete)
49 Laundry house (Tong's house)
50 Three large pits
51 Small brick structure
52-54 Chinese houses
55 Sikh/Chinese house and brick ovens
56 Chinese bunkhouse (two storeys)
57 Farm buildings

Map of the Tod Inlet community showing the cement plant and the villages as they were in the 1920s. Map and key by Philip Wilson and David R. Gray, 2002.

Acknowledgements

The information presented in this book is based on collections of materials in archives in Vancouver, Victoria and Ottawa, and on interviews with people in Victoria and Saanich who remember life at Tod Inlet. Many of my contacts have now passed on. I would particularly like to acknowledge Norman Parsell, who shared his stories with me in a delightful exchange of correspondence in the 1970s and 1980s. Pat van Adrichem and Dem Carrier were particularly helpful, providing information, photographs and artifacts, and spending time at Tod Inlet with me, pointing out locations of various features. Others who shared both information and enthusiasm were Mike Rice, Jim Gilbert, Claude Sluggett, Mary Youlden, Joyce Jacobsen, Lorna Pugh and Joyce Marshall. Dr. Manmohan Wirk, Amrik Singh Dhillon, Nad Lal Pallan, Mukund (Max) Pallan, Mony Jawl, Jeto Sengara, Paul Singh Johal and Jeet Dheensaw helped with information on the Sikh community, and Alan Lowe and Lorelei Lew contributed memories of their grandfathers.

I gratefully acknowledge the Tsartlip Elders I interviewed—Manny Cooper, Beatrice Elliott, John Elliott, Ivan Morris, John Sampson, Tom Sampson and Stella Wright—and also Elder Earl Claxton Sr. of Tsawout.

My parents, Alex and Annie Gray, my sisters Betty Stone and Dorothy Pekter, my niece Nancy Pekter, my long-time friend David Neilson, and his parents, Wally and Eileen Neilson, all helped with the explorations and fieldwork at Tod Inlet in various ways over the years. My mum continued to send me newspaper clippings about Tod Inlet well into her 90s, helping me keep up to date with the Tod Inlet story. My wife, Sally, contributed greatly though her thoughtful editing and encouragement through my years of writing about Tod Inlet. She has actively joined the family of those who love being at this "healing place," as Tod Inlet is beautifully described by author Gwen Curry.[123]

Other original research and new information was gathered from papers found in the old Vancouver Portland Cement Company office at Tod Inlet and from Alex Gray's collections of maritime history. Information on the ships of Tod Inlet came from the files of Robert Turner, Robert Spearing and Frank Clapp; from the City of Vancouver Archives and the Maritime Museum of British Columbia; from the newspaper articles of Norman Hacking and Archie Wills; and the recollections of my parents, Annie and Alex Gray, and my uncle Harvey Gray.

I would also like to acknowledge the assistance, cooperation and friendship of Derrick Mallard, founder of the Citizens Association to Save the Environment (CASE), who was involved with the effort to protect the Tod Inlet area for over 20 years.

Pat van Adrichem and David Gray sharing artifacts from Tod Inlet. David R. Gray photograph.

David Gray measuring the brick oven base at the Sikh village area. David R. Gray photograph.

I also thank the staff of the Royal British Columbia Museum, Library and Archives Canada, the Saanich Pioneer Museum, Saanich Archives, the Maritime Museum of British Columbia, the City of Victoria Archives, the Butchart Gardens and the Vancouver Maritime Museum for their assistance. Though the archives of the Butchart Gardens remain closed to the general public, the owners and staff have always responded positively to my requests for information and for permission to use photographs from the archives collections.

The long-term research that this book is based on was first funded in 1998 by the BC Heritage Trust, the Royal Canadian Geographical Society and BC Parks Branch. The Royal Canadian Geographical Society provided funding for the historical mapping of Tod Inlet. BC Parks Branch provided a contract with CASE in 1998 and with Grayhound Information Services in 2001 to develop information on the ecological impact of the cement plant and the community on the land that is now Gowlland Tod Provincial Park. More recently, the Sikh Heritage Museum of Canada provided some financial assistance for additional research on the Sikh workers of Tod Inlet.

I thank Dr. Nancy Turner and Bob Turner for writing the foreword, as well as providing helpful reviews of the book manuscript. I am also grateful to historians Dr. Peter Rider and Pardeep Singh Nagra for their reviews.

For their most helpful and careful editing of this book, I thank Eve Rickert, Annie Mayse and Grace Yaginuma. I also thank Kelly-Ann Turkington for her work with locating images in the Royal BC Museum and BC Archives, and Lara Minja for her work on the book's design and layout.

Appendix I: A Chronology of Tod Inlet

500 BCE Indigenous people are associated with what is called the Marpole Culture living at S̱ṈIDȻEȽ.

820 CE–mid-1800s Indigenous people of the cultural group called the Gulf of Georgia Culture continue to live here in small family-based villages.

1850 About this time, the last village at S̱ṈIDȻEȽ is abandoned, probably due to raiding by northern peoples. Indigenous people move to what is now Tsartlip Reserve land.

1852 Treaties with Saanich First Nations signed by British Columbia's first governor, Sir James Douglas.

1858 Captain Richards of the steam sloop HMS *Plumper* renames the area Tod Creek.

1859 Thomas Sellick pre-empts land at Tod Inlet.

1861 Bishop George Hills purchases land at Tod Inlet from Sellick.

1866 Bishop Hills sells land at Tod Inlet to Thomas Pritchard.

1869 John Greig purchases land at Tod Inlet from Prichard after discovering lime.

1884 Greig transfers property to his sons.

1885 Joseph Wriglesworth is listed as a lime merchant.

1887 Wriglesworth begins career as lime burner with Greig. Wholesale lime first advertised by the Saanich Lime Company.

1889 Peter Fernie is a lime burner and farmer on 60 acres of land at Tod Inlet.

1890 The Saanich Lime Company is incorporated.

1891 Census lists Fernie as "Manager of Lime Kiln."

1892 Wriglesworth owns 225 acres of land at Tod Inlet.

1895 Lime Kiln Road appears for the first time on a map. CPR cement plant established at False Creek in Vancouver.

1899 BC Portland Cement Company purchases the CPR cement works at Vancouver.

1900 Announcement of the new Tod Inlet cement works.

1902 Butchart visits Victoria and acquires Wriglesworth quarry and old Fernie farm.

1904 Butchart establishes Vancouver Portland Cement Company; work commences on the cement plant.

1905 Cement mill begins to operate; first cement sent to market. Report of the Minister of Mines. *Beatrice* and three scows purchased. First tourist excursion to cement plant advertised. Butchart family takes up residence.

1906 Sikhs come to work in the quarry in the spring. Houses are built in the village, though some families are still in tents in the winter. Parsells buy large rowboat.

1906–1907 Plant expansion; new equipment is unloaded onto the wharf.

1907 Sikh cremation ceremony in April.

1908 Foreman Sing dies in an explosion. Plant closes temporarily.

1909 First listing of Tod Inlet in a Vancouver Island directory—"200 Orientals located here."

1910 *Marmion* purchased. BC Telephone Company installs phone in Tod Inlet.

1911 BC Electric puts grade through for new interurban train. Canada census records Tod Inlet population: Sikhs have left for Golden, Ocean Falls, Vancouver. *Spray* coal shipments.

1912 Brentwood Steam Plant completed. *Leona* purchased.

1913 BC Electric interurban train's first run. The Tsartlip Reserve boundaries established by the McKenna-McBride Commission. *Matsqui* purchased. Plant production max. 500,000 barrels, $1 million. Ship *Bamberton* built.

1914 WWI begins. 300 employed at Tod Inlet. Bunkhouse is used by Red Cross during WWI.

1915 *Leona* lost. Recession, production decreases, deposits near exhaustion.

1916 Heavy winter snow. Bamberton plant temporarily closes. Mrs. Butchart's garden well established, with about 18,000 visitors in 1916.

1917 "Small army" of Chinese gardeners working. Sunken Garden costs $65,000 in 1917.

1918 WWI ends. Norman Parsell on steam shovel in upper quarry (Wallace Drive). Vancouver Portland Cement Company and Associated Cement Company amalgamate to BC Cement Company. *Marmion* sold.

1920 The Butchart Gardens are expanded. *Teco* purchased.

1920s Sam Whittaker holds land at Willis Point.

1921 Tod Inlet cement plant shuts down. Plant continues to make tiles and flower pots.

1925 *Shean* arrives in BC.

1926 First air photo of Tod Inlet: three houses still visible in Chinese village. Upper quarry by Wallace Drive still dry.

1926–1927 Ice on the inlet in winter; kids skate around buoy and back.

1927 First cottages built at Willis Point.

1928 R.P. Butchart awarded Freedom of the City.

1929 *Island King* purchased in Britain and arrives at Tod Inlet. Lime Kiln Road renamed Benvenuto Avenue.

1930 *Kangaroo* to Tod Inlet for boating and fishing.

1930s Coach Lines initiates bus service to Tod Inlet as part of West Saanich route.

1930 or 1931 Fire burns area northeast of Tod Inlet village.

1931 Upper quarry flooded.

1932 Last Chinese workers at tile plant.

1935 Photo of *Teco* at wharf taken by Alex Gray. *Shean* sold. Movie *Stampede* produced.

1936 *Teco* sold. Small boathouse towed to Tod Inlet. Movie *Stampede* in Victoria theatres.

1937 Ice and snow on the inlet.

About 1938 Scrap iron from cement plant shipped to Japan.

1939 The Butcharts give the Butchart Gardens to their grandson, Ian Ross. Start of WWII.

1940–1943 War preparation exercises by Power Boat Squadrons and home guard effort at Tod Inlet.

1941 *Squakquoi* first moored in Tod Inlet.

1941–1943 Power Boat Squadrons organized by the navy.

1943 R.P. Butchart dies in Victoria.

1944 *Island King* sold. WWII ends.

1945–1950 Local logging under way.

1946 Lots at Willis Point subdivided. Tod Inlet Power Boat Owners' Association started.

1947 Wharf and ways constructed.

1950 Jennie Butchart dies in Victoria.

1950–1952 BC Cement Company buys *Hunter* to transport men to Bamberton.

1952 Tod Inlet Post Office closes in October. *Bamberton* sold.

About 1953 Tile plant shuts down.

1955 *Hunter* operates daily to Bamberton until about 1965. Coach Lines bus service to Tod Inlet ends. First exploration of the Chinese midden above Tod Creek.

1958 All houses in Tod Inlet still standing and occupied.

1960s Area by Tod Creek still used as garbage dump.

1963–1967 I collect artifacts from the Chinese area.

1965 The small wooden boathouse sinks.

1966 *Squakquoi* sold. Gate installed at end of Benvenuto Avenue.

1967 Tod Inlet houses still standing in April. Security fence around the cement plant installed.

1968 Aerial photo shows some houses. Laundry building (formerly Tong's house) still standing.

1968–1970 I continue to collect artifacts.

1970s Houses burned by local fire department. The first subdivided land at Willis Point sold to private landowners.

1973 Cement plant still has four stacks.

About 1975 Genstar development proposals.

1978 Three plant chimneys down by December. Tile plant gone; post office building still standing. Only remnant of bunkhouse is the foundation. Continued plans for development; my letters to Victoria *Daily Colonist* and government. Tod Inlet Power Boat Owners' Association using old cookhouse as clubhouse.

1979 Plant buildings still up. *J. Hunter* at wharf.

1980s Most of the cement plant buildings destroyed. Tod Creek watershed enhancement. Genstar continues with proposals.

1983 Tod Creek Water Enhancement Society releases salmon fry into Tod Creek.

1990 Hartland landfill leachate diverted from Tod Creek. FAMA development at Tod Inlet proposed. Information walk and rally at Tod Inlet in September.

1994 Tod Inlet area preserved as part of Commonwealth Legacy. The last of the cement plant buildings destroyed.

1995 Gowlland Tod Provincial Park established.

1996 Management plan for Gowlland Tod Provincial Park published. Archaeology studies initiated.

1997 Ian Ross, owner of Butchart Gardens, dies.

1998 Cement company barn/stable destroyed.

2000 Marine life survey in Tod Inlet. SeaChange Society begins environmental enhancement projects.

2001 My interviews with Tsartlip Elders about Tod Inlet history and cultural importance.

2004 The Butchart Gardens celebrates their centenary and are designated a National Historic Site.

2010 My films *Searching for the Sikhs of Tod Inlet* and *Beyond the Gardens' Wall* produced.

2015 New fishway constructed on Tod Creek.

2016 Tod Inlet designation as Historic Place.

2017 Canada 150 project, Canada C3, visits Tod Inlet. New sand/gravel beach installed.

(*overleaf*) The old cement supports for the boat owners' wharf, built about 1946.
David R. Gray photograph.

Appendix II: Place Names of the Tod Inlet Area

Bamberton. The cement plant and townsite were named after Henry K.G. Bamber, who came out from England for the Associated Cement Company to assess the possibility of opening a new limestone quarry on the west side of Saanich Inlet.

Benvenuto Avenue. The new name for what was Lime Kiln Road since 1929. The name comes from the name of the Butchart's residence, Benvenuto, meaning "welcome" in Italian.

Brentwood Bay. Named for a town in Essex, England, where Mr. Horne-Payne, chairman of the board of directors of the BC Electric Railway, owned a house. At first, only the BCER station was named Brentwood. The name of the post office was changed from Sluggett in 1925 and the community in 1934. The name of the body of water, part of Saanich Inlet, and originally named Tod Inlet, was also changed in 1934.

Butchart Cove. A small cove on the southeast side of the entrance narrows of Tod Inlet. Serves as a docking area for smaller boats associated with the Butchart Gardens. The cove is known to the Tsartlip as "Humsawhut," meaning "Sunshine Bay."[124]

Cole Hill. Cole Hill is located one kilometre south of Tod Inlet, just north of Durrance Lake. A prominent hill of 260 metres in elevation, it was named for a settler, George Cole, who lived in the area in the early 1900s. Early British Admiralty charts called the hill "Mount Fane," a name likely given by Captain George Henry Richards in about 1858, honouring Charles George Fane, mate of HMS *Ganges* between 1857 and 1860.

Daphne Islet. An established local name, "Daphne Islet" was officially adopted in 1934. Formerly called Daphne Island and informally also known as "Skull Island," it was a sacred burial site for the early Tsartlip First Nation people.

Durrance Lake. On some early maps, "Durant Lake"; also Durrance Creek. John (Jack) Durrance was one of the first Europeans to establish a farm in the watershed of Tod Creek.

Fernie Beach. A local unofficial name, given after Peter C. Fernie, farmer and lime burner, who owned the property on the southeast side of the Tod Inlet narrows before the cement plant and the Butcharts arrived. Now part of the Butchart Gardens.

Gowlland Range. Gowlland was a second master on Captain George Henry Richards's 1858 survey of the area on the steam sloop HMS *Plumper*. Several other places in BC also carry his name.

Heal Creek. A small creek that drains from the Hartland landfill south of Tod Inlet into Tod Creek. In 1860 Fred and Charlie Heal purchased a large portion of the Tod Creek Flats from the Hudson's Bay Company. They both farmed and leased the land. A 1914 "Saanich Sheet" map shows a Heal Post Office on West Saanich Road.

Heal's Range. During World War I a proposal to develop the land in the northern part of the Tod Creek Flats as a military range for the Canadian Army was accepted in 1915. This was partly seen as a solution for unemployment. The Heal's Rifle Range began operations in 1916 and has been used for weapons training ever since.

Joylorn Creek. A local name for the creek flowing down into the southeast corner of Tod Inlet. It was named for Joyce Jacobson (neé Carrier) and Lorna Pugh (neé Thomson).

Lime Kiln Road. The road leading from Old West Saanich Road down to Tod Inlet. Also known as the Tod Inlet Road, it was renamed Benvenuto Avenue in 1929.

Malahat Ridge. A long-established local name, "Malahat Ridge" was officially adopted in 1934. The first car journey over the Malahat happened in 1911. The SENĆOŦEN name YOS, meaning "caution," refers to the peak of the Malahat Ridge.

Mount Newton. The tallest mountain in the northern part of the Saanich Peninsula is known as ȽÁU,WELṈEW̱, which means "place of refuge" in SENĆOŦEN. It was renamed to commemorate a surveyor and map-maker in the 1850s. The mountain is part of John Dean Provincial Park.

Partridge Hills. The name appears on the 1861 British Admiralty chart and was in use on maps since at least 1930. The name was given by Captain George Henry Richards in 1857 or 1858.

Quarry Lake. East of the south end of Tod Inlet on the east side of Wallace Drive. Once the third limestone quarry excavated by the Vancouver Portland Cement Company, it was actively excavated between about 1911 and 1921. The quarry began flooding after exploratory drilling to ascertain the amount of quality limestone left and has been full of water since 1931. Once a popular place for bathing, it is now a private water reservoir for the Butchart Gardens.

Saanich Inlet. Saanich Inlet is the body of water extending south from Satellite Channel and Salt Spring Island to Finlayson Arm, the narrow channel leading to the Goldstream estuary. The earliest use of the name by settlers was "Säanich Bay," which appears on the 1855 Pemberton map of southeastern Vancouver Island. "Saanich Inlet" was used on the 1861 Admiralty chart by Captain Richards. Saanich is an anglicization of the SENĆOŦEN word W̱SÁNEĆ, which means "emerging" and refers to the creation story of Mount Newton rising up as the flood waters receded.

Saanich Peninsula. The peninsula stretches from the outskirts of the city of Victoria north to Deep Cove and Swartz Bay in North Saanich. It is bounded by Finlayson Arm and Saanich Inlet on the west and Haro Strait on the east.

Senanus Island. A small island in Bentwood Bay, once used by W̱SÁNEĆ people. The W̱SÁNEĆ name SEN,NI,NES means "chest out of the water."

Sluggett. The former name for what is now Brentwood. The area and the post office were named after an early pioneer, John Sluggett, who bought 700 acres of land in Saanich in 1875.

Sluggett Point. Known to the Tsartlip as ĆIETṈEW̱ÁLE, the "owl place," referring to a site where human remains were placed on a platform above the ground, Sluggett Point is west of Brentwood and marks the southern boundary of the Tsartlip Reserve. (*See* Sluggett.)

SṈIDĆEȽ. The area around Tod Inlet is known to the Tsartlip people by the name SṈIDĆEȽ, which means "Place of the Blue Grouse."

Squally Reach. Captain George Henry Richards of the steam sloop HMS *Plumper* gave the name to the southwestern part of Saanich Arm (i.e., Inlet) between Willis Point (at the north end) and Elbow Point (at the south). The name first appeared on the 1861 Admiralty chart.

Tod Creek. In 1858 Captain George Henry Richards of the steam sloop HMS *Plumper* gave the name "Tod Creek" to the whole area now known as Brentwood Bay and Tod Inlet. The name refers to John Tod (1794–1882), a noted employee of the Hudson's Bay Company who later became a member of the council of government for the Vancouver Island colony in 1851, and eventually a member of the later Legislative Council. Today the name Tod Creek applies to the small stream entering the southeast corner of the head of the inlet. (*See also* Tod Inlet and W̱EĆEĆE.) Tod Creek drains Prospect Lake; other tributary creeks include Heal Creek.

Tod Creek flats. In the 1860s the channel of Tod Creek was moved to the east edge of the flats as the wetland was drained for agriculture, and again in 1915 to accommodate the Heal's Rifle Range. On a 1914 map, the creek is labelled "Government Ditch."

Tod Inlet. The inlet extending southward from Brentwood Bay with a narrow entrance channel opening out to the east. Name of the post office and the village established at the head of the inlet in 1904 and lasting until the late 1950s. *See also* Tod Creek.

Tsartlip. W̱JOȽEȽP, anglicized as Tsartlip, means "land of maples" in the SENĆOŦEN language. The current village came into being after the older village at SṈIDȻEȽ was abandoned.

Wallace Drive. Part of the former right-of-way for the BC Electric Railway, Wallace Drive was apparently named for William Oakes Wallace, who owned the first general store at what is now Brentwood. The southern part of the current Wallace Drive was formerly known as Heal's Range Road.

W̱EĆEĆE. The traditional SENĆOŦEN name for Tod Creek. The word imitates the sound of the creek as it drops down to the waters of the Inlet.

Whittaker Point. A point south of Willis Point on the east side of Saanich Inlet. Named after Sam Whittaker, who first lived there in the late 1920s.

Willis Point. Named in 1858 by Captain George Henry Richards of the steam sloop HMS *Plumper*. The origin of the name is not known. There was no Willis with Richards's BC survey crew or his Arctic exploration crew. The name may have been from a local contact, though there are no Willises listed in the earliest Victoria directories. Willis Point is sometimes used to describe all the land area between Saanich Arm on the west and Tod Inlet on the east. The local SENĆOŦEN name for this whole area is SX̱OX̱ÍEM, meaning "still waters," referring to its appearance at low tide.

Willis Point Road. Most of the roads at Willis Point were based on the logging roads of the 1950s. The road name was only officially adopted in 1993 as the naming was assumed or forgotten at the time of the subdivision construction.

(*overleaf*) The road to the Chinese village, in the fall of 2016. David R. Gray photograph.

Notes

1 P.K. Paul, *The Care-Takers: The Re-emergence of the Saanich Indian Map* (Sidney, BC: Institute of Ocean Sciences, Department of Fisheries and Oceans, 1995), 2–3.

2 G. Keddie, "The Archaeological Remains of Tod Inlet," in Citizens Association to Save the Environment, "Brief in Support of Designation of Vancouver Portland Cement Company Area of Tod Inlet as a Historic/Heritage/Nature Appreciation Site" (unpublished report, 1991).

3 J. Gilbert, interview with the author, September 2001.

4 T. Sampson, interview with the author, Brentwood, BC, 2010.

5 D. Elliott, *Saltwater People*, ed. J. Poth (Saanich, BC: School District 63, 1990), 63.

6 N.J. Turner and R.J. Hebda, *Saanich Ethnobotany: Culturally Important Plants of the W̱SÁNEĆ People* (Victoria, BC: Royal BC Museum, 2012).

7 Elliott, *Saltwater People*, 75, 77.

8 Sampson, interview with the author, 2010.

9 B. Richling, ed., *The W̱SÁNEĆ and Their Neighbours: Diamond Jenness on the Coast Salish of Vancouver Island, 1935* (Oakville, ON: Rock's Mills Press, 2016).

10 *Compact Edition of the Oxford English Dictionary* (1979), s.v. "creek."

11 *Vancouver Island Pilot: Containing Sailing Directions for the Coasts of Vancouver Island, and Part of British Columbia; Compiled from the Surveys Made by Captain George Henry Richards, R.N., in H.M. Ships Plumper and Hecate, between the Years 1858 and 1864* (London, UK: Hydrographic Office, 1864), 50.

12 R.C. Mayne, *Four Years in British Columbia and Vancouver Island* (London, UK: John Murray, 1862), 153.

13 Elliott, *Saltwater People*, 72.

14 *Compact Edition of the Oxford English Dictionary* (1979), s.v. "pre-emption."

15 E. Malladaine, "Saanich Peninsula," in *British Columbia Directory* (Victoria, BC: Malladaine and Williams, 1887), 113.

16 J. Morrison, "Greig, John" (unpublished manuscript based on interviews with Mrs. Bethell in Victoria, BC, June 1982).

17 Morrison, "Greig, John," 1982.

18 "Lime Shipments," *Victoria Daily Times*, November 11, 1890.

19 "The Saanich Lime Company Limited," Victoria *Daily Colonist*, April 19, 1891.

20 Morrison, "Greig, John," 1982.

21 R. Connell, "In the Tod Inlet District," June 27, 1925.

22 "Tod Inlet Now Hive of Industry," *Victoria Daily Times*, July 22, 1905.

23 "President Ward Gives Further Details Regarding the Cement Works," *Victoria Daily Times*, December 4, 1900.

24 D. Clarke, *The Butchart Gardens: A Family Legacy* (Brentwood Bay, BC: Butchart Gardens, 2003).

25 "Street Improvements," Victoria *Daily Colonist*, May 11, 1905.

26 M.L. Parsell, "Reminiscences of Tod Inlet" (unpublished manuscript, 1958), 2.

27 "Local News," *Victoria Daily Times*, September 22, 1908.

28 M. Rice quoted in S. Thompson, "Chinatown Disappeared but Legacy Remains," Sidney *Review*, February 25, 1987.

29 M.L. Parsell, "Reminiscences," 5.

30 M.S. Wirk, *A History of the Sikhs of Victoria, B.C.*, vol. 1 (Victoria, BC: First Choice Books, 2005), 49

31 G. Bilga, radio interview, 1960, Komagata Maru Affair (1964) sound reels 478 #4A—G. Bilga interview, box 994 f.15, Canadian Museum of History Archives.

32 "Hindoos Are Coming," *Vancouver Daily World*, July 20, 1906.

33 G.L. Milne, letter to Laurier, 1907, MG26-G Political Papers, Library and Archives Canada.

34 M.L. Parsell, "Reminiscences," 9.

35 "Hindus Are in Great Distress," *Victoria Daily Times*, August 13, 1906.

36 M.L. Parsell, "Reminiscences," 4.

37 M.L. Parsell, "Reminiscences," 4.

38 "Annual Meeting," *Victoria Daily Times,* April 18, 1905.

39 *Henderson's British Columbia Gazetteer and Directory for 2010* (Vancouver, BC: Henderson Publishing, 1910).

40 G. Sivertz, "When We Were Very Young," Victoria *Daily Times*, May 10, 1958.

41 M.L. Parsell, "Reminiscences," 1.

42 M.L. Parsell, "Reminiscences," 2.

43 "Weird Ceremony at Tod Inlet," *Victoria Daily Times*, April 21, 1907.

44 "Council Deals with Routine," *Victoria Daily Times*, February 9, 1909.

45 "Fell Down Hatch and Was Killed," *Victoria Daily Times*, September 11, 1909.

46 "Cement Works Being Enlarged," *Victoria Daily Times*, May 8, 1906.

47 "Cement Works," *Victoria Daily Times*, 1906.

48 Wirk, *History of the Sikhs*, 127–128.

49 "A Hindoo Cremation," *Canadian Courier* 2, no. 3 (June 15, 1907).

50 M.L. Parsell, "Reminiscences."

51 M.L. Parsell, "Reminiscences."

52 "Local News," *Victoria Daily Times*, August 31, 1911.

53 M.S. Wirk, interview with the author, May 1998.

54 M.L. Parsell, "Reminiscences," 11.

55 "Frankmount Is Due with Steel Shipments," *Vancouver Daily World*, September 10, 1912.

56 "BCER Will Install New Power Plant," Vancouver *Province*, November 1, 1907.

57 N. Parsell, letter to the author, September 21, 1978.

58 "In a Logging Camp," *Vancouver Daily World*, January 21, 1913.

59 N. Parsell, letter to the author regarding *Marmion*, 1978.

60 D. Preston, *The Story of the Butchart Gardens* (Victoria, BC: Highline Publishing, 1996), 43.

61 "Fierce Gale Met Entering Pacific," *Victoria Daily Times*, August 8, 1912.

62 N. Parsell, letter to the author, 1978.

63 H. Ewert, *Victoria's Streetcar Era* (Victoria, BC: Sono Nis, 1992).

64 G. Hearn and D. Wilkie, *The Cordwood Limited: A History of the Victoria & Sidney Railway* (Victoria, BC: British Columbia Railway Historical Association, 1966), 61.

65 "Canadian Casualties," *Vancouver Daily World*, April 1, 1916.

66 "Falls at Front," *Victoria Daily Times,* September 6, 1917.

67 "Wins Belgian Medal," *Vancouver Daily World*, April 8, 1918.

68 M.L. Parsell, "Reminiscences."

69 "Robert Pim Butchart: British Columbia's WWI Director of Wooden Shipbuilding," Victoria Harbour History, https://www.victoriaharbourhistory.com /harbour-stories/enterprisers/robert-pym-butchart/.

70 "Blacksmith Wanted," *Vancouver Daily World*, May 8, 1918.

71 N. Parsell, letter to the author, July 27, 1978.

72 N. Parsell, "A Nostalgic Excavation," *Islander (Daily Colonist Magazine)*, 1980.

73 "Sidney Notes," *Victoria Daily Times*, October 8, 1920.

74 "*Mary* Brings Cement from Tod Inlet to This Port," *Vancouver Daily World*, May 6, 1921.

75 "Present Parting Gift," *Victoria Daily Times*, June 14, 1921.

76 N. Parsell, letter to the author, 1978.

77 B. Wright, *The History of Willis Point: A Unique British Columbia Community* (Central Saanich, BC: Willis Point Community Association, 2018).

78 Wright, *History of Willis Point*.

79 Wright, *History of Willis Point*.

80 Ewert, *Victoria's Streetcar Era*.

81 M.L. Parsell, "Reminiscences," 9.

82 L. Pugh, *Brentwood Bay and Me, 1930-1940: A Brief History of Brentwood Bay*, 2nd ed. (Saanich, BC: Saanich Pioneers' Society Archives, 1997), 4.

83 Pugh, *Brentwood Bay and Me*, 2.

84 Pugh, *Brentwood Bay and Me*, 3.

85 Pugh, *Brentwood Bay and Me*, 19.

86 Pugh, *Brentwood Bay and Me*, 14.

87 Pugh, *Brentwood Bay and Me*, 18.

88 R. Connell, "Rambles Round Victoria," *Victoria Daily Times*, May 16, 1924.

89 Connell, "Rambles," *Victoria Daily Times*.

90 R. Connell, "October's End in Highlands Where Ravens Fly," *Victoria Daily Times*, November 7, 1931.

91 Elliott, *Saltwater People*, 73.

92 Elliott, *Saltwater People*, 73.

93 "The Venerable Chinese Loves the Famous Gardens," *Islander (Daily Colonist Magazine)*, April 2, 1961.

94 BC Cement Company advertisement, *Nanaimo Free Press*, March 22, 1937.

95 "Church Parade for Soldiers," July 4, 1932.

96 H.A. Halliday, "Preparing for the Past," *Legion Magazine*, November/December 2004.

97 Clarke, *Butchart Gardens*.

98 D.R. Gray, "Power Boat Squadron Patrol," *Port Hole* 16, no. 3 (September 1989): 40–41.

99 "Reserve Army Stages Early Morning Raid," *Victoria Daily Times*, July 24, 1943.

100 Gray, "Power Boat Squadron Patrol."

101 Tod Inlet Power Boat Owners' Association, *Constitution of the Tod Inlet Power Boat Owners' Association*, October 25, 1964.

102 "SENĆOŦEN Home Page," FirstVoices, https://www .firstvoices.com/explore/FV/sections/Data/THE%20 SENĆOŦEN%20LANGUAGE/SENĆOŦEN/SENĆOŦEN.

103 "Annual Meeting," *Victoria Daily Times*, April 18, 1905.

104 "Hungarian Partridges Released Around City," *Victoria Daily Times*, November 17, 1908.

105 "Blue Grouse," *Times Colonist*, August 27, 1925.

106 L. Neff, interview with the author, 1994.

107 Wright, *History of Willis Point*, 17.

108 R. Carver, letter to the author, 2018.

109 Ker & Stephenson, *Appraisal of BC Cement Property, Tod Inlet, Municipality of Central Saanich*, December 20, 1957.

110 Sivertz, "When We Were Very Young."

111 S. Lang, "Weather Reduces Fishing Pressure," *Victoria Daily Times*, November 29, 1968.

112 S. Lang, "For Anglers This Weekend," *Victoria Daily Times*, May 8, 1970.

113 G. Curry, *Tod Inlet: A Healing Place* (Victoria, BC: Rocky Mountain Books, 2015).

114 L. Dorricott and D. Cullon, eds., *The Private Journal of Captain G.H. Richards: The Vancouver Island Survey* (1860-1862) (Vancouver, BC: Ronsdale Press, 2012).

115 S. Down, "Park Designation Means Big Changes for Tod Inlet Group," Victoria *Times Colonist*, December 8, 1994.

116 D. McLaren, *Gowlland Tod Provincial Park Archaeological Inventory and Impact Assessment*, report prepared for Saanich First Nation and BC Parks (Victoria, BC: Millennia Research, 1996).

117 "Old Native Agreement May Stall Tod Proposal," Victoria *Times Colonist*, March 31, 1982.

118 "Halt Sale of Tod Inlet Lots until Land Claim Settled—Band," Victoria *Times Colonist*, July 20, 1994.

119 *Interim Reconciliation Agreement between Her Majesty in Right of the Province of British Columbia and the Tsartlip First Nation*, March 23, 2017, https:// www2.gov.bc.ca/assets/gov/environment/natural -resource-stewardship/consulting-with-first-nations /agreements/tsartlip_interim_reconciliation _agreement_-_signed_by_mjr_2.pdf.

120 Citizens Association to Save the Environment, "Brief in Support of Designation of Vancouver Portland Cement Company Area of Tod Inlet as a Historic/Heritage/ Nature Appreciation Site" (unpublished report, 1991).

121 K. Bill, K. Bunting and T. Heeley, *Seabed Imaging and Mapping System Survey of Tod Inlet: A Baseline Inventory* (Victoria, BC: Camosun College Environmental Technology Program, 2001).

122 "Butchart Gardens National Historic Site of Canada," Parks Canada Directory of Federal Heritage Designations, https://www.pc.gc.ca/apps/dfhd/page _nhs_eng.aspx?id=10910.

123 Curry, *Healing Place*.

124 G. Keddie, "Piecing Together Outsiders Views," Royal BC Museum, November 3, 2016, https://staff .royalbcmuseum.bc.ca/2016/11/03/david-latasse-of -saanich-and-songhees-heritage/.

Bibliography and Sources

Alexander, M., and A. Brown. *Bamberton: From Dust to Bust and Back.* Mill Bay, BC: Bamberton Historical Society, 2012.

BC Parks South Vancouver Island District. *Gowlland Tod Provincial Park Management Plan.* Langford, BC: BC Parks, 1996.

BC Minister of Mines. *Report of the Minister of Mines for 1904.* Victoria, BC: Government of BC, 1905.

Beebe, F., dir. *Stampede.* 1935; Central Films.

Bill, K., K. Bunting and T. Heeley. *Seabed Imaging and Mapping System Survey of Tod Inlet: A Baseline Inventory.* Victoria, BC: Camosun College Environmental Technology Program, 2001.

British Columbia Cement Company. *Community Song Book: Song Book for Use at Community Functions at Bamberton, B.C.* Victoria, BC: Colonist Presses, n.d.

Capital Regional District Parks. *Preliminary Study of Lands Owned by Fama Holdings Ltd. for Regional Park Purposes (Tod Inlet/Creek).* Victoria, BC: CRD Parks, 1992.

Castle, G., ed. *Saanich: An Illustrated History.* Saanich, BC: Corporation of the District of Saanich, 1989.

Citizens Association to Save the Environment. "Brief in Support of Designation of Vancouver Portland Cement Company Area of Tod Inlet as a Historic/Heritage/Nature Appreciation Site." Unpublished report, 1991.

Clarke, D. *The art Gardens: A Family Legacy.* Victoria, BC: The Butchart Gardens, 2003.

Claxton, E., and J. Elliott. *The Saanich Year.* Brentwood Bay, BC: School District 63, 1993.

Cooper, R.W. "Cariboo Candles in Douglas Swamp." *Islander (Daily Colonist Magazine)*, September 21, 1980.

Curry, G. *Tod Inlet: A Healing Place.* Victoria, BC: Rocky Mountain Books, 2015.

Dorricott, L., and D. Cullon, eds. *The Private Journal of Captain G.H. Richards. The Vancouver Island Survey (1860-1862).* Vancouver, BC: Ronsdale Press, 2012.

Dougan, R.I. *Cowichan My Valley.* Cobble Hill, BC: R.I. Dougan, 1973.

Elliott, D. *Saltwater People.* Edited by J. Poth. Rev. ed. Saanich, BC: School District 63, 1990.

Ewert, H. *Victoria's Streetcar Era.* Victoria, BC: Sono Nis Press, 1992.

Gray, D.R., dir. *Beyond the Gardens' Wall: The Immigrant Workers of Tod Inlet.* 2010; Grayhound Information Services. 30 min.

———. "Cement Boats of Tod Inlet." *The Resolution* 17 (September 1989): 1113.

———. "Deep and Sheltered Waters: The History of the Community of Tod Inlet, B.C." Unpublished draft report submitted to BC Parks Branch, 2002.

———. "A History of the Chinese and Sikh Workers of Tod Inlet, BC, 1904 to 1921." Presentation at National

Council on Public History Annual Meeting, Ottawa, April 18–22, 2001.

———. "Mapping the History of Tod Inlet." Unpublished report submitted to the Royal Canadian Geographical Society.

———. "Pigs' Teeth, Pottery and Portland Cement: The Story of the Chinese Workers of Tod Inlet, BC." *This Country Canada* 9 (Autumn 1995–Winter 1996): 56–67.

———. "Power Boat Squadron Patrol." *Port Hole* 16, no. 3 (September 1989): 40–41.

———, dir. *Searching for the Sikhs of Tod Inlet*. 2008; Grayhound Information Services. 48 min.

———. "The Wartime Origins of the Power Boat Squadrons." *The Resolution* 9 (Fall 1986), 3–4.

Greig, J. Affidavit sworn before notary public in Victoria, BC, December 26, 1930.

Halliday, H.A. "Preparing for the Past." *Legion Magazine*, November/December 2004.

Hearn, G., and D. Wilkie. *The Cordwood Limited: A History of the Victoria & Sidney Railway*. Victoria, BC: The British Columbia Railway Historical Association, 1966.

Henderson's British Columbia Gazetteer and Directory for 2010. Vancouver, BC: Henderson Publishing, 1910.

Keddie, G. "The Archaeological Remains of Tod Inlet." In Citizens Association to Save the Environment, "Brief in Support of Designation of Vancouver Portland Cement Company Area of Tod Inlet as a Historic/Heritage/Nature Appreciation Site." Unpublished report, 1991.

Malladaine, E. *British Columbia Directory*. Victoria, BC: Malladaine and Williams, 1887.

May, T. 1988. "Earning Her Keep (*Beatrice*)." *The Resolution* 16 (August 1988): 2–3.

Mayne, R.C. *Four Years in British Columbia and Vancouver Island*. London, UK: John Murray, 1862.

McCormick, J.A. *Cruise of the Calcite*. Everett, WA: B & E Enterprises, 1973.

McLaren, D. *Gowlland Tod Provincial Park Archaeological Inventory and Impact Assessment*. Report prepared for Saanich First Nation and BC Parks. Victoria, BC: Millennia Research, 1996.

Morrison, J. "Greig, John." Unpublished manuscript based on interviews with Mrs. Bethell in Victoria, BC, June 1982.

Parsell, M.L. "Reminiscences of Tod Inlet." Unpublished manuscript, 1958. BC Archives collection

Parsell, N. "Before Butchart Gardens." *The Review*, May 4, 1988.

Paul, P.K. *The Care-Takers: The Re-emergence of the Saanich Indian Map*. Sidney, BC: Institute of Ocean Sciences; Department of Fisheries and Oceans, 1995.

Preston, D. *The Story of Butchart Gardens*. Victoria, BC: Highline Publishing, 1996.

Pugh, L. *Brentwood Bay and Me, 1930-1940: A Brief History of Brentwood Bay*. 2nd edition. Saanich, BC: Saanich Pioneers' Society Archives, 1997.

Richling, B., ed. *The W̱SÁNEĆ and Their Neighbours: Diamond Jenness on the Coast Salish of Vancouver Island, 1935*. Oakville, ON: Rock's Mills Press, 2016.

Tod Inlet Power Boat Owners' Association. *Constitution of the Tod Inlet Power Boat Owners' Association*. 1964.

Turner, N.J., and R.J. Hebda. *Saanich Ethnobotany: Culturally Important Plants of the W̱SÁNEĆ People*. Victoria, BC: Royal BC Museum, 2012.

The Vancouver Island Pilot: Containing Sailing Directions for the Coasts of Vancouver Island, and Part of British Columbia; Compiled from the Surveys Made by

Captain George Henry Richards, R.N., in H.M. Ships
Plumper and Hecate, between the Years 1858 and 1864.
London, UK: Hydrographic Office, 1864.
Victoria Daily Times, 1885–1905. "Of Age" edition.
Victoria, BC: *Victoria Daily Times*, 1905.
Wirk, M.S. "Cremation Rituals in Victoria, BC."
Unpublished document, ca. 1998.

———. *A History of the Sikhs of Victoria, B.C.* Vol. 1.
Victoria, BC: First Choice Books, 2005.
Wright, B. *The History of Willis Point: A Unique British*
Columbia Community. Central Saanich, BC: Willis
Point Community Association, 2018.

(*overleaf*) The barnacle-encrusted
cement pilings of the old wharf, now over
100 years old, 2019. David R. Gray photograph.

Index

Alex Gray standing near the entrance to the tunnel between the cement plant and the first quarry, 1967. David R. Gray photograph.